MOURNING DAYZE: A WISCONSIN GARAGE BAND
Rockin' Since 1965

Published by McIver Publishing
Text copyright © 2016 by Rick Pfeifer

ISBN-13: 978-0-9962846-7-7

Published in the United States by
McIver Publishing
Freeport, IL 61032

FOREWORD
Lyle Ernst-Freelance Journalist

Gear Fab records has just released a CD entitled "Mourning Dayze the Lost Recordings," with a brief history of the band from 1967. National and international interest in "garage bands" from that era appears to be the force behind the interest in these lost recordings. It's a collection of the groups very first attempt at writing and recording original songs. It's a historical document more so than a musical statement.

Mourning Dayze is a well-known band in the Whitewater/Edgerton area. They currently do a mixture of soul, Motown, R&B, Pop and reggae. The group has been performing since 1965 and over the years, they've played in states as far east as New York and as far south as Florida . The band also toured extensively in the Western U.S and Canada .

This "garage band" gained success and recognition during the late 60's and 70's. They played teen bars which were popular venues during that time, and traveled to gigs in a 1957 Cadillac hearse pulling a trailer with their equipment. Their signature song, "Fly My Paper Airplane" was released in 1967 and received critical acclaim and radio airplay.

The band was also popular on college campuses, not only for its music, but for its light show. Mourning Dayze was one of the first rock and roll bands in the state of Wisconsin to include a traveling "state of the art" light show which included a strobe light. The band also became known throughout the Midwest due to its props. These included a large banner featuring their name, an umbrella on a mic stand, a siren, an old fashioned pole lamp with a yellow light, and the familiar Taj Mahal on the kick drum.

In their early years, prominent musicians passed through the band leaving a long - lasting impression. Curly Cook, an early guitarist with the Steve Miller Band, introduced Mourning Dayze to the power of the blues and soul of the guitar. Berry Oakley played bass guitar with Mourning Dayze shortly before the formation of the Allman Brothers Band.

During their first five years, Mourning Dayze opened for many well-known bands, including The Music Explosion, Ohio Express, The Lemon

Pipers, The Trashmen, and The New Colony Six.

From the summer of 1972 to the spring of 2000, they played a portion of every year at Alpine Valley Resort in East Troy , Wisconsin . They began performing as a house band for the winter ski season and on weekends during the summer. In the mid-70's, Alpine Valley Music Theatre became a major stop on the national tour for rock, pop and contemporary styles of music. The band was in the perfect setting to meet, jam, and listen backstage to national touring acts every weekend.

ACKNOWLEDGEMENTS

This book was written for those who have enjoyed this band and have wanted to know a little more about it. We are humbled and honored to have shared this life with you. To our wives, husbands and significant others, without a doubt there have been many, many times when you've needed us, wanted, longed for us while we have left you alone due to the band's need to rehearse, gig or do something. It's so much more than a "thank you" that we extend to you; that just falls so short. It's something we can only share from each respective heart. Thanks to all former bandmates who became involved with this project-your heartfelt, enriching contributions are appreciated and so needed, they are invaluable. Anyone who enjoys any aspect of this project has Doug Henry to thank. Doug's vision, steadfastness and determination was the driving force behind completing this project. Without him, there would be no book. Thanks to family, friends and neighbors for your constant love and support. It has meant so much to us, and your tolerance for our two-days a week, sometimes more, rehearsals! We are grateful for all of the club owners and agents who've provided us with places to play. Thank you. A special thanks to Betty (nothing new there!) for keeping a life long collection of our band photos, newspaper clippings and promotional material. This book would not be nearly as much fun without them. (And thanks to Rise for keeping them organized!) Thank you, "Sea Monster" Alan Luckett for your dedicated work on the DVD and book cover, neither of which, would have happened without you. A very special thank you to Robert (Bob) Burrows, UW-Whitewater, professor emeritus of English for your professional eye in making corrections and suggestions while engaged in the slow and tedious task of proofreading the first half of our story. Your work has helped to clarify our story to its readers and enlightened those who wrote it. Thanks to free-lance journalist and author Lyle Ernst for spending countless hours in attempting to write our story, which included two drafts of the story which we relentlessly critiqued and questioned, only then to have realized we'd given Lyle an impossible task. This project had to be written by those who had been there. Lyle, your drafts and expertise in editing and publishing have been a vital contribution to the completion of this project. We couldn't have done it without you. Thanks, Lyle!

The biggest thank you we have is to all of the wonderful people who have supported us for over 50 years! You're amazing! From our hearts to yours, THANK YOU!

Lyle Ernst is a freelance journalist and award-winning author from Davenport, Iowa. His journalism background includes contributing news stories, feature stories, and columns to newspapers in Illinois, Iowa, and Wisconsin.

Lyle has had articles published in *Radish Magazine*, *Our Iowa*, and *Women's Edition* magazines. He has contributed essays to three books edited by Robert Wolf: *An American Mosaic, Heartland Portrait*, and *River Days: Stories from the Mississippi*, along with an essay in *Make Hay While the Sun Shines*, edited by Jean Tennant.

His non-fiction work includes *ForeWord Review* **Book of the Year Silver Award Winner**, *Native Writers, Voices of Power*, co-written with Ojibwa author Kim Sigafus. In addition, he and Ms. Sigafus co-wrote *Native Elders, Sharing Their Wisdom*, and *The Life and Times of the Ojibwa People*.

He and Kim Sigafus have published two novels: *The Mida* and *The Mida Book Two, Finding Genny*.

I must thank my dear friend, Joyce Godwin Grubbs, for the review she wrote of this book. The Mourning Dayze musicians where so enamored with it, they chose to put it on the back cover. As usual, Joyce, you came through with flying colors.

A special thank you to my wife, Pat, who put up with me handing her pages of text to proofread, of which she is unmatched.

And, to my daughter Cindy, a huge "thank you." Without her this book may never have seen the light of day.

~Lyle Ernst

Lyle Ernst died September 30, 2016 only several weeks after being diagnosed with cancer and before his beloved Chicago Cubs would find themselves in the World Series. Doug and Rick had spoken with Lyle less than one month before his unexpected death. Lyle was so upbeat and enthusiastic about starting the work necessary to get our story into print that Doug began to get excited thinking about traveling with Lyle while they promoted the book. It was not meant to be.

We are deeply grateful to Kim Sigafus, Lyle's long time co-worker, for her energy, love and respect for Lyle's art and craft. Kim did not hesitate to say yes when asked if she would be interested in finishing what her friend Lyle is unable to do. We deeply appreciated Kim's knowledge and expertise and investment in this project. Most of all we appreciate her heart.

Lyle Ernst

Lyle Ernst was a freelance journalist who took wonderful pictures that captured the essence of the stories he wrote. An author and editor, he co-authored several fiction and non-fiction books with me, his writing partner, Kim Sigafus, and edited many books, helping authors on their self-publishing journey. He is known by many and loved by everyone who knew him.

He was kind, had a sharp wit, and a sense of humor that would either make me laugh or cringe at his crude jokes. Lyle saw the world as it really was, and didn't like some of it. He was vocal and supportive of the Chicago Cubs, whether or not they were winning or losing. Never sanctimonious, he told it like it was and you always knew where you stood with him.

He was my best friend, but that doesn't mean we didn't fight once in a while, pick on each other, or let each other get away with much. I respected his opinion, his writing, and his editing. You could call him whenever you needed his opinion, sure he would tell you what he really thought whether or not you were ready to hear it.

Lyle grew up along the Mississippi River in Iowa. He was proud of where he'd come from and never moved too far from the river. When I met him, he was living in Prairie du Chien, Wisconsin, and eventually he would move to Davenport, Iowa.

We lost Lyle on September 30, 2016 when he lost his battle with lung Cancer. Not a smoker, family and friends wondered how this could be. Suddenly the world became a little quieter and a little less sunny, now that his laugh and quick grin was gone.

This book meant a lot to him and was his last bit of writing before passing away. It is with a glad heart I finish this project up for him. I wish the rest of the world could have known him the way I did.

So, Lyle…rest in peace, my friend. This project is done.

~Kim Sigafus

DEDICATION

This book is dedicated to Ray and Betty Pfeifer, and to all parents and guardians who helped young musicians follow a dream of being in a band and performing in front of live audiences. The 1960's was a time in history of social change, political unrest, and civil rights and war protests. We, as musicians, would not have been able to achieve our goals and be able to enjoy the continuous pleasure of performing without Ray and Betty. At a time of social challenge, not all parents and guardians were willing to sacrifice their traditional ways and support young musicians, as well as allowing them the freedom to pursue their musical ambitions and dreams. Not all parents and guardians were willing to compromise their financial positions by giving young musicians monetary support in the purchase of musical equipment and transportation with no guarantee of monetary return. Not all parents and guardians were willing to share their personal dwellings and meals, or offer moral support to garage band musicians. Ray and Betty Pfeifer did all of this, and more.

~Doug Henry

Ray and Betty

The Heart and Soul of the Band
Lyle Ernst
"The one constant was mom and dad"

Ray and Betty did whatever it took to help their children realize their ambitions regardless of the impact it had on their own lives. They were the "sixth man" on the team, as much members of the band as the members themselves and maybe more. Each was always there for emotional support and advice. They were also, bar none, our biggest fans. Doug: "Vehicles belonging to band members always needed repair work of some type, and when they did, Ray was there for us." Rick: "I can't even guess how much money Dad saved us by working on all of our vehicles. We would have been in trouble financially if it weren't for him." Betty paid the bills accrued by the band and also paid the band members, as well as handled financial matters when they were on the road. (They also let us use their Skelly credit card when we were out of town, which was nearly always.) Betty washed and ironed everyone's clothes and cooked all the meals for the boys and their friends. She also made sure everyone was comfortable when spending the night; this could mean upwards of twenty people dropping in to spend the night without notice! But, It was done with ease and always great fun. And, Betty laid down the law. "Someone had to," she always said. All the members of the band and their friends, hangers on and girlfriends, loved Betty. Everyone called her Betty, even Rick. They still do.

During their second year, the band rehearsed in Betty and and Ray's newly carpeted living room. When neighbors, friends and girlfriends heard about it, they would all come and crowd into Betty's living room. There were people all over the house, sometimes as many as fifteen or more.

While the band rehearsed (and these guys were loud) Betty's two year old daughter Renee would sleep peacefully upstairs. (This was actually great practice for Renee, who later in life, would find herself participating in high profile meetings and able to stay focused while filtering out the noise.) Several years later they would begin to rehearse in "the barn" out back and have continued to do so for over 50 years.

Ray took Rick and Rise to music lessons in Waukesha once a week. Ray drove the 76-mile roundtrip, returning to Whitewater at 9:00 p.m., which left Ray with no more than 11/2 hours to sleep before having to return to work. Ray worked two jobs. It's amazing he never missed a day of work in his entire life.

Rick was only fifteen when he joined the band. He had no problem getting into bars for out of town gigs, but Ray and Betty would go with him in Whitewater or he couldn't get in.

The night of a gig, Betty would stay up until the boys returned home in the wee hours of the morning. The next morning, usually a Sunday, Betty would find fifteen to twenty people spread all over her house, sleeping wherever they could find room. Betty would feed them all, and she made everyone feel like they were just part of the family.

Betty: "I wonder how we did it. I don't know how Ray and I afforded it all. There was always food for anyone who wanted some. It was a lot of fun, and I'd do it all over again."

Betty and Ray

How This Project Got Its Start...

Rick: One night while sitting at home in front of the computer, with too much time on my hands, Google's search engine box began calling me, like a genie that has granted me an unlimited number of wishes, asking me if I had anything I'd like it to search for. "Hmm...? Wonder what would pop up if I searched Mourning Dayze? Never tried that before." Until February of 2005, none of us had ever "Googled" the name Mourning Dayze, let alone our record "Fly My Paper Airplane!"

I typed in Mourning Dayze and hit "search." I almost couldn't believe what I saw. There were many references to Mourning Dayze. One in particular stood out, Gear Fab Records had rereleased the Mourning Dayze 45 "Fly My Paper Airplane" which was recorded in Chicago, on an album called "The Psychedelic States: Illinois in the 60's!" Man, I flew to the phone and called Doug, telling him the story of what I'd found. Then I called Steve, who let out a patented "WHAT?" He couldn't believe it either. Doug was as blown away as Steve and I, but with one big difference-as usual, he saw the significance of the moment and all the possibilities it held regarding our history and story. Just like our music, our story could be shared. It was Doug who said we should buy a hearse as well as make a record. I knew he meant this when he said, "we should write a book about the band."

We wrote this story for those of you who have ever wondered about the history of Mourning Dayze or have been interested in what's gone on behind the scenes. Check this book out..."The story of Mourning Dayze, A Wisconsin Garage Band!"

PART ONE:

THE ORIGINAL MOURNING DAYZE

MOURNING DAYZE

A Wisconsin garage band rockin' since 1965.

INTRODUCTION

Have you ever played in a garage band or wondered what it would be like to play in a garage band? Especially if you're from Wisconsin! The story of Mourning Dayze is familiar story to thousands of musicians and bands. It's not the story of a band that's been on Billboard's Top 100, or made any significant contributions to the world of pop music or had any "star" status. This is the story of everyday people individually growing up with a desire to play the rock 'n roll they'd heard on the radio. Then, by some marvelous bit of fate, 1. finding each other, 2. loving the weapons of rock 'n roll, 3. singing from their hearts, and 4. having a "not to be denied", desire to perform on stage.

Mourning Dayze has been performing since 1965 to the present, 2017. One member of the original band has kept Mourning Dayze "alive and well" for all of its 50 year plus history, that is Rick.

The band's story was written by Rick and will often be told using his perspective, (sometimes told in the first person, other times in the third person, speaking from the band's point of view) as he has been the one constant member through its history. Writing that is done in italics indicates perspective from the present day. So, let's get started by providing you with the back ground on Rick. This will give the reader insight into events that led up to the very beginnings of the band, as well as some historical background. "Roots mon" know your past!

Before the Beginning or "How'd you guys get started anyway?"

Rick: Musical memories help me keep track of where I've been in life. Here are some early highlights. I was four years old in 1953 and loved sitting in front of our family's 78rpm record player listening to and singing along with Patti Page as she sang, "How Much is that Doggie in the Window?" I sang along with Patti, over and over and over again. I loved to sing but I must have driven my family absolutely crazy!

I enjoyed watching Gene Autry and Roy Roger's television shows, not for the action, but for the music. Like my singing cowboy heroes, I too wanted to play the guitar, sing, get the "bad guys" and get the girl!

2

IT'S SO EASY TO
BE POPULAR

When You
PLAY TODAY'S
MOST POPULAR INSTRUMENT
THE GUITAR

Mom and dad had a real love for country and western music. Mom not only played the Hawaiian guitar but also strummed a guitar and sang (once while riding a horse in a local show!) Dad had a "one note fits all" approach to singing and didn't play an instrument, except the radio. I guess they wanted me to carry on the legacy. One Christmas morning I found a guitar under the family Christmas tree. WOW!, was I excited, my very own guitar. This must be what heaven is like! I couldn't play a lick, but I could hold that guitar and pretend that I was playing and singing songs just like my heroes. My parents signed me up for guitar lessons with local teacher Shirley Stone. At this time accordion and Hawaiian guitar studios were the rage it wouldn't be long for the guitar to dominate the scene. I took a few lessons but soon lost interest. I didn't want to learn about music or play songs from a book, I wanted to learn the songs I was hearing on the radio, rock 'n roll don't 'cha know. My mother said I'd learned enough to play " Billy Boy" and "The Midnight Special," which I played over and over.

On our neighbor's radio in 1954 I heard Bill Haley and the Comet's record, "Rock Around the Clock." The beat and groove blew me away and I'd never heard anyone play the guitar like that. I was floored. A few years later Ricky Nelson sang Fats Domino's hit "I'm Walkin'" on the TV show "The Adventures of Ozzie and Harriet." I thought that was so much cooler than the singing cowboys. People were dancing to his music and the girls loved it. It was such a great vibe. From then on at school during Show and Tell, I would sing a Ricky Nelson song or something rock 'n roll related. I was hooked on rock 'n roll.

By the fifth grade I had the opportunity to choose an instrument to play in the school band. I had no trouble choosing mine. I chose the drums and still have a passion for the percussion section. That was also

3

the same year my choir teacher told me that rock 'n roll would never last, saying it was just a fad. He said that in a few years no one would remember Elvis or rock 'n roll.

In 1959/1960 the Ventures released their version of "Walk Don't Run," a remake of the Chet Atkins version of the tune jazz guitarist Johnny Smith had written and recorded in 1954. "Walk Don't Run" was one of the first surf tunes to make Billboard's top 100, making it all the way to #2. In 1961, I heard the Ramrod's instrumental version of "Ghost Riders in the Sky" and I was "blown away" by the guitar sound on that record.

In sixth grade, I began delivering newspapers; that would change everything...

Before There Was a Band, There Was Ron Wolfe...

Rick: Ron Wolfe was the first "real" rock 'n roll musician I'd ever met. I began delivering newspapers in the spring of 1962; I was in the sixth grade. On my route there was a house on Jefferson Street from which I could here someone, it seemed like every day, playing his heart out to rock 'n roll music on a drum set. (It shook the neighborhood!) I thought that was so cool-"rock 'n roll, right here in Whitewater!" I knew the guy's name who was playing those drums, but didn't really know him. It was drummer and artist Ron Wolfe. Ron seemed much older than I was; man, he was in high school! He even had a car, which looked like a hot rod! Cool eh? Ron's sister Barb and I were in the same sixth grade class at the Eastside school. My father worked with Ron's dad Jack at Hawthorn Melody dairy in Whitewater. Ron's dad was also quite an artist. Several years later, during the summer of 1964, Ron had found out I had an electric guitar and amp, which may have been communicated between our fathers. Then one life-changing day, to my absolute amazement, Ron asked if I'd like to go to a jam session he was part of and sit in with the group. I'd never done anything like that before but sure jumped at the chance. Luckily my parents were ok with the idea. Ron picked me up at home and I put my amp and guitar, which was in a cardboard case, in the back of his hot rod. Off we went. So cool! I felt like I was part of the birth of rock 'n roll. We played in the living room of his friend, guitarist Bill Wade. We played popular rock tunes of the day by reading the music from books and sheet music that was written for piano. I don't remember there being any singers; the melody was played on the guitar like the "Ventures" or "Shadows". I was pretty shaky and only did this once. That was my first real rock 'n roll experience. I was in heaven!

In 1964, southern California represented a lifestyle that was the dream of many teens throughout the country and the world. Surfing, hot rods and muscle cars, the music of Dick Dale, Jan and Dean and the Beach Boys, skateboarding, the beach, and slot car racing, were all part of a growing "youth culture." Many teens identified with and wanted to be part of that movement. Whitewater didn't have ten foot waves to "shoot the curl", but it did have rock 'n roll, hot rods and slot car racing. Ya, right here in Whitewater! We had a 50' oval slot racing track which supported organized races in the basement of the local Gambles store where Robert E. Lee worked part-time; more on Robert E. later. The track had been moved to Whitewater from neighboring Palmyra. Palmyra was the home of "The Matadors," a popular area band, which occasionally hung out at that track, parking their slick cars in front of the store and dressing "cool," like they'd just come from the "big" stage. They sounded great and looked like rock 'n roll stars. (During the mid 60's Whitewater High School's Larry Black would play organ for the Matadors and was one of the first to wear "Beatle boots" to school. I'd heard, but can not verify, that after Janis Joplin died, Larry became the organist in her band.)

The "Beatles" appeared on the Ed Sullivan Show on February 9, 1964. It 's been reported that an estimated 73 million people watched the show that night. Kids loved the "Beatles." Parents were bewildered. The following Monday, it seemed like every kid in Jr. High was singing "I Want to Hold Your Hand" with a lot of the guys trying to comb their hair just a little different than they did the day before.

It was at Whitewater's slot-racing track that I'd met Ralph Wells, Jr. Ralph loved slot-racing, fast cars, pop music and playing electric bass guitar. Ralph was six years older than I, and also worked at his father's music store, "Wells' House of Music" which was located in downtown Whitewater.

Ernie Wells, Ralph's dad, owned and operated the music store as well as another shop in town, where he made and repaired violins. Ernie Wells studied music and the violin at Julliard and spent one winter living on park benches in order to continue his studies. He was a repair man so renowned, that Eugene Ormandy of the Philadelphia Philharmonic, on several occasions flew, with his violin, to Whitewater to have Ernie make necessary repairs on his instrument. Ernie also worked for the Gibson and Martin guitar companies. Later in life Ernie would often plan a summer vacation to visit the Martin factory to spend time with his friend Fred Martin.

Ralph Wells Jr.

Ralph Wells Sr.

When Ralph and I were at slot-racing events our conversations always turned to bands and pop music. One day Ralph asked me if I would like to play guitar in a band he was trying to put together with drummer Ron Wolfe and a lead guitarist. I didn't feel I had enough experience, but Ralph and Ron had heard me play and felt that if I worked on the material I'd be just fine. They were five or six years older than I

7

was. I was beginning my sophomore year in high school,1965. Ya, there was a big age difference , but the draw and the chance to play rock 'n roll negated any issues regarding age. Ralph and Ron didn't have any issues with it, so why not? We practiced in Ralph's dad's violin repair shop which was located on the second floor of a Main Street business. It was a long haul, lugging our amps and equipment up that seemingly endless flight of stairs, but it never bothered us we wanted to play!

During our first week together, we had two rehearsals, then played our first gig, which was at the *Richmond House* on highway 89, just outside of Whitewater. The band didn't have a name, but we knew twelve or fifteen songs, all instrumentals, and played them over and over to fulfill our four hour night. We played songs like *Walk Don't Run, Green Onions, and Wipe Out.* The people at the bar enjoyed us. We didn't get paid for playing, but it was so much fun, I could have cared less.

Our lead guitar player left the group after that first gig. Ron, Ralph and I still wanted to play, so the three of us continued to rehearse at Ralph's father's violin repair shop and began looking for a lead guitar player.

On a Thursday night, early in September, we were practicing downtown in Mr. Well's repair shop. It happened to be , *Freshman Night,* a night when local merchants welcomed the incoming UW Freshman class to downtown Whitewater. The small downtown area was packed with freshmen. The three of us decided to take advantage of the situation. We opened the windows facing Main Street and placed our amps and the drums as close to them as we could, then began playing every tune we knew. We were hoping to get some exposure, land some gigs, meet girls, or just have fun. (Maybe someone would even discover us!) Well, nothing like that happened, but we did find a guitar player, or did a guitar player find us?

Fall 1965 - The Band Comes Together...

Doug Henry – Lead Guitar
The only problem was, I played cornet

Doug: "I grew up in South Milwaukee, Wisconsin. I began playing the cornet [trumpet] at age eleven in the 6th grade, and have been playing musical instruments ever since. I continued playing the cornet throughout high school in South Milwaukee and in my senior year I added the baritone at the request of the band teacher because there was only one baritone player. While playing the cornet and baritone I was asked to play in the *South Milwaukee Municipal Band.* This was an honor as I was the youngest member. The band was made up of South Milwaukee alumni past the age of 60. I got to travel with the band and played in a concert at the *1964 World's Fair* in New York. That was really exciting.

My friend and neighbor, Don Schmidt, played saxophone in the high school band at South Milwaukee, and also in a rock band. Don invited me to join him at practices and eventually to their gigs because we hung out together and it gave me something to do. I would help them set up and tear down. The band even gave me one of their cream-colored blazers to wear. I thought that was really cool.

They had worked up a song by Eddie Cochran called "*Summertime Blues*" a big hit in 1960. There was a low verbal bass part in the song. One night after practice Don and I were riding home and I told him, "That verbal bass part isn't low enough. I can do it lower." He told me to go ahead and try it at the next practice. So at the next practice I got my real low voice going and the band went nuts. From that time on I got to go up on stage wearing my blazer and do that one song with the band. I was hooked on this "rock thing." The only problem was, I played cornet.

I told my mom I wanted to learn to play a guitar so I could play in a band. With money I had saved from delivering newspapers, and with the help of my mom, I bought a 3-pick-up Kay electric guitar for $100.00. This was 1963.

I bought a beginner's guitar book and learned three chords very quickly. I thought I was ready for my buddy Don's band that had lost its rhythm guitar player. Unfortunately, only knowing three chords and not being able to change chords real fast didn't cut it, and they found someone else.

But I was determined to play in a band, so I went out and bought all the band books I could find, then took guitar lessons, and played and played. A guitar playing friend who had a rock band agreed to give me lessons. One year from the time I bought my first guitar, I was teaching at a guitar studio in South Milwaukee."

Memories From Doug's Brother and Sister

Gayle Henry-Kay, Doug's sister: *"I liked it when my brother's band would play in our basement because our floor would vibrate from* the loudness. I remember my Mom cringing when the hearse, that carried their equipment, would pull into the driveway. I also remember my Dad yelling at Doug to get a haircut. I really did like "Fly My Paper Airplane," and I still have the 45. It was cool to say my brother made a record."

Brian Henry, Doug's brother: "As far back as I can remember Doug had a guitar in his hands and an old reel-to-reel tape recorder filled with his "practice" sessions. I remember "winning" a guitar drawing at a local clothing store and it quickly became Doug's guitar. All his practicing and dedication evolved into his high school band known as the Crescents. It was really cool for me having the older high school kids (including two varsity basketball players and a cheerleader) hanging around our house for the practice sessions.

Once he got to college it was obvious The Mourning Dayze was a very high quality band with talented and dedicated musicians. It was quite a sight and very exciting to see the guys pull up to our home in blue collar South Milwaukee in the band's converted hearse.

The one thing that sticks out in my mind is how much fun the band always seemed to be having, both when they were playing and when they were just sitting around. One could sense there wasn't anything they would rather be doing than singing and playing music.

I'm five years younger than Doug and on two separate occasions The Mourning Dayze played at special event dances at South Milwaukee High School. It made me very proud when my fellow classmates told me how impressed they were with the band.

I always enjoyed the stories of the band's travels around the country and the various artists who were performing at the same venues.

To this day, Doug has never lost his enthusiasm for putting on the guitar shoulder strap and playing some of his favorite tunes. Everyone should be so lucky to have something they love doing so much."

Doug: "Next, I hooked up with my first band called *The Crescents*. In the fall of 1965, I entered the University of Wisconsin at Whitewater, Wisconsin. My goal was to join a rock band, or start one ASAP.

This takes me to Freshman Night in downtown Whitewater and meeting Rick, Ron & Ralph. I heard them from the street, and went up the stairs to the room where they were playing. I introduced myself and gave them some info on my music experience. Ron volunteered to take me to

11

my dorm to get my guitar and amp."

Rick: "Ralph and I were pretty excited while waiting for Ron and Doug to come back. Here was a guy from Milwaukee who had experience playing in a band, knew instrumentals, had his own equipment and was looking for a band to work with. Wow! Just what we were looking for. When they came back, we were full of anticipation and getting more excited by the moment. Doug came up the stairs carrying a beautiful Gibson Invader amp and when he opened his guitar case, wow, there was a guitar that had three pick-ups on it! Doug knew lots of instrumentals and began to show us his stuff by playing some of them for us. Ron, Ralph and I looked at each other and we didn't have to say a word- man, this guy sounds great! Doug sounded just like the guys on the records we were listening to! Some of the tunes Doug played were, Pipeline, Wipe Out, Moon Race, Sleep Walk, Tear Drop, Lariat, and Let's Go Trippin'. Then we took some tunes we all knew and played them together as a band. Hey, I think we even surprised ourselves by just how good we sounded!

As our first night together came to an end, it was clear that we'd like to have Doug join our band and that Doug wanted to play with us. We scheduled another rehearsal to begin to really learn Doug's instrumentals; our band was coming together."

Doug and Rick performing at the Best Western Convention
Monona Terrace, Madison, Wisconsin, 2008

In December, 2007, Doug was attending a Best Western conference in Montreal, Canada. Surf songs were being played and Doug is thinking, " I could do better myself." He then got an idea. He approached some Best Western corporate personnel and requested permission for Rick and

12

him to play at the upcoming Best Western convention to be held in May, 2008 in Madison, Wisconsin. (They played some of the same songs they played that very first Freshmen Night.)

    Rick: "At our next rehearsal we began to talk about the need to have a singer in the band. We all knew it would take more than us playing instrumentals to get the kind of bookings we hoped for. I was able to sing three songs which we learned, but we needed more than that. An experienced singer is what we really needed. Well, check this out...

    A couple of weeks after Doug came on board, Steve Ellmann, like Doug, a freshman at the University of Wisconsin at Whitewater, stopped in "Wells' House of Music" to check out the local music scene. They began talking about their musical backgrounds and interests. Steve began talking about being a drummer and singer in bands prior to coming to Whitewater. Ralph could hardly contain himself because the band needed a singer and this guy could be it! Ralph began talking about the band he was putting together and the fact that he had a drummer, and was now looking for a singer. Ralph invited Steve to come to our next rehearsal to see if he'd be interested in joining us. Steve accepted.

    Steve made the long climb up the steps to "Wells' Violin Repair Shop" which was our rehearsal hall. Ron, Ralph, Doug and I were pretty excited about the possibility of us working with an experienced singer. When Steve arrived, introductions were made; then it was down to the business of what kind of music do you like and "what songs do you know, that we would know?". Ron, Ralph and Doug were familiar with nearly all of the songs Steve knew. Ok, well that's good, but what songs can we play that Steve can sing? Steve asked if we knew "Love Potion #9." Doug, Ralph and Ron knew it but I didn't, so I got a quick lesson from Doug. (something that would be repeated many times our first year together) *Now, before a singer can sing and be heard over the decibel level of a live band, he needs to use a microphone. Simple enough, and that mic has to be plugged into some sort of amplifying system, yip, got that. Most bands at that time, did not have dedicated P.A. Systems, they would plug their mic's into their guitar amplifiers. Tone wasn't much of an issue, volume and being heard were. Many bands playing large venues in the 60's would often complain that their crowds were so loud, they would drown out the band. Sound reinforcement was in its infancy.* Steve plugged his mic into one of our amps, then spoke those words... "testing, testing, one two three." We were ready. Ron counted the tune off, Doug

13

hit the opening chord, Ralph and I came in and Steve began singing......Wow! He sounded fantastic, had presence, attitude, a bit of an edge as well strong leadership qualities. If you're going to perform in front of people these traits are indispensable; it's no place to be shy. Steve enjoyed what we were doing as well.

It was a fun, loose, let's take care of business atmosphere. Steve agreed to join the band as lead singer.

We had a band!

Steve Ellmann   Ron Wolfe   Ralph Wells   Doug Henry   Rick Pfeifer
Rehearsing in Wells' Violin Repair Shop

Steve Ellmann – Lead Singer/Drums
Dad saves the day

Steve: "I grew up in Oconto, Wisconsin, which is part of the Green Bay metropolitan area. My influence in music was very diverse. I grew up with the music of the 40's while listening to my dad's band. Later, I played in his band. I always liked big band music-Glen Miller, etc., as well as the alternative stuff like Cab Calloway.

All the kids in my family were required to begin learning the piano in 1st grade, and then a band instrument in the 3rd grade. I played piano until 8th grade. I chose the trumpet as my band instrument.

I had respect for classical music. I grew up singing Bach and Beethoven in a male church choir where I was the featured soloist. I also liked Perry Como and Andy Williams My pop music favorite was the Dave Clark Five. My introduction to rock 'n roll was a DJ from Green Bay named, "Johnny Sax; the Sax with the wax appeal". I used to put my transistor radio under the covers and listen to all of the new tunes late into the night. I knew, already then, what I would be doing soon. I spent my adolescent years playing music, and to this day, I am more comfortable playing on stage than I am dancing on the dance floor.

My first musical group was a trio called PEP's. It consisted of a guitar, bass and drums. I played in that band between the ages of 12 and

15

15. We played our first "gig" on a flatbed trailer for a fashion show. We only knew three songs, and played them over and over throughout the show as the girls paraded by in their new fashions. Before the "gig," I was in the basement of our house getting my drum kit "looking good." My kit consisted of a huge bass drum (taken from a merry-go-round), a thin wooden snare, and a marching cymbal wired to a metal music stand. I was very nervous as I was getting ready to bring the kit upstairs to load into my buddy's car for the "gig." My father appeared at the top of the stairs, and in a very firm voice said, "Where are you going with those?" I answered, proudly, that I was going to my "gig." He said, "You're not leaving this house with those drums." I was devastated. His face softened, and he said, "You can use mine." He owned a brand new set of Slingerland Blue-Pearl Finish drums. I thought I had died and gone to heaven.

Throughout my musical career, my father promoted my playing, except when I was practicing licks from the great rock drummer, Sandy Nelson, in the basement at 10:00 or 11:00 in the evening. My father co-signed a loan for my first drums-a Rogers Mardi Gras Pearl Finish set. This is the set that I played while with Mourning Dayze. I have used several other sets, but , to this day, I still have my original kit, and was given my dad's set when he passed away.

After that I joined a band called "J and the Tempests." I stayed with them until I turned 18. With "J and the Tempests" after our first set at a club the owner came up to the whole band and said, "come here you guys, I'm buying you all a shot, drink up! You sound great but you've got to loosen up and have some fun up there!" We drank up, loosened up, and had some fun playing, the club owner and patrons could tell the difference. Thanks to that club owner we learned there was more to being a successful band than just sounding good and playing tunes people enjoyed: you also needed to genuinely have fun on stage. We played all over Central and Northern Wisconsin. When I went to college at Whitewater the band dissolved. While at college, before I connected with Ralph, Ron, Rick and Doug, I played gigs with all types of bands set up through the musicians' union. I played with "old time" bands that featured standards from the 40's as well as a polka band, my father's band, and several others."

The Coachmen

Now that we'd agreed to become a band, we needed to work on building our set list, figure out what equipment we'd need, how we'd get ourselves and equipment to gigs and most importantly, give our band a name. We rehearsed four times a week for the first two weeks at "Wells' Violin Repair Shop." Steve and Doug, having experience playing in their respective bands, found themselves knowing many of the same songs; this allowed us to build our set list quickly with songs that had been road tested on the dance floor. Ralph, Ron and I contributed to the growing set list as well. "As lead singer and frontman, Steve brought a lot of personality and stage presence to the band. On occasion, he wore white gloves while performing, even rehearsing. (check out the pic of us rehearsing at the violin shop!) We razzed him about that, and still do. We would soon find that Steve was a natural at handling the business end of the band as well as the dealings with club owners, which is an art as well as a skill. Steve fell very naturally into the bands leadership role. We still needed to name the band.

During a rehearsal we spent some time trying on different names and just couldn't agree on anything. It was Doug who offered up the name "The Coachmen." *Which may have had something to do with Doug's love of fine luxury automobiles. Several years later with Doug's eye and initiative, the band would buy a 1957 Cadillac hearse. At that time he was driving a 1958 Buick Roadmaster, silver. Doug, "with air shocks, which were something when they deflated, a radio scanner and a back seat that was displaced from the front seat just like a limo."* We all liked it, the name stuck, we were "The Coachmen."

Rick Pfeifer   Ron Wolfe   Steve Ellmann   Doug Henry   Ralph Wells

After two weeks of rehearsals, we suddenly found ourselves landing our first gig at Nora's Store on highway 12 between Cambridge and Madison. Our second gig was at Whitewater's Hawk Bowl, thanks to Dave Kachel. Man, were we excited! We each made $15.00, I could not believe we were getting paid to play music! "Money for nothin' and the chick's for free." This would be the first of many gigs played at the Hawk between 1965 and 1974. We were on our way. *The Hawk Bowl, a local venue during the 60's and early 70's, regularly ran some of the best live entertainment in the area and drew great crowds from the university and surrounding area.*

Whitewater's icon, Dave Kachel, supported us throughout our history. Not only did Dave give us our start, legendary Wisconsin booking agent Ken Adamany credits Dave with helping him as well. "He helped me get started with live music at The Hawk Bowl in 1959. I remember him with great respect, as a tough, but fair negotiator who didn't seem to mind loud Rock and Roll." (1)

Kachel, a 1948 UW-Whitewater graduate, donated millions of dollars to the university over the years, supporting building projects for athletics, arts and academics. These include the DLK/Kachel Fieldhouse, the Kachel Family Sports Complex, the Kachel Center in the Young Auditorium, and the Kachel Center for Entrepreneurship. Gifts from the Kachel family support numerous student scholarships annually. Mr. Kachel truly loved Whitewater and the university. (2) Dave's son Jon, who's followed in his father's footsteps with his own vision, asked one day if I knew that "Bill Haley and the Comets" had played the Hawk Bowl. I didn't, but thought it was a great piece of Whitewater's diverse and interesting musical legacy.

Our gig at the Hawk went well, people were dancing and having fun, the owner liked us and we had a ball. We had no P.A. system at that time. We plugged our mics directly into our guitar amps. As long as the singing could be heard over the music, we thought we were doin' just fine. Soon after our debut at the Hawk, we got a gig to play at one university dorm party, then another. Word was getting around, "there's a new band on campus." We were playing fraternity and sorority parties on and off campus. Having a live rock 'n roll band at your party meant you were "hip," "in the know," part of "the scene," and "where the action was." The demand for live bands was often greater than the supply. When word of mouth got around an area that a good band was playing that meant big crowds, it was the place to be. Word of mouth is how much of the popular culture was spread. Sure, there were the radio DJs, posters and ads in the papers, but the word of mouth had real power to inform and persuade. Doug, "I could see a lot of potential in our little group, and after Steve joined the band as the lead singer, things began to happen. We got more gigs, and soon we were playing on campus. It was a natural high for me being recognized as a "rock musician" on campus. The guys in the dorm nicknamed me "Elvis." I was on my way."

We played anywhere we could, for anyone who would have us. We used Ralph's fathers van for a while to get us and our equipment to gigs, for which we were grateful. Once we all froze going to a gig at Appleton's Darboy Club; those early vans didn't have much for heat in them. We even took the cowl off the engine to try to warm up, but we really didn't mind, we had a gig. During those first few months we gigged a lot. I'll never forget the frat gig we played in Johnson Creek. When we went to set-up, there was no riser for Ron and his drums, instead, there were tables put together for him to set his kit on! Somehow Ron found a way around that one.

To avoid climbing all those stairs at "Wells' Violin Repair Shop" and to accommodate everyone's schedule we rehearsed at Ron's parents house one Saturday afternoon. In order for me to rehearse with the band, my mom (usually known as Betty) delivered all 82 papers on my paper route. And yes, Ron's house was on my route. Betty no doubt heard us practicing. *Throughout her lifetime and dad's, each would give all they could, no matter what it might be, to support their children's hopes and dreams. The band and all of its members and friends were also part of their family. Regardless of circumstances everyone was always welcome and loved. Mom and dad could see we were having fun and just loved to play. They could see that we really took care of business and that our playing was making other people happy.*

It was common for us to check out other bands that were playing in the area. We were lucky, not only did the Hawk Bowl run some great entertainment, we also had the University, which brought in national acts, the biggest in regional names and the best from the area. We could watch how these successful groups went about their business and incorporated what we could, into our group. It was a great way to get a feel for the "scene" in talking with other bands about what was "hot" regarding equipment, music, agents and places to play.

The night we, the band, saw Milwaukee's "Sam McCue and Legends" play at the University in Whitewater was a game changer. I was familiar with the "Legends" through my cousin Melody who lived in Waukesha WI. and like many, loved being a hip teenager. One of her loves was dancing; she always seemed aware of the latest dances and hottest tunes to dance to. She owned the "Legends" Capitol LP release "Let Loose," released in 1962. Mel would play and dance to it over and over when she came to Whitewater to stay with Betty for a few days. Mel would talk of the "Legends" consistently packing the Muskego Beach Ballroom and how they were, without a doubt, the best band in the area. And to think the "Legends" were, right here in Whitewater. They played at the UW student union and the house was rockin': they sounded like stars and looked like it too! I had just bought a new amp which my mom and dad had co-signed for. It was a Silvertone 1485 six ten 100 watt amp which Ralph had in his store. On this night, Sam McCue's amp stopped working in the middle of their set. We went right to the stage and began talking with Sam to see if we could lend a hand. Sam ended up playing through my Silvertone amp for the rest of the night: it never sounded better! Sam was very thankful for our help, and we had made a connection. Ralph and I would travel to watch, listen and talk to the "Legends" whenever we could. That group made a huge impression on me. It demonstrated to me what an elite, live band sounded like, plus I could see how a bands dress made a huge statement about the group itself, and best of all what a great a live guitar player sound like.

We were getting to be well known on campus and were getting a lot of local work, but all too aware that in order to get ourselves on a bigger stage, we'd need a booking agent. Why? Because all of the top area bands had an agent. Smiles. We knew many of the working bands in the area were using the Ken Adamany agency out of Janesville WI. It seemed like a very logical step for us to talk with him and see what the world of talent agents was all about. It was probably Steve, our leader, who called Ken to introduce himself and the band to get a feel for the culture, environment and expectations.

SAMMY McCUE AND THE LEGENDS

Teen Bars

What made Wisconsin rock? *Doug: "The "beer bar" or "teen bar" as they were called in Wisconsin in the 1960's was an open avenue for garage bands to be able to perform in front of enthusiastic audiences, be monetarily compensated for their performances, and allowed them to develop an identity regarding their style of music to thousands of fans across the state. This ultimately led to recording offers and opened doors with booking agents to explore boundaries beyond Wisconsin. Such was the case with our band, The Mourning Dayze.*

Teen bars were bars in which only beer was served and you had to be 18 years of age. Not all cities/counties o.g., Milwaukee and Whitewater (Walworth County) had this law to be able to serve patrons under the age of 21. You had to venture out to surrounding counties to patronize these establishments and witness live entertainment. Most of these establishments would run entertainment 3 to 6 nights a week. And there were hundreds of these bars across Wisconsin. Neighboring states did not offer this venue, a situation which only added to the draw of patrons crossing the state lines to the teen bars and the entertainment they provided.

In the 60's hundreds of bands were formed. Bands such as ours were able to "crack the circuit" by means of a booking agent, Ken Adamany, of whom the Grim Reapers (later Cheap Trick) was part of the agency. To stay in an agency and remain in the teen bar circuit was entirely dependent upon the popularity of your group which translated into how many dollars the club owner was bringing in the door.

You could not ask for a better venue. Depending on the town your audience could be college students or young adults that were already in the work field. They were totally knowledgeable of the current national music scene and were appreciative of your sound if you were current and performed well. Several times we were approached and thanked for the West coast tunes we performed. This was a little ahead of the times, so to speak, for a Midwest group. Most groups at the time were playing good rock n' roll and soul music. We were able to do that and more.

When it came time for high schools to have special occasions, such as proms or homecoming dances, bands like ours were contacted through our agency because of the popularity that we created at the local teen bars. This also led to gigs at county fairs, city celebrations, and even the State Fair. As confidence grew within the agent we found ourselves

22

performing in Chicago, including the Pandora Box television show which was Chicago's local version of Dick Clark's American Band Stand.

As musicians developing our own sound and exploring more musical challenges it would have been hard to do without the live performances that the teen bars offered. In my opinion there is nothing close to the magnitude of venues and opportunities such as are available today. For us it was never a question of "when we were going to play." It was "where are we playing next!" It wasn't a summer circuit. It was an all-year-round circuit.

The band stayed together for 5 years. This was an exception at the time. Most bands didn't make it to 2 years. This only enhanced our popularity and opportunities which in turn put us in states such as Florida, New York, Nebraska, and Missouri, plus the states that bordered Wisconsin. The teen bar, plus practicing every week and every day on the road, was the initial "ticket" to our success."

One of the unique settings was Woodley's Country Dam in Amery, WI, located in the far north corner of Wisconsin. This unique setting offered a "teen bar" with a liquor bar (21 years of age) connected to each other. This was our encounter with the "Trashmen" of "Bird Is The Word" fame. They performed in the 21-year-old bar while we performed in the "teen bar." We would hang out and talk during our respective breaks. John Valentine, our rhythm guitar, actually bought a used Fender reverb from one of the Trashmen!

This venue attracted a lot of groups from the Twin Cities which played a lot of good old Rock'n Roll. We were doing a lot of Beatles and Yard Birds along with west coast tunes from Spirit, Jefferson Airplane, and The Strawberry Alarm Clock. The "teen" crowd really appreciated this sound along with our psychedelic light show! We believe it was a change from the "blue collar rock'n roll" they were accustomed to.

Several times we played in the Appleton area at the local "teen bars" and also Lawrence University. In most cases it was the same clientele. Because of the age requirement for the "teen bars" many of the students had heard us before we played at their university as was also the case in Oshkosh, Stevens Point, Eau Claire, and Whitewater. The Whitewater students did have to travel out of town and county to patronize "teen bars" because of the local laws.

Baraboo and Sturgeon Bay were not college towns at the time but their clientele consisted of local working people and several college students that were often home for the weekend. It was a good mix which

23

allowed us to perform our west coast sound, British sound, and Rock'n Roll.

When we did Cream, Hendrix, and The Doors we really stood out among other groups that came through these towns.

It was just another example of how the "teen bar" scene allowed us to expand our horizons regarding our repertoire and our ability to perform it in front of enthusiastic crowds. When we spent many hours practicing, we knew we would be rewarded because we knew the "teen bars" would appreciate our efforts. I don't think this would have been possible for us and other groups if it was not for the "teen bars" across the State.

It was not always a guarantee our sound would be accepted by all "teen bar" crowds. Two venues I remember in particular were Nora's Store outside of Cambridge and Weiler's outside of Port Washington. Nora's was close to Madison but did not attract a college crowd. In fact it was just the opposite. But we were accepted and actually invited back. Weiler's was not the same situation. It was a crowd of what at that time we called "greasers" or "hoods" or in other words a rough crowd. We did fine but I believe we decided on our own not to return to that venue!

All garage bands didn't take advantage of the "teen bar" circuit for one reason or another. Some were happy to just stay in their hometown and play the local schools, churches, and private parties. The Mourning Dayze on the other hand "Had Band Will Travel" philosophy. I believe bands that "stayed at home" didn't have the commitment and in some cases the talent to expand their horizons. It took work beyond musical skill to travel to all corners of the state to perform and to engage with agents to send us to these places. It required having a well kept vehicle that could travel 52 weeks a year, staying in motels, practicing on the road, and last but not least it had to be a group effort and commitment or none of this could have taken place. We would hear of bands "fighting and arguing" amongst themselves and never were surprised when we heard of their break-ups. Again, two years together was considered good at the time for garage bands. We were together just over 5 years! Who knows how long the original group would have performed without Vietnam stepping in!

From Monroe to Eagle River to La Crosse to Green Bay the "teen bar" circuit kept us and our music going. Our music went from "Love Portion # 9" to the unique sound of a Wisconsin group called "Soup."

24

From there we started to write and incorporate our own tunes as we were "instructed" to do by our lead guitar player, Rick. Rick assigned us to write at least one song and bring it to the next practice; thus today we have the story and CD of "Lost Recordings."

From Marinette to Marshfield to Manitowoc to Nekoosa there was just no stopping us if there was an opportunity to perform our music in this "teen bar" circuit. It might have been in the heat of summer at Hop's Modernaire outside of Eagle River or below zero temperatures at the Mount View by Rib Mountain in Wausau, not to mention the 25 degrees below zero we encountered in Nakoosa one Christmas day night. It would be interesting to determine the number of thousands of miles we traveled in Wisconsin alone "hitting" the "teen bar/beer bar" circuit!

Afternoons were interesting at the "teen bars." Usually the crowd was big enough to only occupy the stools at the bar and at the game machines. This was the 60's, so pin ball was big-with such games as "Cow-Poke." We would appear about 1PM or so the following day after the gig and prepare to practice. Numerous times we were questioned by the attending patrons "what are you guys doing?" When we informed them we were about to begin to practice and work on some new tunes their reaction was "oh, wow!" Again, this wasn't common practice among other bands and again another example of how we used the "teen bars" to further improve our sound and repertoire.

There were exceptions. If there was a local festival, such as we encountered in Sturgeon Bay, at times we would "skip" the practice and attend the festival and have a "few pops" before the gig. At least I would!

As I stated earlier, the "teen bar" circuit was such a unique venue for garage bands during the 60's that it will probably never be witnessed again. Because of the times and laws of today we will never experience this type of era again. This is not to say that current laws are wrong. It is to say that many musicians will not have the opportunity to expose their music and talent to the live audiences that was available way back in the 60's!"

Rick: "Our practices began to incorporate the sounds, ideas and looks of many of the groups we admired. Thinking that we were just as good as they were and just needed to hone our craft, this often meant "imitation" at this point in our lives. I remember how we all got excited when Ralph lent Doug a "Fuzz Tone" to play the lead line to the Stones "Satisfaction," it was a mystery how they got that sound. When Doug plugged the "Fuzz Tone" in and played the line, sounding "just like the record," we were all smiles. And ya, we got group pictures taken in matching burgundy suits with black pants for our promo pics, just like everybody else. But there was something a little different with our group. We had no fear of taking chances or of trying something new, and we followed through with our ideas. By our second or third job we had already begun to play tunes that were popular on the radio and on stage without ever rehearsing them. We were always listening to each other and had fun while working at playing together. This would prove to be big later on when we began to improvise and interpret other people's music and began writing our own stuff. It's amazing to think that, even then, the needs of the band out-weighed the needs of its members. It seemed like we all knew we were doing what we were supposed to be doing and in all phases understood and did what it took to get it done. One thing for sure about us and most other groups-we loved playing for a full dance floor. It also became a real mission for us to do whatever we could to keep the dance floor packed from start to finish.

Doug's instrumentals were a big draw for us. People would often come to see us, just to hear Doug play his guitar. Steve fronting the band gave us a "look." Steve was bursting with personality and was very comfortable talking to the audience over the mic, which really helped to develop and cultivate a rapport with the audience and build a fan base. Steve could always handle the usual banter back and forth between the band and crowd as well as the hecklers and disruptors whom he handled with tact and ease. Steve had a presence that people enjoyed and remembered."

Rick was fifteen at this time, and a sophomore at Whitewater High. In order for him to play with these guys, it took the band's bassist, Ralph Wells, who was 21 and the oldest member of the group, to convince Rick's parents that he would take full responsibility to be sure that Rick didn't get involved with drinking, drugs, gambling, or women. Rick's parents believed Ralph would tell them if Rick wasn't following "the rules'" (and Ralph did do that). Rick was mindful of these "rules," because he was told if he didn't follow them, he would not be able to play in the band. Rick said, " It was rare that I was asked for my I.D. in the bars we played. Occasionally it became an issue. Sometimes before we played a gig we would know we would be "carded." We got around that by having my mom come along with us. Betty probably had more fun than any of us!"

Rick Pfeifer – Rhythm Guitar/Vocals
Sorry coach, I'd rather play guitar

Rick: "As I became drawn to the electric guitar, I began to look
for someone who could teach me how to play the music I was hearing on
the radio. My mother's sister lived in Waukesha and knew of a place that
gave guitar lessons, the Waukesha Music Center. My teacher was Floyd
Jester, who could teach contemporary styles of the day. Other students
had told me that he had taken some lessons from the legendary guitarist
Les Paul. Floyd proved to be the perfect teacher for me. Not only was he
a very fine guitarist, he also played in a band, could read and understand
music, and could learn to play songs by ear by listening to records and
songs I wanted to learn that were played on the radio. This was an eye
opener for me. I thought you learned to play music by learning to read
music. I had no interest in playing lead guitar at that time. I wanted to
play rhythm so I could accompany myself while I sang. It wasn't until
later in life that I learned to play instrumental music on the guitar.

My first electric guitar was recommended to my mother by Floyd.
He felt a Les Paul Jr. would be a good electric guitar for me to begin with.
It cost $179 and came with a cardboard case. (I don't think it came with a
pick, strap or easy chord picture chart!) My mom paid for it with her
earnings from her waitress work. I did not appreciate then how much she
sacrificed for me I didn't have a clue, I do now. She and my dad took
turns driving me to Waukesha for guitar lessons every week, regardless of

27

the weather.

Dad worked at a local gas station, Williams' Cities Service, where the radio was always on playing country/western, pop music and Milwaukee Brave's baseball. Many times I went with him Saturday nights and he'd be listening to the WGN Barn Dance. I'm sure I must have begged him to change the station to WLS in Chicago, but it didn't happen on those nights. It wasn't until later in life that I was grateful for the exposure.

In sixth grade, I began delivering newspapers. The first thing I bought with my first paycheck was a transistor radio. Then I could listen to rock 'n roll radio while I delivered papers and after hours at home.

I not only met Ron Wolfe on my paper route but also Robert E. Lee. The Lee house was the home of the three Lee kids, Bob, Dick and Ellie. We used to talk together while I delivered papers, but we never "hung out." Their father was a professional clown with Ringling Brothers Circus and did clowning locally as "Cousin Otto." Little did I know then, but beginning in 1972, Bob Lee would play drums with Mourning Dayze for the next five years.

In seventh or eigth grade, I met Denny Ketterman. Denny and I became friends; we also played in the percussion section throughout High School. In years to come, Denny would also play drums with Mourning Dayze.

My seventh grade band director, Mac Davidson, would prove to be an inspiration for my entire life. He was always supportive of my musical pursuits and seemed to understand the inner part of me that wanted to do nothing but play and be involved with music. He was someone I trusted and believed in. Unlike many well educated musicians at that time, who often didn't have much good to say about rock and roll, Mr. Davidson took it as another form of music. Mr. Davidson played a house gig at the Sterlingworth Resort on Lauderdale Lakes located in Elkhorn, Wisconsin, for a dozen years or so. Little did I know then that one day Mourning Dayze would share the stage with him and his band for nearly five summers. We played Sunday through Thursday and his band played Friday and Saturday. He often came to hear us play, and would always appreciate and comment on the finer points of our sound, which we had worked quite hard on to achieve. He was so encouraging and always square with us. That meant a lot.

In Junior High, my choral teacher introduced me to the world of international music. I've been in love with it ever since. The variety,

28

diversity, freshness, and depth is a never-ending source of inspiration and creativity. The infinite ways which one can use to express oneself through music are amazing. They demonstrate time and time again that we are only limited by our imaginations.

Another huge musical influence was Phil Suzie, a college student who rented a room from my parents. Phil loved classical music and played it all the time. I couldn't help but hear it. I used to tell him it sounded terrible and that he should listen to rock 'n roll 'cause that's where it's at. Later in life, I came to love classical music. I wonder if Phil's record collection impacted my taste in music? I'm sure it did.

Dale Spencer, also a student at Whitewater, rented a room at Queen Street. Dale has been a life- long friend of the family, a great guy. Dale asked me if I knew the jazz great Wes Montgomery. I didn't have a clue. Dale told me I needed to become familiar with him, which I did. I've been forever grateful. Not only did I become aware of Wes Montgomery, but I also became aware of jazz. Thanks Dale!

Ollie Klogne was another college student who rented a room at our house. Ollie loved to sing in choirs and barbershop quartets. He taught me this: "When a person can read music, it provides an access point to nearly all of the world's music." It was quite a revelation, and really made an impact on how I approached written music."

Looking back...2014

Rick: *"For anything I've accomplished, I have my family to thank. I was born into a family whose unconditional love was always present. I experienced love without fear and knew pure joy. It was how we lived. I was never discouraged with trying to find who I was and what I was about. No matter what path I chose, I was always encouraged. I've been in love with music as far back as I can remember. That love has never stopped. It has only continued to grow and expand. I feel if each of us does our very best in sharing what we love, it will surely, in some way, on some level, make our world just a little bit better.*

To my band mates. I've learned from each of you. When you listen to my sequences or me playing solo, with Rise or the band, you will find part of you in what I play. I am sincerely grateful to all I've worked and crossed paths with. Thank you."

The Coachmen

This photo of the "Coachmen" was taken at the Whitewater armory New Year's Eve, December 31, 1965. The headstock of Ralph's bass guitar can be seen on the far left. Ron is on drums, Doug is in the center playing lead guitar, Rick is to his right and playing his Gibson Les Paul Jr., Steve is singing and fronting the band. The band has yet to purchase a PA system and is still singing through their guitar amps. About this same time, Rick and Ralph went to watch a band "from Chicago" play this same venue and to their amazement, they had a PA system dedicated to vocals. They couldn't wait to tell the rest of the band. Rick, "now this was "big," we really felt if we were going to compete, we needed to keep up technologically and use the best equipment we could afford." As a band we wanted to stay on top of current musical trends-that included equipment. We needed a PA. system.

I'm not sure where we bought our first PA, which was a Gibson, with 2 ten inch speakers per side. It proved to be a controversial purchase. Ralph's father, to the best of my memory, would no longer let us rehearse in his shop because we had bought it from another dealer, or because it was a Gibson or something. Regardless, we could no longer rehearse in his shop. We did rehearse in Ralph's father's living room after that, Ron's house, my family home and later on Steve's family home and Doug's as well. Having rehearsal space is as important as having gigs. (We were yet to rehearse in a garage, but that was coming!)

The Coachmen playing at UW-Whitewater's student union using their first PA.
Ralph, Doug, Rick. Steve and his drum kit are fronting the band.

Ron left the "Coachmen" in maybe January or February 1966. Ron has run off to tour with Uncle Sam. Ron has been part of the Mourning Dayze family ever since. His love and enthusiasm for music and drumming has not dimmed. Occasionally Ron will stop in to see the current version of Mourning Dayze, and it's always very good to see him. Ron is a founding member of our family.

Ron Wolfe playing with the Whitewater High School Alumni Band

So...we began to discuss our next move, we needed a drummer.

But, hey, we have a drummer, who's also our lead singer. Steve brought up the idea right away that he could sing and play drums. (odd, I never knew drummers sang!) Wow, what a cool idea! Steve seemed to know just how it would be done and jumped right on that horse. He was a natural at singing and drumming, which requires high levels of concentration and physical endurance. It's work enough just to play drums; now think about it; add aggressive singing along with that, now that's a man load-o-work. Steve did it with ease and made it look easy.

Rick: "With Steve singing and playing drums, the band began to develop its own sound, its own way of playing and working together. We were always able to talk with one another. We were open with each other and put the group's needs before our own. It was always, "what's best for the band?" musically and business-wise. All of us were dedicated to almost business-like rehearsals. We were on a mission. This attitude seemed part of our collective experience as to how to be successful. It was a very natural way for us to be. We also had a whole lot of fun!"

Getting Gigs

Doug: *"A garage band from the '60's creates a long trail before "making it." Playing for any crowd or gathering in any venue is the initial goal of a garage band. But first you actually have to form a band that is capable of the feat. It all starts with days and nights of practice in a "garage" or "basement" or "storeroom" or "living room" as was the case with the Mourning Dayze. The best sound that follows this commitment is "we have a job!" This means we are going to perform for an audience and get paid for it!*

This is the start. It comes from somebody that knows somebody that is looking for a band to perform. The first gig you perform for dollars is really scary. You don't know if you are ready for this reward and the entity hiring you has never heard you because you haven't played anywhere. But you have to take the offer and that's the start! You get paid in cash for this at the end of the night and now you feel you have "made it! Little did we know what we had started and how far we would actually end up going. What a great journey it was!

We were all fired up after our first gig and wanted more gigs and enjoyed the monetary reward that came with this neat "job." But gigs don't fall out of the sky. You need somebody out there "knocking on doors" as you do in any business. A booking agent (talent agent) isn't interested in

*you because you haven't played anywhere so to speak so they can't sell
you to club owners and other venues that hire bands. So you start with a
manager that believes in you and has the skills to "sell your goods" and
gets your foot in the door. This is the route we took with a person we met,
Wally Jones.*

*From Whitewater we started playing in Milwaukee at "Papa
Joe's", and the Wisconsin Dells at "Vans." All this because we had a
person that believed in us and was "knocking on doors." At times we
asked Wally, "are you sure we are ready for these places?" "Oh yeah,
they'll love you!" he would respond. I don't believe we had ever met a
person with the energy and support that was provided by Wally. It seemed
that these gigs started to "snowball." We didn't play every week but we
always had a gig on the horizon."*

It's uncertain how we met him, but one day we met Wally Jones.
Wally became our self appointed "manager." Wally introduced Doug to
Jerry Walker and they quickly became friends. This is significant because
Jerry was from Baraboo, Wisconsin, enjoyed live music and highly
encouraged the band to come up and play the great clubs in the
Wisconsin Dells and Baraboo area. Which we did.

Lyle Ernst: "Mike's Teen Bar" and "Fischer's Teen Bar" were
"The" places for teenagers in Baraboo in the '60's. But the Highway
House proved to be the most memorable for the boys from Whitewater.
Traveling the highways and byways of Wisconsin under the banner of the
Coachmen, the guys played one of their memorable gigs in 1966. The
occasion was the birthday of Dave Dembroski, owner of the liquor store in
Baraboo. Betty and Ray drove all the way from Whitewater for this
momentous occasion. Doug was out in the audience playing his guitar
that was strung with a 35-foot bright red cord. Those were the days before
cordless. The next day, Jerry Walker, a friend of the band who lived in
Baraboo, reported that 23 half-barrels of beer were drunk that previous
evening." The band woke up the following morning in a tiny house trailer
in the middle of the field where the party had been. There was not a soul
around, just the remains of a great party. Somewhere in the background
someone was playing Johnny Rivers' "The Poor Side of Town."

This would be the beginning of a remarkable relationship between
the Coachmen/Mourning Dayze and theWisconsin Dells/Baraboo area.
Over the next four years during the tourist season, but not exclusively, the
band was a regular fixture in the area. We played to packed houses at
Van's, Chula Vista, The Del View, the youth center, and street dances for

summer festivals. They played to full houses at Baraboo's Highway House. Years later Rick would go to the Highway House to see Doug play with Myrtle Moon Pickle in the upstairs bar. One night after a gig at Fischer's Bar in Baraboo, the band was driving down highway 113 and had bottles being thrown at their hearse. The band reported the incident and it was in the paper the following day. (And we thought the crowd loved us!)

Doug recalls one of their many great gigs in the Dells. "In March of 1967 Jimi Hendrix released a single called "Purple Haze" in the UK. It made it over to the US in June of that year. It was a psychedelic tune that would become one of most famous psychedelic tunes of all time and end up on the Jimi Hendrix Experience album. There was also a new Beer/Teen Bar about to open in the Wisconsin Dells area just west of Lake Delton on highway 23 called the Purple Haze in the summer of '67. We, the "Mourning Dayze," were booked to open this club. Our reputation as a psychedelic band had spread throughout Wisconsin by this time. With our psychedelic light show that included our strobe light we headed to the Wisconsin Dells area to open this club. Because of our several appearances in this area we were no strangers to the locals and were quite popular in the area. The club had a sunken-dance floor about six feet below the stage and bar area that was circular. They had a good light system of their own in the club. The club was packed as we prepared to play our first tune. You guessed it. We opened with "Purple Haze"! After 40 plus years I can still remember the "electricity" in the room from that night!"

Rick: "In the summer of '66 the Coachmen played Palmyra for a city-wide festival, on the back of a flat bed truck. The people that we played for seemed to think we were "stars" and treated us accordingly. Hmm? The crowd went crazy when they played "Summer in the City" and "Wild Thing." Papa Joe's on Bluemound in Brookfield was the first gig we played six nights in a row and long hours, the first of many."
Doug: "I'd get home at 3 in the morning and had to be on a mission row for my fruit market job at 5a.m.!" *The band's un-relentless drive to gig was never hampered by the obstacles or responsibilities life would confront them with. This attitude prevailed for the lifetime of the band in all they did.* We thought this gig would be our "breakthrough" gig in Milwaukee. The band played Majestic Hills ski resort, Lake Geneva, playing inside the chalet, not in the music theatre. This would be a memorable gig for two reasons. Once Rick convinced his mother to let him take her prized organ out of the living room and to the job. He also

convinced the band he would be able to seamlessly play on a select number of tunes, even though they'd never rehearsed with an organ. Betty's organ was used for the job, which went well. The organ expanded the group's sound. The band soon bought an AceTone compact organ from Crown Music in Milwaukee, doing, once again, what ever they could to improve themselves.

The Ace Tone compact organ

Lyle Ernst: "This first summer the band was together, Rick and Ralph went on a road trip to book gigs. They started in Milwaukee and worked their way up the coast to Green Bay. "We didn't have the money to stay at a motel," says Rick. "We slept in Ralph's car and cleaned up in gas station bathrooms. We got quite a few jobs for our efforts." The most significant place they got a gig was a place called "The Old House" near Port Washington, just north of Milwaukee. One gig they booked they'll never forget was "Weiler's Teen Bar". **Doug:** "The expression, "this was a rough place" is an understatement." The owner hired about two dozen sheriff's deputies on a nightly basis because the crowd was made up of mostly "greasers" from Milwaukee. This was one of the infamous bars that had chicken wire surrounding the stage to protect the band from flying beer bottles. There were numerous fights. Doug recalls one night when two guys broke their beer bottles and went after each other. "We kept on playing, as we were instructed to, when fights broke out." Thank you deputies! Rick was 16 and was told by Doug to sit back-stage during their breaks to avoid the chance of being "carded."

On Freshmen night 1965, Ralph, Ron, and Rick were in "Wells' Violin Repair Shop" trying to figure out how to keep their band together.

One year later; as the "Coachmen," Ralph, Rick, Doug, and Steve, were hired by the City of Whitewater to play downtown for Freshman night. The band was beginning to generate a "buzz" and their popularity was growing. Social change was making its presence felt in all aspects of life. The pop music scene was spreading "the word," promoting and supporting the ideals-freedom for all individuals, the basic right of being told the truth and to question authority. Musical creativity was happening everywhere. Dylan went electric in '65. The Beatles and the Stones and the Byrds played a style that would be labeled "folk rock." Simon and Garfunkel were popular, and the Beach Boys released "Pet Sounds" in 66 to list just a few new groups. It was an amazing time.

Wikipedia says-"The Sixties", as they are known in both scholarship and popular culture, is a term used by historians, journalists, and other objective academics-in some cases nostalgically to describe the counterculture and revolution in social norms about clothing, music, drugs, dress, formalities, and schooling. Conservatives denounce the decade as one of irresponsible excess, flamboyance, and decay of social order. The decade was also labeled the Swinging Sixties because of the fall or relaxation of social taboos, especially relating to racism and sexism that occurred during this time." (3)

The band was not politically driven but did embrace the ideals of social change regarding personal freedom and equality. We enjoyed wearing "mod" clothing, mainly because it was so radically different than anything we'd ever seen before and just another way to break free from social constraints. It looked cool and we loved having fun.

The "Coachmen"
Ralph, Rick, Steve, and Doug

This picture was taken in UW-Whitewater's student union nearly one year after their first pro-mo shot for their "Coachmen" 8x10's. What a difference in style, clothes, some of which are "mod", dress and hair!

INTRODUCING
The
Coachmen

TIME:

DATE:

PLACE:

The same photo was used for a band poster in which the band's name was written in psychedelic lettering. Pretty cool, eh?

Ken Adamany Music Enterprises, LTD.

Doug: *"We weren't expecting more than we had for gigs at this time as we were attending college and Rick was still in high school. Steve was from Oconto, Wisconsin, and was living with his grandmother in Whitewater and I was living in a dorm. Steve's grandmother went out of town for a long weekend and Steve and I decided to invite a couple of girls we met over for a little party. It was a Thursday night which is a normal party night in a college town.*

We were all feeling pretty good and the phone rings. It was about 11:30PM. I heard and saw Steve talking on the phone and it looked pretty serious. He cuffs the mouth piece and turns to me, "do you want to play in Marinette, WI tomorrow night and Saturday?" I said, "yeah, sure!" I heard Steve say, "yeah, Ken, we'll do it." I asked Steve who was that? It was Ken Adamany! Ken Adamany was the number one and best known booking agent in Wisconsin. This opened a whole new world to us and was the start of playing on a weekly basis.

The Adamany Agency was actually located in his home between Milton and Janesville, Wisconsin. He was booking over a hundred bands throughout Wisconsin and the Midwest and beyond. It was a great home with a swimming pool and a room to jam in and I believe he had recording equipment set up in the room also. One time in the summer of '67 we were picking up our contract (legal agreement to perform) for our gig in Clearwater, Florida and ran into Steve Miller and his band and were invited to jam with them.

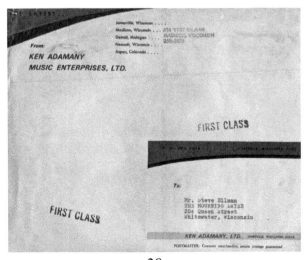

NORTH CENTRAL PRODUCTIONS, INC.
TALENT AGENCY

P. O. BOX 1232
MILWAUKEE, WIS. 53201

STEVE ELLMANN
PHONE 271-0480

During this time Boz Scaggs, The Steve Miller Band, The Grim Reapers (later changed their name to Cheap Trick) and the Mourning Dazye were all in the Adamany Agency. (Cheap Trick and The Steve Miller Band were inducted into the Rock & Roll Hall of Fame April 8, 2016.) I like to tell the story that all these groups are still performing today but the only one that didn't make it "nationally" was the Mourning Dayze! And I also like to tell everybody that Rick enjoys what he is doing with the Mourning Dayze today as much or more than our fellow colleagues of the '60's.

The Adamany Agency really kept us busy but with the number of groups in his agency we weren't sure how long this would last. We were approached by the North Central Agency in Madison that was run by two individuals who took us "under their wing," providing us gigs and professional advice for our song writing and recordings. From North Central we moved on to the Phil Dutcher Agency located in Madison and in the same building. From the Dutcher Agency the Mourning Dayze ended their first five years with a long time established agency out of Milwaukee, A.C.A. Our final long distance travels with this agency ended in Ogdensburg in up-state New York.

This journey started in a "garage" setting and developed into a lifetime experience. It took the dedication of all the members of the group to work hard to create a sound that would be recognized as an entity that could succeed. It took a person that went "door to door" to let others know about us and who would want us to perform for their venue. It took people in the talent agencies that would hire us and continue to hire us for their clients. It took several decisions by the members of the Mourning Dayze to "follow the path" that we thought best fit our long term future in the business. In other words, "it didn't happen over night!"

Late September of '66, we were off to Marinette. Rick was in High School, and the principal let him leave early, for which we were grateful. The gig went well; the dance floor was packed both nights, plus we'd made solid contact with Ken Adamany. Maybe we'd be discovered!

The week-end we played at "Mike's" we spent the night in Oconto at Steve's parents' home. We were treated like kings and got to meet Steve's family for the first time. The following day, Steve gave us a tour of the city complete with history lesson. (I don't think any of us had any idea just how popular Oconto beer was! It was, wasn't it?)

We got more work through the Adamany agency after that gig. We weren't signed exclusively but were getting a lot of bookings and club owners were asking the agency to have us come back once we worked their club. One thing to note about this band is this-we didn't turn down gigs because they were too far away, didn't pay enough, or because it "wasn't our kind of crowd." We said "yes"....and just did our thing. We did not change our style of music when it came to where we were playing. We went into clubs knowing we'd win people over; if we didn't that would have been fine, but I don't remember that ever happening.

We may not have realized it at the time but the way we looked also made an impact on marketing the band as well as on our drawing power. Live musical performance was big and when a band was wearing trendy cloths playing hip tunes and sounding good, that was a formula for a big draw in the clubs. For those in the audience, it was a way to feel part of the music and identify with others having similar tastes and interests. It was clearly a way to be part of the sub-culture. How one looked could be very defining.

In the fall of '66 we performed live on Channel 9 television in Wausau. Doug remembers us playing "Last Train to Clarksville" by the "Monkees." We also were wearing every piece of "mod" clothing we had. We wanted to look good for our fans, don't 'cha know! We again played in Wausau a few weeks after our TV appearance. The manager of a local men's clothing store had made a point to come and talk with us. His store was doing a "mod" clothing promo the following day, Saturday, which involved the local radio station. He'd seen us play on Channel 9, loved our sound, saw we wore "mod" clothing, and wondered if we'd be interested in coming to his store as part of his promotion. His promotion would include being live on the radio. We felt it would be good exposure for us and a lot of fun. So away we went! Check out these pics!

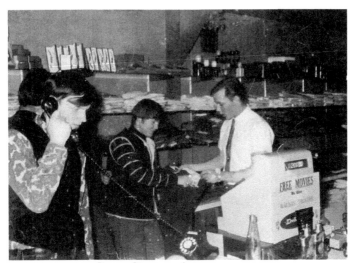

Doug, Steve, and store manager

Ralph, unknown, Steve, Rick, Doug

Doug's Hitchhiking Adventure
As told by Doug

Doug: "The year is 1966. Hitchhiking was popular in those days. Everyone around Whitewater hitchhiked on Highway 12. We'd even hitchhike to Madison on weekends.

UW-Whitewater was having an outstanding year in football and was scheduled to play in the NAIA (National Association of Intercollegiate Athletics) championship game in Tulsa, Oklahoma. Our agent wasn't sure if we has a gig that weekend so Steve, Rick and I couldn't plan anything. The school had twenty buses full of students and drove them to Chicago where an entire train was reserved for the trip to Tulsa. My roommate, Ken Frost, had signed up. It turned out that we didn't have a gig so my only choice was to hitchhike. I bet Ken twenty dollars that I could hitchhike and get to Tulsa before him.

Some of us were hanging out in Ft. Atkinson at a bar called the Point. Another friend, Mike Rittleman, didn't have a ticket to the game either. I talked him into hitchhiking with me and he agreed, but said he had to hitchhike back to his dorm to get some money. I told him if he wasn't back by 1:00 a.m., I was going without him. He didn't get back by one, so I left. A group of nurses from Janesville picked me up. I told them I was going to Tulsa and was gonna beat the train, and asked for a ride to Janesville. I had only about four or five dollars on me.

They dropped me off in downtown Janesville. It was between 1:30

43

and 2:00 a.m. I called a cab. I had no idea what street I was on so I had to run down the street to the corner and read the street sign, then run back to the phone booth to tell them where to pick me up. When the cabbie got there, he asked me where I was going. I told him Tulsa, Oklahoma. He said he'd give me a ride to the edge of town. It cost me a couple bucks. From there I hitched a ride to Darien on Highway 14. It was then well after 2:00 a.m. in November and I had no gloves and no hat.

I began hitchhiking. A city cop gave me a ride. Every time I got into a car I told the driver the complete story. After the cop left me off, I stood in an outdoor bathroom to keep warm. Later a guy driving a big straight truck picked me up. He took me down Highway 14 to Harvard, Illinois, and dropped me off around 4:00 a.m. From there I got another ride. It's now around 6:00 a.m. and beginning to get light. Two gals took me to route 66.

By then it was about 7:30 a.m. I was somewhere south of Chicago. My next ride was in a two-tone brown '56 Caddy driven by a construction supervisor who lived south of St. Louis. I got in and he pulled out a brown paper bag with a bottle of brandy in it. I took a couple swigs and brought him up to date on my travels so far. Like everyone else who picked me up, he got excited about my bet. I mentioned that I was getting hungry so he stopped and bought me a sandwich. He also bought a pint of brandy, which we finished off. It was then around 8:30 or 9:00. We continued on, and around noon or so he dropped me off right before the bridge that crosses the Mississippi river in St. Louis.

I walked over the bridge. After the brandy I wasn't walking normal. I remember seeing Busch Stadium. Next, a guy driving an old '49 or '50 pick-up truck took me a few miles. He bought me a piece of pie and a cup of coffee and got me out of downtown St. Louis. I walked for quite awhile before two guys in a '59 chevy convertible with a broken plastic window in the back, picked me up. I was a little leery about them. They had long oily hair, were unshaven and spoke with a strong southern accent. The interior of the car was littered with trash, but they seemed to be nice enough guys.

Next, I hopped on a city bus, getting off right before it turned off Route 66. I began hitchhiking again. But what I didn't realize was the fun was coming to an abrupt end. No one was stopping for me as I stood in the parking lot of a truck stop. The waitress told me that the owner didn't want anyone hitchhiking on his property. The owner came outside and yelled, "I don't want you hitchhiking out there!" I said, "ok," and went into the cafe next door where I began asking people for a ride. I would go outside for a while, until I got cold and then go back inside to get warm.

It was then getting close to midnight. The owner of the truck stop returned. He was drunk and began cussing at me. I couldn't make him listen. It was then around 2:00 a.m. on Saturday.

Eventually, he left, but there was no traffic. It was then almost 6:30 a.m. and I'd been stuck at this truck stop for twelve hours. A nice guy came along and asked me where I was going. I told him my story and he gave me a ride to Joplin, Missouri. I rode with him for about an hour. From there I got a couple more rides, one with a guy who didn't understand English. He was going to El Paso, Texas, which took him through Tulsa. He left me off at the outskirts of Tulsa. It was then 10:00 or 10:30 on Saturday morning and I haven't slept.

A professor from the University of Tulsa picked me up. And, of course, I gave him the entire story. I had about one dollar left in my pocket. I'm thinking, "By golly, I'm gonna win this bet. I'm gonna be standing in front of the football field waiting for that bus to arrive." That was before the professor decided to give me a tour of the University of Tulsa campus. He was a real nice guy, but I was getting very nervous. Finally, he let me out. I ran up to the main gate just as the buses came down the street.

Ken couldn't believe it. He said, "I can't believe you got here first." They had been partying on the train, at the hotel, and on the bus. We got into the stadium and got our seats, then along came Steve. "Jesus, Henry! I can't believe you're down here."

I had been hitchhiking for a total of thirty-four hours. I kept track of the number of rides I got. It came to twenty-three.

After the game, which UW-Whitewater lost, I got on the bus with Ken for the ride to the hotel. The hotel was like an open house with people coming and going with their booze. Pretty soon Ken passed out on the floor. He was good at that. I didn't have any money or booze of my own so I ordered room service and told them to charge it to Ken's room. From that time on until I returned to Whitewater, I don't think I ever was sober. Thank goodness Ken paid for everything.

Sunday morning came and I needed a ride. By now I was sobering up. I got on the bus with the guys and took it to the train where I snuck on. When the conductor came by to collect the tickets, I hid in the bathroom. By now the whole campus knew about my hitchhiking adventure, and it so happened that the head of the Student Council lived

45

upstairs in the same house that Ken and I lived in. He threatened to turn me in, but instead charged me forty dollars, which was half of the cost of the roundtrip.

Looking back, I really enjoyed that trip."

Author's note: Doug's adventure resonated with Bob Burrows who while proofreading, making corrections and suggestions to the first five years of this project commented on a three day hitchhiking adventure of his own. Doug and I both smiled at Bob's heartfelt comments because this is exactly why we wrote this story. It was to share our love of life with others and to remind us just how similar and beautifully connected we all are.

We soon found ourselves needing another PA. Our current PA was just not big enough to cover the rooms we were playing. Doug, being from South Milwaukee, was familiar with the music store that many of Milwaukee's bands used, West Allis Music. As a band we went to West Allis Music in search for a new PA. Doug Tank was our salesman, who was also a guitarist with Milwaukee's fabulous "Royal Lancers." This would be the beginning of a terrific relationship between Doug, West Allis Music and the band which would continue until the original band dissolved. The band always appreciated that we were able to get "loaners" and try equipment on the job to see if it met our demands before we would consider purchasing it. West Allis Music was much more than just a store, it was a great place to network and to get a feel for "what was hot" in the world of music, nationally and locally. Word of mouth was our "social networking" device. We bought a PA, 3 Lansing 12s on a side, a small mixer powered by a Fender Bassman amp. Common today, sound reinforcement departments were not to be found in the music stores we shopped in 1966.

WEST ALLIS MUSIC CENTER INC.

Gibson • Rickenbacker • Fender • Kustom • Sunn • Lansing • Martin • Ludwig • Slingerland • Zildjian • Shure • Roberts

8924 W. GREENFIELD AVE.
WEST ALLIS, WISCONSIN 53214

Ken Polacheck – Lead Guitar

We played "The Old House," a teen bar just north of Milwaukee.
Rick: "On our way to "The Old House" a AM radio station disc jockey
announced he was about to play the Beach Boys' newest release, "Good
Vibrations." Man, I could not believe what I was hearing. I can easily and
vividly recall this moment. I didn't understand what was going on, just
knew I wanted to be part of that kind of musical energy. I didn't want to
be a "Beach Boy." It wasn't that; it was the electricity, the vibe, the energy
that was in that tune-it was so much more, more about attitude." This gig
proved to be significant. As a band we'd been beginning to work on
material that was targeted at the college crowd rather than playing "the
hits" heard on the radio or bar room standards.

Ken Polacheck introduced himself to us while on break at "The
Old House." Ken talked about how much he liked our sound, feeling we
had a lot to give and seemed to have a genuine feel for what we were
musically about. Ken was also a musician and guitar player from
Shorewood. He told us if we ever needed a guitar player that we should
consider giving him a call, stating he'd love to play with us and felt he
would be a strong addition to what we were doing. As a band we had
many people approach us because they wanted to play with us. We'd
politely listen but had always been satisfied with our group as it was. We
exchanged phone numbers with Ken. He made a positive impression on
us all, but figured we'd stay as we were. Or did we?

Two to three weeks after meeting Ken at the "Old House" we
found ourselves playing "Jack's 23 Club" in Wausau with a new lineup.
Rick and a memory from playing "Jack's": *"I was not old enough to
drink and was told if I did I wouldn't be able to play in the band. One
night we were playing at "Jack's." We had rented a room in a motel
directly across the street from the club. Doug enjoyed drinking blackberry
brandy after a gig. I wanted to join in and enjoy the after-hours fun. I
told Doug I would go halves with him on the brandy. That way, I could
have some too. I had never drunk it, and wanted to see what it was all
about. We bought the brandy, and after the gig I was excited about trying
it. Well, to my surprise, Doug wouldn't let me have any. He drank it all
himself after telling me that if I had some he'd tell my mother. I believed
him! Hmmm. I thought Doug was on my team. Ha!"* Ralph and the
band parted ways. Ralph then joined "The Opposition" which was a local
soul band. Letting Ralph go was not easy for Rick. "He was my friend I

47

liked his dad very much, and he gave me my start in the business. Although I knew at this point we had different priorities, I wanted to be with a group that put "being their best" as a priority regardless of personalities or life situation." There would be other times when we had to let someone go because it was best for the band. Ken was called and agreed to join us as our lead guitar player. Doug would switch from lead guitar to bass guitar, which he really enjoyed almost immediately. Ken had a friend who had a bass for sale that Doug bought, and seemed destined to play. He's been playing it ever since. Rick continued to play rhythm guitar and Steve was drumming and singing as usual.

Ken Polacheck – Lead Guitar

Ken was not with the band for more than four months but made a real impact on us. He left us to do studio work in California. Ken was a very progressive player, always trying to figure out the latest guitar licks from anywhere he could find them as well as working on his own licks and chops. Ken was always more than willing to show anyone how he was playing a tune or a lick that he played. He very much emphasized the importance of a band's doing their own material, and that if we were serious about being a band, we needed to do our own stuff, that we'd be just one of a million other cover bands if we didn't. He was right of course. While Ken was with us we began to play downtown Racine fairly often at the Nitty Gritty and Ivanhoe.

There was another very popular group that regularly played in the Racine area also called "The Coachmen." This would prove to confuse club owners as well as fans. We were aware of the situation and in a few months time we changed our name for this and other reasons.

The Mourning Dayze

How did you come up with that name anyway?

   Lyle Ernst: "The guys always tried to keep their expenses to a minimum, which meant driving home the same night from most gigs, regardless of how far away they were. Often, the band was coming back to Whitewater in the early morning, long after the sun had come up.

   One morning, driving home from a gig in Wausau, Wisconsin, the guys were so tired, that they got a little "slap happy," as Steve would say. This particular morning it was slightly foggy when the fog hangs in five to ten foot banks off the ground, and the sun is blocked out by a low ceiling of clouds. The guys were tired. Their eyes were burning from the cigarette smoke after the night's gig.

   The guys had been discussing a different name for the band. There was another band named "The Coachmen," and they wanted to separate themselves from them. The times, they were a changin'. The name "Coachmen" was no longer cool, but more importantly, it did not reflect the times, their music, or their image.

   As they traveled down the road they began brainstorming for a new name for the band. Somehow the name "Mourning Dayze" came up and everyone agreed on it. They decided to change the spelling of the name just to be "different"-or was it being the same?

   One of the main reasons "Mourning Dayze" was successful in those first five years was because they played one-nighters and traveled long distances. They did whatever it took to play as many gigs as they could. They never missed a gig because the weather might be bad, or because they weren't in the "right" or "their" demographic group."We wanted to play," says Rick, "because we wanted to share our love for music with others."

   They had fun playing music, and this rubbed off on their patrons. That, and the fact that the guys got along famously. They shared private thoughts and lives; they argued, and they talked things out.

50

One memorable gig we played with Ken was New Year's Eve, Dec. 31, 1966, at Riolo's Restaurant in Whitewater. Rick's mom, Betty, had worked there for years and was best of friends with Rio and Fran Achilli, the owners.

Betty and Fran showing the band how it should be done!

Betty had convinced them they needed live music for New Year's Eve, it should be rock 'n roll and it should be us! Thanks to you Betty, we landed the job!

Doug   Steve   Rick   Ken

51

This was the night we would meet John Valentine. John would soon be with the band for the next two years. These would be some of the band's most creative and memorable years. A remarkable time! John Valentine, a Whitewater guitar player and folk singer, was making a lot of positive comments about the band, and he suggested that if we ever needed a guitarist and singer, we should consider him. John had a terrific personality, a huge, genuine smile, and lots of creative energy. He liked to have a good time and live in the moment. He made a lasting impression on all of us. We exchanged phone numbers, and we always kept our options open. We weren't looking to add any new members; we were happy with our current lineup.

But on a night in February, 1967, Ken told us he was leaving us to go to California to pursue an opportunity to do studio work. We were happy for him; we would not do anything that would hinder any of our band mates from pursuing what they felt they needed to do. We wished him success and felt grateful for his having been with us. Ken left without much of any forewarning. The night he left, Ken showed Rick as many of his guitar parts as he could. Rick had no real interest in being a lead guitar player, but it seemed like it was his turn to do what was needed to keep the band moving forward. It was the logical thing to do. He did what he could and borrowed any licks he could from Doug, while trying to remember all that Ken had showed him.

We'd always worked with a rhythm guitarist and now we needed one. *The thought of a power trio had not crossed our mind, it took Cream, Hendrix and Soup to do that!* Hey? What about that guy who introduced himself to us at Riolo's New Year's Eve?

It had almost been two months since we met John; we had not forgotten the genuine interest he demonstrated in wanting to play with us. We gave him a call to see if he was available and still interested in working with us. John was ready and willing; the group was set. Mourning Dayze was about to embark on an amazing two year journey.

John Valentine – Guitar/Vocals

John Valentine – Guitar/Vocals
Artistic, Creative, Curious, Inventive, Fully Engaged in Life

John: "For the first ten years of my life I lived with my family on a farm near Whitewater, Wisconsin. When the family moved into the city of Whitewater, I was very shy and introverted, and spent most of my time by myself building model airplanes, rockets and radios. There was a piano in the house and I liked to pick out tunes on it. My mother thought I should take piano lessons, so I did. However, I hated my piano teacher, and after about four lessons I refused to go anymore.

My mother knew that if I liked something I would excel at it, and if I didn't like it, there was little chance it would hold my attention. One year, when I was still in grade school, I got a Silvertone guitar for Christmas. It came from Sears. In those days, if Sears didn't have it, we didn't get it. After about two weeks I figured out how to tune it, and I was off and running.

By the time I was in high school, I was what would come to be referred to as an audiophile. I loved anything to do with sound reproduction. I had built a massive stereo amplifier system from a kit. I had also built stereo bass reflex speakers in my shop class, and I listened to all types of music. The school even used my stereo system for sock hops in high school. I leaned toward classical music, but as my guitar playing matured, I began listening more to Chet Atkins and flamenco guitar music.

During my senior year, two of my friends, Dick Krenz and Mark

Sullivan and I decided to start a group to sing folk music. "The Kingston Trio" was hot then. We patterned ourselves after them, calling ourselves "The Kingsmen Trio." We did the usual birthday parties, Fourth of July gigs, and anything else that provided exposure.

After graduation, we auditioned for a television show on Channel 3 in Madison, Wisconsin. For the next year we did a weekly guest spot on the Lorraine Rice Show. We were doing well until folk music vanished almost overnight. With the war in Vietnam going on, we all were potentially cannon fodder. Dick decided to get it over with and joined the Marines. Not long after, Mark received his draft notice and he was gone.

From top to bottom: John Valentine, Dick Krenz, Mark Sullivan

I don't remember exactly how I connected with Mourning Dayze, but one day I found myself in Rick's living room trying to learn rock and roll. I didn't have an electric guitar, but I had a friend who had bought a new Gibson Barney Kessel model jazz guitar. He needed money so the deal was that I would buy his guitar, and whenever he could scrape up the money, I would sell it back to him. So, there I was, a fingerpicker trying to play rock and roll on a jazz guitar. Doug, Steve and especially Rick, were incredibly patient, and eventually they molded me into a rock guitar player. I thoroughly enjoyed those couple of years with Mourning Dayze.

54

After I left the band, I missed not being off on another gig, but it didn't take long to get over that.

Not long after, Dick Krenz returned home after being wounded in Vietnam. He married his sweetheart and moved away. Then Mark Sullivan returned from Vietnam, and he and I talked about getting back into music as a duo. So we auditioned at a big club in Fontana on Lake Geneva, Wisconsin and the owner called me and said we had the gig. Mark was living in Milwaukee at the time, and when I called to tell him the good news, he had decided not to go back to traveling again. I called the club owner to tell him we were unable to do the gig, but he convinced me to come in and do a single. Never, ever, did I see myself performing as a single, but I did it, and loved it. It was the best gig ever, right in my back yard. My equipment never left the stage. I would walk in with my guitar, plug it in, and the place was always packed.

The "Stevensen Three" was a unique place. The owner had modified a large dairy barn. He and his family lived upstairs, and the entire first floor was converted into a bar, a stage and a dining area. He even converted the silo into a dining room. It was located very close to the "Abbey Resort."
A lot of clientele came from there.

That lasted for about six months until my draft board finally caught up with me. On my last gig, I walked in and the entire club was filled with banners wishing me good luck. It was a tough night, but one I will never forget."

Mourning D with Johnny V
The Summer of Love

In the spring of '67, Mourning Dayze found themselves quickly approaching the "summer of love". The world of music and art was bursting with excitement and creativity. John not only brought a love of music to the band, but also a love for photography, art and had the creative drive to pursue his interests and also integrate them into the band.

The word, "psychedelic" was freely used to describe the music and art of this era. Here's a brief overview of the word thanks to Wikipedia:
1) "A psychedelic experience is characterized by the striking perception of aspects of one's mind previously unknown, or by the creative exuberance

of the mind liberated from its ostensibly ordinary fetters. Psychedelic states are an array of experiences including changes of perception such as hallucinations, synesthesia, altered states of awareness or focused consciousness, variation in thought patterns, trance or hypnotic states, mystical states, and other mind alterations. These processes can lead some people to experience changes in mental operation defining their self-identity (whether in momentary acuity or chronic development) different enough from their previous normal state that it can excite feelings of newly formed understanding ranging from revelation & enlightenment to the opposing polarity of confusion & psychosis.

Psychedelic states may be elicited by various techniques, such as meditation, sensory stimulation or deprivation, and most commonly by the use of psychedelic substances. When these psychoactive substances are used for religious, shamanic, or spiritual purposes, they are termed entheogens. Psychedelic artists use highly distorted visuals, cartoons, and bright colors and full spectrums to evoke a sense of altered consciousness. Many artists in the late 1960s and early 1970s attempted to illustrate the psychedelic experience in paintings, drawings, illustrations, and other forms of graphic design.

The counterculture folk music scene frequently used psychedelic designs on posters during the Summer of Love, leading to a popularization of the style. The work of Robert Crumb and others doing posters for hippie bands, such as Big Brother and The Holding Company, spawned interest in the artwork among their followers. Peter Max's psychedelic poster designs helped popularize brightly colored spectrums widely, especially among college students.

One example of this experimentation is seen in Mati Klarwein's painting *Annunciation*, which was used as the cover art for Santana's Abraxas (1970). The cover of Pink Floyd's album A Saucerful of Secrets (1968) is also of this type.

The Beatles' album cover for The Magical Mystery Tour album has features common in psychedelic art, such as a wide color palette and surreal visuals.

The fashion for psychedelic drugs gave its name to the style of psychedelia, a term describing a category of rock music known as psychedelic rock, as well as visual art, fashion, and culture that is associated originally with the high 1960s, hippies, and the Haight-Ashbury neighborhood of San Francisco, California. It often used new recording techniques and effects while drawing on Eastern sources such as the ragas

56

and drones of Indian music.

One of the first uses of the word in the music scene of this time was in the 1964 recording of "Hesitation Blues" by folk group the Holy Modal Rounders. The term was introduced to rock music and popularized by the 13th Floor Elevators 1966 album *The Psychedelic Sounds of the 13th Floor Elevators.* Psychedelia truly took off in 1967 with the Summer of Love and, although associated with San Francisco, the style soon spread across the US and worldwide.

The counterculture of the 1960s had a strong influence on the popular culture of the early 1970s. It later became linked to a style of electronic dance music, or rave music, commonly known as psychedelic trance." (4)

The Summer of Love

"The Summer of Love was a social phenomenon that occurred during the summer of 1967 when as many as 100,000 people converged on the Haight-Ashbury neighborhood of San Francisco, initiating a major cultural and political shift. Although hippies also gathered in major cities across the U.S., Canada, and Europe, San Francisco remained the epicenter of the social earthquake that would come to be known as the Hippie Revolution. (5) Like its sister enclave of Greenwich Village the city became even more of a melting pot of politics, music, drugs, creativity, and the far greater lack of sexual and social inhibitions that it already had. As the hippie counterculture movement came farther and farther forward into public awareness, the activities centered therein became a defining moment of the 1960s, (6) causing numerous "ordinary

57

citizens" to begin questioning everything and anything about them and their environment as a result.

This unprecedented gathering of young people is often considered to have been a social experiment, because of all the alternative lifestyles which became more common and accepted, with more gender equality, communal living, and free love. (7) gender equality, communal living and free love. (7) Many of these types of social changes reverberated on into the early 1970s, and effects echo throughout modern society.

The hippies, sometimes called flower children, were an eclectic group. Many were suspicious of the government, rejected consumerist values, and generally opposed the Vietnam War. A few were interested in politics; others focused on art (music, painting, poetry in particular) or religious and meditative movements. All were eager to integrate new ideas and insights into daily life, both public and private. (8)

As a band, we loved the music, dress and artwork that was coming from California as well as the energy and freedom that came with it. We were equally captivated by the music coming from Great Britain. These album releases in 1967 would be monumental in shaping the band's sound and direction for years to come. "The Doors," "The Grateful Dead," Tim Buckley's "Hello and Good-bye," Jefferson Airplane's "Surrealistic Pillow," The Beatles, "Sargent Pepper's Lonely Hearts Club Band," Hendrix album "Are You Experienced," 1966, "Fresh Cream," "Buffalo Springfield" and "Chet Atkins' "Picks on the Beatles."

We soon found out just how much John loved to sing; he really wanted us to work on singing three part-harmonies-and we did. (In the car, before the gig, at a party, where ever the opportunity presented itself, John wanted us to work on our vocals!) The contemporary music we were playing, was being played loud. Loud, so people in the audience could physically "feel" the music vibrate in their bodies. This made them "feel" part of the live performance. The audience wanted more than a "listening" experience. In short, we needed to play louder than we'd ever played before...very cool!. This meant we needed guitar amps that would handle playing at louder volumes. We went to West Allis Music, as usual, but this time it was different-we had John with us. John understood the in's and out's of amplification. (John would continually stress that, as electric guitarists, we should know how our amps worked, and how they should be cared for. In those days, all we were interested in was plugging in and playing.) John, with Doug Tank's help, got us on solid footing for our new amp purchases. John and Doug used Bogen amps with JBL

15inch cabs and Rick bought a Twin-Reverb. We were set-and louder than we'd ever been! Cool!

Doug with John's Barney Kessel

John with Steve's drums

At all hours of the day or night, the band was packing or unpacking, setting up or tearing down, getting to rehearsal or driving to the gig; it's just part of daily life for a band. Those dues are never paid. The above pic's were taken in front of Queen Street.

Lyle Ernst: "The end of the night usually meant a long ride back to Whitewater in the wee hours of the morning. The guys shared the driving chores so one person wouldn't have to drive three or four hours straight through. To determine who drove in what order, they had a "rule," and a little "game" they played on a nightly basis. The first driver always had it the easiest because they all were still wound up from the gig, and less likely to be tired, not to mention having a few more beers to put down. At the end of the gig, when they were all present on the stage, the first person to think of driving would yell "first." The rest of the guys would yell "second, third, fourth" as fast as they could, which determined the order in which they'd share the driving chores on the way home."

Our first gig with our brand new equipment was at "Harold's Club 23" in Sheboygan Falls. The club was packed and the beer was flowing (kinda sounds like Stagger Lee doesn't it?!). Steve was fronting the band singing a ballad, Rick was on drums, Doug on bass and John was closing his eyes, getting lost in the song. All of a sudden and out of no where, some guy from the dance floor walks over to John and punches him in the face. And, ya, all hell broke loose; including a couple of our brand new amps falling off the stage! Fortunately, a group of uniformed sailors jumped in and hustled the drunks away from the band and dance floor and then out of the club. The club owner felt worse than we did about the incident and bought the band, along with girls they'd met from the club, drinks until early morning. On our way back to Sheboygan we had to drop one of the girls off at her apartment, (At this time, we are using John's Comet and a U-Haul trailer to haul us and our equipment around) John is behind the wheel, and asks one of the girls for directions to get to her apartment. She tells John to turn right at the railroad tracks...well, we came close, John turned right all right, right on the tracks! It was pandemonium...none of us could stop laughing...even to this day!

John lived in Delavan, Wisconsin, worked at Southern Lakes Printing, and was hip as to how advertising and the newspaper could be used to promote the band. John stressed the need for us to be promoting ourselves when we could, and to be prepared when agents or club owners requested promotional materials from us. Throughout John's time with the band, photo shoots were considered as important as rehearsals.

This was the first poster John created for us...cool eh? Ya, it really is...so cool in fact it was used for the cover of this book. Thank you, Roland, for advising us regarding all of our options, that this is the poster we should use for the book's cover

The band rehearsed at a minimum of two times a week every week. During this period, the band was rehearsing in Betty and Ray's living room, brand new carpet and all! This was never viewed as a "problem" or something that was not welcome. In fact it was just the opposite; these were occasions that were looked forward to. **Rise:** "I would listen to them practice in my parent's living room. They were so loud you couldn't hear yourself think. Yet, our little sister, Renee, who wasn't quite one-year old, would sleep right through it. It was always fun sitting in the living room with the college girls. I was only 13, so that was the cat's meow."   Doug, Steve and John's friends would often come to rehearsals in the living room. It was not unusual for 8-12 people, and sometimes more, to be at our rehearsals. There was always room for everyone and everyone was welcome. The more people in the house, the better the vibe at Queen Street! On the weekends, coming home from a gig, you'd find friends of the band sleeping at Queen St. wherever they could find a spot. Later in life Betty and Ray would often wonder just how they did it, and also agreed they would, without a doubt, do it all over again. We all felt like one big family! ah... truly the summer of love!

Due to our success in the clubs and willingness to travel, the Adamany agency kept providing us with more and more work-and we were loving it. We hadn't exclusively signed with him at this point, but in a few months would. The summer of '67 began with us playing Memorial Day weekend at Hassie's Bar in Sturgeon Bay. Hassie, "Bear," could see that we were the perfect band for his crowd, which was a mix of terrific locals, and vacationers who loved to party. For two consecutive summers we played "Hassies" all three major summer holidays to overflow houses.

Some Fun Stories

Doug: "One night after the gig at Hassie's the gal with the "funeral home car" let me drive it back to our motel with her and her friends aboard while Steve, John, and Rick drove to the motel with our hearse. The hearse arrived first and it was about 2:30 in the morning. As I pulled up to the motel I turned on the red light and the siren! The girls got real nervous and the boys came running out of the motel, "Henry, what the hell are you doing?" It was always a great trip to Sturgeon Bay. Most of these same girls attended UW-Oshkosh and always came to see us play our gigs in Oshkosh. We mostly played at the Ralph Hotel, which was downtown, when we played in Oshkosh."

The morning of this same night, we were sleeping in past check out time after being up all night. The owner of the motel began knocking on our door, to get us up and out of our room, stating, "Dayze, it's morning." *Doug, "I'm sick already."*

Lyle Ernst: "Mourning Dayze had a big following in college towns, and Oshkosh was no exception. The Ralph Hotel, downtown Oshkosh, was a favorite of college students who attended the University of Wisconsin at Oshkosh. Doug became "real" friendly with Mary Smagel, a UW student from Sturgeon Bay, so friendly that she came to the lake house at Whitewater to visit Doug. All of this took place after Doug and Kathy (later his wife) broke up again. According to Doug, he and Kathy's breaking up seemed like an every-other-week occurrence. After a while Doug sort of lost track of Mary. He was too busy being a musician to remember to contact her on a regular basis. He realized she had gotten tired of waiting around for him when, a few years later, while Mourning Dayze was playing a gig in Sturgeon Bay, Mary Smagel and wedding party, was next door from where the band was staying, enjoying her wedding reception.

Another "Doug happening" took place in Oshkosh. Doug wanted to stay at the bar and listen to "Twistin' Harvey Scales and the Seven Sounds," who were playing after Mourning Dayze had finished their gig.

Rick and Steve didn't want to stay; they'd been through this before, so they took off for home in the hearse. (It was painful, "HENRY!," for them to watch their bass player ask someone to get him a chair so he could sit down and enjoy the band in the middle of a packed dance floor!..smiles) Doug had met a guy who said he would give hime a ride to Whitewater in a Volkswagen bug. What Doug didn't know is this guy didn't ask the owner if he could drive his VW. Doug was a bit "wasted," so it took awhile before he realized he was riding in a stolen car. At about the same time he came to this realization, he noticed a police car following them. Doug suggested to the driver that he drive the speed limit in order to not give the cop a reason to stop them. The next day Rick's father, Ray, was reading the newspaper, and commented on an article that said the Whitewater Police had located a car that was stolen in Oshkosh."

The band received its share of heartfelt fan mail: here are a couple...

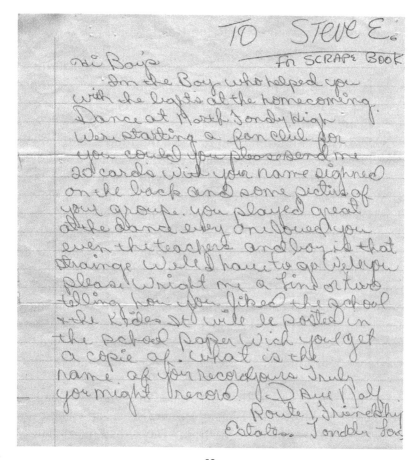

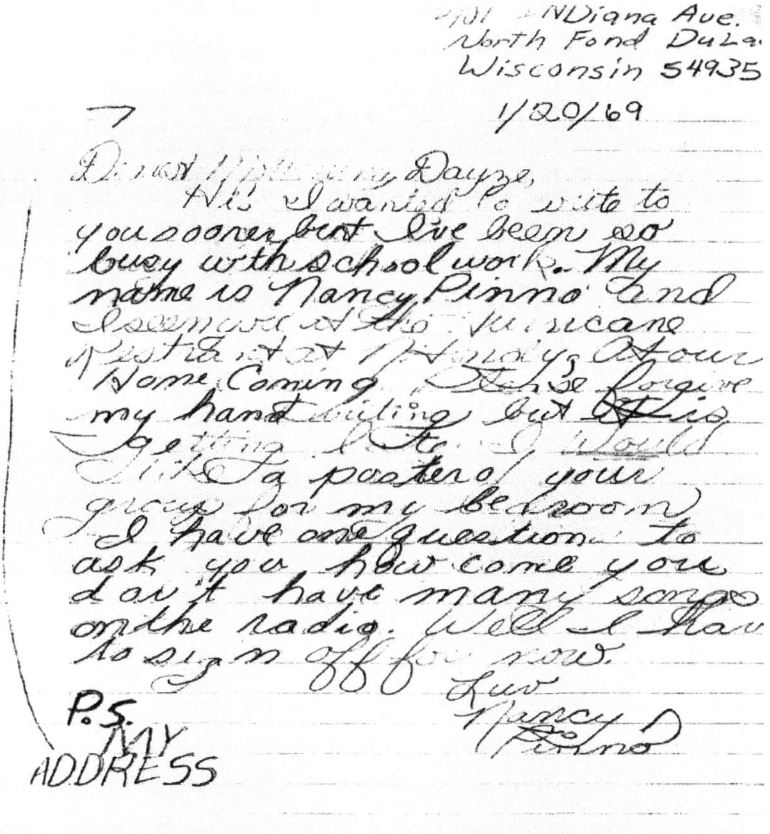

[illegible] N Diana Ave.
North Fond Du La.
Wisconsin 54935

1/20/69

Dear [illegible] Dayze,
Hi! I wanted to write to you sooner but I've been so busy with school work. My name is Nancy Pinno and I seen you at the Hurricane Restaurant at [illegible] At our Home Coming. Please forgive my hand writing but it is getting better. I would like a poster of your group for my bedroom. I have one question to ask you, how come you don't have many songs on the radio. Well I have to sign off for now.

Luv
Nancy Pinno

P.S. MY ADDRESS

More Fun Stories!

Steve: One cold winter night we were staying at a motel in Manitowoc. I had driven my Alpha Romeo (silver convertible with red leather bucket seats). It was low on anti-freeze, so Rick and I went to get beer and anti-freeze; we left Doug at the motel... without beer. We didn't find a store with anti-freeze, so we bought some beer and headed back. Everything was cool until we went over a hill and found the road had turned to ice from rain earlier in the day. Cars were sliding all over the road. I did a 360' and landed in the ditch. A tow truck came along, but before he could stop, he slid into the ditch right across the road from us. The driver of one of the wrecked cars had a broken leg, and a cop had put him in the back seat of his squad car. Just then, another tow truck came over the hill, did a donut, and spun into the ditch near us. The cop went over and gave the truck driver a ticket. Next, he gave us a ticket. Rick and I are trying to convince the cop to take the guy with the broken leg to the hospital. We kept saying "You have to take that guy to the hospital. He has a broken leg." Finally, he left. In the meantime the two trucks managed to wrench each other out of the ditch. One of them pulled us out, and we continued back to the motel.

When we got back there, Doug was all pissed off. He said, "What took you guys so long?" I said, "We were in an accident." He said, "It doesn't take that long to get into an accident."

Doug: We were going to play a gig in Wausau, Wisconsin, and I asked my girlfriend to go along. She said yes, and the guys had no objections So Rick and I got packed up and Rick said, 'Do you have some rubbers?" I said, "Yup, got 'em in my billfold." "O.k.," he said, "then we're ready." Whenever we stayed out of town, the band paid for two hotel/motel rooms. Usually Rick and I stayed in one room and Steve and John in the other. But this night, the guys were good enough to stay three in a room so I could bunk with my girlfriend.

When the time came to use a rubber, I couldn't find them. Then I remembered; for some unknown reason I had taken them out of my billfold and placed them on top of my golf bag. From that time on, whenever Rick and I were packing up for a road trip, Rick would say, "got your golf clubs?"

Lyle Ernst: "On one of their trips to Sturgeon Bay, Doug met a girl who was running a basketball hoop game for her uncle at the local fair. Doug asked her if she wanted to go for a ride in a hearse. She told Doug he was nuts, but agreed. It could be said that, by the time the afternoon rolled around Doug had quaffed a few cans of Schlitz, so off they went to a quarry where they made out in the hearse. Doug had to place a briefcase between the floor and gas pedal to keep the hearse running, or it wouldn't have started for a long, long time. On their way back to the fairgrounds a tire went flat. They were only about half a mile away, so she walked the rest of the way. Doug changed the tire while the briefcase kept the hearse running. The guys were pissed at Doug when he finally got back."

Rick: "Hassie's" was located about two miles outside of Sturgeon Bay and right across the street from Door County's Cherryland Airport, which got John thinking. Along with having a real love affair with RC airplanes, John was also working on getting his single engine pilot's license and working out the logistics to fly to the gig at "Hassies"! Which was way cool...

While with the band, I don't believe any of us realized how much interest Doug had in flying. So much so, that Doug would get a pilot's license which allowed him to fly for the business he was in, flying cross-county to play golf or see a Packer game, fly skydivers, fly for fun, and (most important of all) fly to Palmyra for the annual Father's Day Fly-In and breakfast!"

Palmyra Father's Day Fly- In and Breakfast
Betty and Doug

Nashville Trip To Visit John

One magical day Doug called Rick and asked him if he'd like to fly to Nashville and visit John.   Here's the story per Doug: *"I was always interested in airplanes so when John Valentine was in the band in the 60's I thought it was really cool that he was taking flying lessons. I attended junior high and high school in South Milwaukee and lived just a mile from Billy Mitchell International Airport so I would ride my bike to just to hang out and watch aircraft takeoff and land and walk around in the terminal which was very easy to do back then. After John left the band in the late 60's I had virtually no contact with him. Rick had kept in touch and would see John from time to time when he came back to visit his family in Whitewater. In 1999 Rick informed John, who was living in Nashville, that I just obtained my Multi-Engine rating along with the Commercial*

66

and Instrument rating which I had for single engines for several years. John said to Rick, "give Doug my congratulations on his new rating and tell him I am green with envy!" He also said, "tell Doug that in a hot twin, Nashville ain't that far away and I will buy the burgers!" Rick and I decided that this was a trip we had to take.

In 2001 my wife Cheri and I were vacationing in Vienna, Austria on September 11th waiting for our friends Nick and Cathy Ryan to meet us there because they were scheduled to fly in from Chicago but then the Twin Towers' tragedy broke. They never made it that year and after that the Air Traffic system was changed forever. We did the trip 5 years later and were able to meet up with our friends in Vienna and had a great vacation with them!

Before our European trip in 2001 I told Rick we had to do our Nashville flying trip to see John, which we hadn't done to this point. I informed Rick that I had two friends, Jon Hart and Curt Zimmerman, who would like to do the trip to Nashville. They also had friends in Nashville that they could visit while we visited with John. Rick contacted John and he set a date in October that we would fly down to visit John.

The date was set for October 13, 2001. We would fly a twin engine Piper Seneca from Watertown, WI to Nashville. John would pick up Rick and me at the John C. Tune airport in Nashville while my other two friends would go in another direction and meet us back at the airport in the morning for the return flight. Because of "9-11" I had to check our route and arrival for TFR's, Temporary Flight Restricted areas. TFR's were set up after "9-11" and indicate the President is in the area or any other level of VIP's are present. If you penetrate these areas they send up the F-16's to escort you to the nearest airport which "ruins the rest of your day and trip!' Because it was only a month after "9-11" I called the airport directly to be sure there were not any local procedures I should be aware of. There were none and there were no TFR's scheduled for our trip.

The morning we left the weather was IFR, instrument flight rules, meaning we would be making the entire flight in the clouds or just above them in light rain and I would be using the instruments in the plane to conduct the majority of the flight. There would be no scenery to view on the way down. In fact, we had to use an instrument procedure to land, meaning we didn't see the runway/airport until we broke out of the clouds one mile from landing! We also encountered a strong headwind on the way down so our flight time was just under 4 hours. The return trip was almost all clear with favorable winds giving us a flight time of just under 3 hours.

Watertown, WI
Jon Hart   Doug Henry

Nashville
Chet Atkins   Doug Henry

The visit with John was great. I hadn't seen him for over 30 years since he left the Mourning Dayze. He gave us a great tour of Nashville and pointed out several historic sites. We walked the downtown area and had a couple of beers. We went to the Chet Atkins statue situated on one of the corners downtown and had pictures taken "with Chet!" Rick had

68

been to Nashville several times and attended Chet Atkins' seminars several times over the years. He actually had "one on one" sessions with Chet, but was never able to hook up with John on these trips. John treated Rick and me to dinner (he "bought the burgers") downtown while we reminisced about the "old days" and several years in between.

From downtown we went to John's home where we continued an enjoyable evening and where John put us up for the night. At the time John was editor of a remote control aircraft flying magazine. He was also in the process of building several remote control aircraft which he had on display in his workshop. He also talked about the "real" plane he owned, a Cessna 172. As we retired for the evening a good storm was brewing overhead. But as morning arrived it brought a calm atmosphere and sun for our trip home!

2016...John and Doug sharing their love of flight while heading to Carrolton MO, 10-13-15.

That same summer we played extended stays in the Wisconsin Dells area which were always a blast. We met so many terrific people in the Dells, many of whom would do all they could to promote the band. (Doug and I met WGN's Franklin McCormick in Lake Delton doing his all night radio broadcast, complete with Meister Brau in hand!) Many people we met sincerely felt we were destined for bigger things and did all they could to help us on our way. We shared their belief in our future.

Promo shots taken in the Dells by friends of the band.

Doug

Doug   Steve   Rick   John

While rehearsing at "Van's" in the Dells, John happened to have his "flat top" with him, a gorgeous Martin D-18. John introduced Rick to the world of "finger-pickin" that afternoon.
(Finger-picking, also called thumb-pickin', or fingerstyle, is a term used to describe both a playing style and a genre of music)
Rick: *"When I began playing guitar, I was given a flat pick. A flat*

pick is held between the thumb and index finger, or thumb and the middle finger. I never was comfortable with a flat pick, and am not to this day. It had a habit of getting tangled up in the strings and landing on the floor, still does! But being the innovator I am, I figured that was the only way to play the darn thing. I played all through high school and college using just flat pick.

John Valentine had a great love for music and was a good finger-picker. He would constantly tell me I should learn how to finger-pick, and should explore that style as well as the dazzling stylings of the great flatpicker, Doc Watson. John had many Chet Atkins albums in his collection. I think I told John that Chet sucked. I was so "brill" and open minded, eh? I was too arrogant and naïve to really give it a try. When I finally did try, it didn't come easily to me so I just blew it off. I did not realize that I was denying myself another approach to playing the guitar as well as another way to look at music and the guitar. John had a Martin D-18 that had a sound that I can still hear to this day, it was so beautiful! I'm so grateful John introduced me to that style of playing. Thanks, John!

With long time encouragement from "Well's House of Music" owner/operator Ralph Wells Sr., after Doug and Steve left, I began to dabble in the world of classical guitar playing and contemporary solo guitar playing. I stumbled onto an album by Stephen Grossman which was full of blues and ragtime tunes played solo on the guitar. That album also included accurate transcriptions of every tune. I'd never seen anything like that, I was amazed and tried to learn as much as I could from it. It was an ear-and-mind opener to say the very least! More guitar heaven! The music that was written for pop music at that time was geared toward piano players with the guitar chords written as symbols above the staff. There were no accurate transcriptions of the guitar work in pop music at that time that I was aware of. You were on your own to figure it out, which has its benefits as well. Stephen Grossman's work helped me tremendously in my quest to play solo guitar.

The band was playing in Bemidji, Minnesota, and as always, the band was checking out the local music store. I was thumbing through learning materials in the guitar section when I spotted a book entitled "Chet Atkins Goes to the Movies." It was a note for note transcription of an entire album by Chet, transcribed by some guy named John Knowles, who I'd never heard of. Years later, John would be a major player in my musical life. So now I'm thinkin', "at last, I can finally learn to play like

Chet." Well, I soon learned that even though I had an accurate transcription of Chet's work, I still wasn't going to sound like Chet or even really come close. It did, however, give me an example of what world class fingestyle guitar playing was all about plus a deeper appreciation for the playing of Chet as well as insight into how he approached the guitar and handled arranging for the guitar. More importantly, I learned just how much there was to learn!

In August 1986, the American Fingerstyle Festival, was held on the UW campus in Milwaukee, WI. Many of the finest fingerstyle guitarists in the world were there; it was a an amazing line up.

Throughout the day, these great guitarists were easily available to talk one on one with. I took full advantage of the opportunity, it was guitar heaven! It was a wonderfully open and friendly environment, where learning, love for music and the guitar, were at the core of everything. One of the workshops I attended was lead by John Knowles. John was musically very close to Jerry Reed, Lenny Breau and Chet Atkins, working with each, one on one, to accurately transcribe their work, so it could be shared with the world, elevating the level of fingerstyle guitar playing. John can take what may seem absolutely impossible to achieve and make it accessible to all who are willing to put in the time. It was through John's workshop that I learned of the CAAS, the Chet Atkins Appreciation Society.

The CAAS meets in Nashville once a year. Once I learned of it, I participated every other year. I got to meet Chet, which was a great moment for me and got to hear and learn from some of the finest players in the world. Guitar players come from all over the world to this convention it's four days and nights of non stop guitar playing. It's a great place to share and learn. Stylistically you'll hear traditional, contemporary, pop, jazz, classical, alternative and innovative. Everything you can imagine...and then some! It's sooooooooo cool!

The impact Chet Atkins has had on music and the world is well documented and truly an amazing story. His musical gift to the world is unparalleled. He will continue to inspire guitarists and musicians throughout history. I remember him not only for being such a major player in the history of music and the guitar, but also because he was such a wonderful and kind person. I'll steal or borrow any licks I can from him!

Rick meets Chet Atkins

Author's note: *In 2001 Rick recorded a CD called "Influences." One of the tunes on it was "Thankin' Marcel." This tune was Rick's tribute to Marcel Dadi, a Jewish/French guitarist known for his finger- picking style. Marcel patterned himself after his idol, Chet Atkins, and also re- created the instrumental styles of Merle Travis and Jerry Reed. "Marcel was a tremendous influence on me," says Rick. "While my sister Renee was studying in Paris in the early '80's (you were studying weren't you, Renee?), I asked her if she would go to Marcel's music store and purchase several of his albums. (I'm forever grateful that she did!) I wanted these specifically because these were solo albums of Marcel and included transcriptions of the music." In 1996, Rick was fortunate enough to meet Marcel at the CAAS in Nashville, just prior to Marcel being honored at Nashville's Country Music Hall of Fame. One week later Marcel was killed when the Boeing 747 on TWA flight 800 exploded off the coast of Long Island, July 17th, 1996. "At least I got to tell him how much I loved his work, and to thank him for what he has contributed to the world of fingerstyle guitar playing and to my own life," Rick said.*

One early June afternoon in 1967 Doug, Steve, and I found ourselves at Queen Street. Out of the blue, John comes stormin' into the house with an album in his hand, and he's excited, real excited! John, "You guys have to hear this, and hear it now, you won't believe what you're about to hear!" John put the album on the turntable and played us, "Sargent Pepper's Lonely Hearts Club Band" by the Beatles. And yes, we like so many others were "blown away" by what we heard, not just the songs on the record, but also because it was a concept album, that was brilliantly packaged. That album revolutionized popular music.

*Flower Power! Doug's future wife was getting into the era too;
she had a painting party with her girlfriends. They painted flowers all
over her car. It was a beautiful sight to behold. (A secret, I believed in
people with flowers, still do.)*

Lyle Ernst: "One memorable gig played in the summer of '67
was in Amery, a little town sitting alongside the Apple River in the heart
of the St. Croix Valley. A large venue, the Woodley Country Dam, near
Highways 8 and 46, north of Amery, featured many popular bands from
the Twin Cities. Mourning Dayze played in a teen bar, while The
Trashmen played in the over 21 bar. Based out of Minneapolis, The
Trashmen was another rock 'n roll band that would be known as a "one hit
wonder." Their biggest hit was a tune called "Surfin' Bird" that made the
top ten nationwide early in 1964. The song was a combination of two
songs, "The Bird's the Word," and "Papa-oom-mow-mow."

Now, here's why the gig was so memorable. "John didn't have a
reverb for his amplifier and one of the guitarists with The Trashmen had
one for sale. It was a Fender stand-alone reverb and John paid the guy $20
bucks for it. At a gig at the "FogCutter," just outside of Whitewater, John
plugs in his reverb, but it's not working. (John has always done his best to
stress to his bandmates the importance of understanding how their
equipment works as well taking quality care of it.) Then gives it a good
old fashioned, "kick," and watch as amp and reverb topple over. It still
doesn't work. Rick then checks the "lock" on the reverb unit and finds
that it's in the off position. He releases the lock and the reverb works just
fine."

The Mourning Dayze Light Show

John Valentine: *"*As the band matured, we decided we needed a
lighting environment that we could control ourselves. Most of the venues
we played had very basic psychedelic lighting facilities. I had a
conversation with Boyd Mefferd, an art professor at University of
Wisconsin-Whitewater, and we discussed building a system for the band.
*Boyd had spent a portion of this summer in California observing the major
"light shows" that would would often be as big a draw as the headlining
bands. These would include "The Brotherhood of Light" at San
Francisco's Winterland Ballroom and Fillmore West and "The Single
Wing Turquoise Bird" light show troupe in L.A. In 1968 Boyd was*

commissioned to do a huge light sculpture at Milwaukee's Summerfest. The project, while under construction, blew down during a wind storm. At the time, I was holding down a full-time job, but had been a student in Boyd's art class, and still hung around with the art crowd, including some of the professors. Along with a professor of arts, Boyd was a wizard with electronics and lighting as well, and produced "light art," which was relatively unknown at the time. He and I kicked around some ideas and came up with a ballpark cost, which was not cheap. The guys in the band were completely on board with it, so we went ahead with the project.

I built all the mechanical enclosures in my brother's basement cabinet shop, while Boyd set about designing and building the amps, filters, and electron tube controllers that we would use. Boyd settled on using "thin film filtered" lights that produced extremely pure colors. We were controlling about 1,500 watts of lighting with sound that required some heavy-duty components. Simply put, we used the sound from the band, amplified it, and split it into three channels of high, medium and low frequency. The volume of the sound controlled the brightness of the lamps. We added a foot switch panel that would allow us to switch from this system to a random flashing mode, or a solid on-or-off mode.

The effects were mesmerizing, to say the least, and the audiences loved it. Without a doubt, we had the coolest lighting system of any band around. We were definitely "state of the art."

Steve   Strobe Light   John
Ft. Atkinson Municipal Building

75

Doug used the large multi-functional foot controller John had made to engage the multi-faceted light show. The lighting was used to enhance and highlight each individual song, maximizing the audience's enjoyment. It was quite a show! There was none other like it.

Lyle Ernst: "Boyd Mefferd moved on from Whitewater to become a renowned sculpture of "light art." Not only did Boyd design sculpture for Milwaukee's Summerfest, in later years he built displays for light shows in Dallas, Kansas City, Minneapolis, New York City, St. Louis, and other major cities across the United States."

John was always building, creating, inventing, or designing something. We had written an "attention getting" loud instrumental to begin our shows. John built an electronic siren, which sounded just like a police siren, which he "played" and coordinated with our opening song while playing his guitar part. The first time we played at Fort's Municipal Building and used the siren the police and fire department members came rushing into the building because they weren't quite sure what was going on. (Was there a fire or and emergency?) Then they figured out it was us...the band! hmmm.

76

At a recent gig, May, 2011, as Mourning Dayze played, a man came up to Rick on break stating... "I couldn't believe it when I saw the name Mourning Dayze on the marquis. My wife and I came here for the fish fry and wouldn't leave until I was able to talk with some one from the band..." Are you the same band that played at the Fort Municipal building in the 60's? I used to see you guys back then, and you were great. And, I just couldn't believe another band would have that same name!"

Mourning Dayze in the summer of '67, played at Majestic Hills, Lake Geneva's premier music venue which featured national/international acts like The Who, Beach Boys, regional acts like REO Speed Wagon and Cryan Shames, plus solid area bands. The following photos were taken from a featured article in the Delavan Enterprise.

Majestic Hills, Lake Geneva

Doug   *John*   *Steve*   *Rick*

We'd been working regularly with the Adamany Agency for nearly a year. We would soon sign an exclusive contract with him. In August '67, Ken asked us to play a one-week gig at Rudy's Surf Side, Clearwater Florida. You bet we would; sounded like a paid vacation to us!

Doug's wife Cheri and Doug at Rudy's, February 2015

The one catch to playing this club was that we had to "clean up" a bit and wear suits. We also had to send promo material to the club with us wearing suits. hmmm... Well, we did. We felt doing so would provide us with increased opportunities.

This is the publicity photo we used for the Florida gig.
Doug, Rick, John and Steve

Lyle Ernst: "The boys left Whitewater headed for Rudy's Surf Side Lounge, Clearwater Beach, Florida in August, 1967. All four were packed into John's '64 Comet, which was pulling a U-Haul trailer, with no room to spare." **Steve**: "It was a rainy night and we were on our way to play a gig in Florida, Doug was driving. Without any warning, he stopped the car and told me it was my turn to drive. I asked him where we were. He said, " I don't know; probably somewhere in Georgia." I looked around and saw that we were on a gravel road between two cotton fields. Doug got in the back and went immediately to sleep. I decided to find a place to turn around, but the road was narrow with deep ditches on both sides. I drove forward to find a road to turn into and turn around on. As soon as I put the car in gear, the radio began blasting, " A Rainy Night in Georgia." There was nothing I could do except laugh." **Lyle Ernst**: "Rick spent much of the week playing John's flat-top guitar, writing music and lounging on the beach." Meanwhile, Doug and John hooked up with a couple of good-looking local chicks, who worked at the club, one of whom drove a bright red T-Bird convertible. The guys ended up hanging out with the gals all week long, even getting invited to their homes. One night, while Doug and John were tooling around town in the T-Bird with the gals, Steve and Rick drove up to the same stop light in downtown Clearwater and couldn't believe their eyes when next to them were John, Doug and the girls! The T-Bird belonged to John's girl, while Doug's girl drove a VW Bug that she let him drive anytime he wanted. John, Doug and the girls spent a wonderful week together. Steve in the meantime was busy spending time with a little dark-haired cutie. "We spent time together at the beach and at her place. It was a memorable ride home, specially over Look Out Mountain, but they made it. There were some phone calls exchanged in the following weeks, but soon everyone went their separate ways."

Give me a head with hair!!

This is the iconic photo you've been waiting for!
Rick Pfeifer's hair is touching his ears which is proof he wore his hair long!

Lyle Ernst: "In the late 1960's, public schools across the nation still had strict codes of dress and conduct. These included rules against the wearing of long hair by boys, no wearing of blue jeans by girls during school hours, no chewing gum in school, and on and on. To violate such rules was considered an act of defiance and a discipline problem punishable by everything up to and including suspension from school. In the school year of 1967-68. Rick Pfeifer was a senior at Whitewater High School. By that time Mourning Dayze had been playing professionally for two years, and Rick was wearing his hair long like all the other rock and roll musicians. In Rick's opinion, his hair was really not that long; "it only touched the top of my ears."

Long Hair Evokes Headaches, Ask Any School Board Member

Lyle Ernst: "In the August 24, 1967 edition of the Janesville Gazette, reporter Bonnie Moody wrote a 4-column story on the "long hair incident." In it, she interviewed Superintendent P.A. Piddington, two school board members, two parents and a member of the high school faculty."

Moody's story: "One of the teachers suggested that "Ricky" cut his hair and take advantage of a "Sears" sale on wigs. Russell Wessels, father of two teen-age sons, felt that the board should look upon it as a "fad," and exercise some tolerance. He said he remembered how crew cuts were frowned upon during his teen years.

Two board members, Don Grosinske and Norman Anderson took a hard line stance against the "girlish" haircuts. Grosinske said no boy would play on the local school's basketball team with long hair. It's this writer's opinion that Mr. Grosinske failed to note that Rick was not trying out for the basketball team. To further explain the mood of adults during the '60's Anderson said he had fired a youth at his mill that summer because the boy refused to get a haircut. Dennis Conway, a member of the high school faculty, was quoted as saying, "Ricky Pfeifer is one of our best behaved students."

The newspaper article also stated that wearing wigs while playing

81

in a band would not cut it, especially, on the East Coast where the band was scheduled to play for the Brown University Homecoming in Providence, Rhode Island. The article said that the *Supremes,* a popular Negro girls' trio would headline the show."

The school superintendent at that time was P.A. Piddington. Following is a letter recently sent to Rise by Richard C. Haney author and Professor of History at the University of Wisconsin-Whitewater. Rise had asked Professor Haney if he'd like to contribute "something" to the book and he submitted this terrific perspective regarding the "long hair incident," Whitewater High School's Superintendent Piddington was Mr. Haney's step-father. Check this out!

Richard C. Haney, Professor of History, University of Wisconsin-Whitewater: "In the late 1960's, school principals and administrators also were trusted to make decisions on such disciplinary matters based upon their good judgment, and were not required, as is now the case, to strictly enforce every rule violation without exception because failure to do so could lead to a lawsuit. (Consequently, today you read of nutty cases such as an eight-year-old girl being suspended from school for violating the rule against carrying knives because she had a nail clipper in her school bag—the principal had to strictly enforce a rule even though in the particular instance it was ridiculous to do so. (In the late 1960's, such would not have been the case because most administrators would have had both the power and the good judgment to make an exception to the "no knife" rule for the little girl with the nail clippers.) Because it was the late 1960's and he was the leader of his very successful band, he wore his hair long because band members were expected to wear long hair in those days. One of his teachers reported to the principal that Rick Pfeifer's long hair violated school rules. The principal said that Rick would need to get his hair cut to an acceptable length, or else face suspension from school, and possibly even not be able to graduate unless he got his hair cut. (Is this like the fable of the bee that stung the rat that scared the lion that jumped on the back of the elephant that started the elephant stampede that trampled the village!!)

Rick Pfeifer's mother, Betty Pfeifer, made an appointment with my step-father School Superintendent P.A. Piddington, to appeal the matter. I should add that P.A. Piddington was a large man with a poker face (Mom always called it his "school face"), and he could appear rather ominous to most high school students! Betty Pfeifer explained to him that the reason Rick wore his hair long was not to be defiant or to deliberately break school rules, but because his very active and popular band played to audiences which expected band members to wear long hair (it was the late 1960's remember).   In other words, Rick's long hair was part of his job requirement and had a very real impact upon his income. Betty Pfeifer even brought Rick's checkbook along to show to Superintendent Piddington, to prove that Rick's band provided a very nice income for a high school boy.

Dad picked up the telephone in his office and made two calls. He informed the high school principal and the school board president that Rick Pfeifer's job required that he wear long hair, and that as superintendent he was exercising his authority to make an exception to the "long hair rule" in the case of Rick Pfeifer. Rick could keep his long hair, he could not be expelled from school or disciplined in any other way because of it, and he would of course be allowed to graduate. End of discussion. Case closed! (When he needed it, Dad's "school face" could appear ominous to principals, teachers, and school board members as well as to teenagers!) That evening, dad came home and told the story to my mother and me. As I recall, he very much sympathized with Rick Pfeifer, felt sorry that the situation had even gotten so far that Betty Pfeifer had to appeal to the superintendent as a last resort, and was glad that the matter came to his attention so he could help the young man out."

Author's note: "In 1965, Phil Lesh was fired from his job at the local post office in the Haight/Ashbury neighborhood of San Francisco, California for wearing his hair too long; it barely grazed the top of his ears. A few months later, Lesh joined a rock 'n roll band called *The Warlocks*, later changed to *The Grateful Dead.*"

Fall of "68, Whitewater High School

Doug, far left, had to buy a new amp a Kustom black tuck and roll 200 and two black tuck and roll speaker cabinets, each with two 15 in. speakers, to handle the drive and volume he needed. In helping Doug purchase the amp, Doug's dad co-signed for him while Milwaukee's famous Ralph Hanzel signed the bill of sale. John is playing his beautiful Gibson Barney Kessel through a Bogen amp and 15" JBL. Steve is on his drum kit and singing lead, complete with the Taj Mahal on his kick drum. Rick is singing harmony under the shelter of his umbrella, (an idea he "borrowed" from Milwaukee's "Shag"). In front of Doug and Rick, you can see the enclosures for part of the band's light show. Behind Doug, the curtain has been pulled open for the lights designed to work vertically, and in this case, to the side of the band, had a backround to display their vibrant colors. Behind Rick is the band's banner, made by a friend of John's and one of three TVs used as oscilloscopes. Each guitar was connected to its own "TV" and gave the viewer a visual interpretation, via wave form, of what each instrument was playing. Audiences just loved watching the amazing display of patterns which coincided with the music.

NEW OR USED	MODEL	SERIAL NO.	DESCRIPTION OF GOODS OR SERVICES (IF GOODS, GIVE MAKE OR TRADE NAME)	CASH SALES PRICE
NEW	Kustom	19175	Model #4-150 Bass Amplifier	$

DEBTOR STATES THAT THE ABOVE GOODS ARE PURCHASED FOR:
☐ PERSONAL, FAMILY OR HOUSEHOLD PURPOSES; ☐ BUSINESS OR COMMERCIAL PURPOSES; ☐ FARM EQUIPMENT; ☐ FIXTURES.

INSURANCE COVERAGE		MOS.	PREMIUM
			$
CREDIT LIFE INSURANCE ONLY			$
CREDIT LIFE AND DISABILITY	LIFE		$
	DISABILITY		$
TOTAL INSURANCE PREMIUM (ENTER AS ITEM 4)			$

The person proposed for credit insurance by Notice of Proposed Insurance on Debtor's copy, is the person whose name first appears as signer of this agreement, if premium is included.

10. The Debtor(s) agrees to pay said total Time Balance in __18__ successive monthly instalments of $ __37.82__ on the __11th__ day of each succeeding month, beginning __Jan. 11, 1968__ at the office of the Secured Party or Secured Party's Assignee, with interest thereon after maturity at the highest legal rate at which parties may contract, together with a reasonable collection fee in event of default, or in lieu of interest after maturity Debtor agrees to pay such delinquency charges as are permitted by law, and if the services of an attorney be employed for the enforcement of any of the obligations of Debtor, or rights of Secured Party, by suit or otherwise, Debtor agrees to pay reasonable attorney's fees, court costs and disbursements.

DEBTOR ACKNOWLEDGES THAT THIS AGREEMENT WAS COMPLETELY FILLED IN PRIOR TO ITS EXECUTION AND THAT HE RECEIVED A TRUE COPY THEREOF.

This __11th__ Day of __December__, 19 __67__

DEBTOR X _John Henry_
(PERSON TO BE INSURED AS ABOVE)

DEBTOR

SALES TAX . . . . $
1. TOTAL CASH SALE PRICE . . . . $ 397.00
2. LESS DOWN PAYMENT . $ __320.00__ $ 320.00
   CASH + TRADE-IN
Bogen Amp-Cab W/2-Lansing Spks.
(Description of Trade-In if any)
3. UNPAID CASH BALANCE . . . . $ 577.00
4. INSURANCE TO BE PROCURED BY ☐ DEBTOR ☐ SECURED PARTY
   If no insurance premium shown, no coverage will be procured $
5. OFFICIAL FEES _____ $
   (DESCRIBE)
6. UNPAID (PRINCIPAL) BALANCE (ITEMS 3 + 4 + 5) . . $ 577.00
7. TIME PRICE DIFFERENTIAL (SERVICE CHARGE) . . . . . $ 103.76
8. TIME BALANCE (ITEM 6 + 7) . . . . $ 680.76
9. TIME SALE PRICE (ITEM 2 + 8) . . $

SECURED PARTY _Ralph Manzel Enterprises, Inc._

BY _Ralph Manzel_ TITLE President

Joseph Stradinger, Whitewater High School, Class of 1970: E-Mail dated July 14, 2010;

Dear Rick,
I know you could have charged us a lot more, but you didn't, and I'm very grateful. Rick, you are an ageless wonder and Rise looks younger that she did in high school, only a little bit taller. You guys must be on a high vitamin intake to maintain the level of energy you show. Whitewater and the State of Wisconsin can be proud to have a talent like yours. Thanks from all of us from the class of "70."

Lyle Ernst: "The band was popular on college campuses, mostly for its music, but also for its stage props and light show. It is believed they were the first rock and roll band in the State of Wisconsin to include a traveling strobe light."

The Green House

When John joined the band he was living in Delavan; after he moved to a house behind Riolo's on Lauderdale Lakes and then moving again to a house on Whitewater Lake. Finally he settled in Whitewater for several years at the "Green House." The band stopped rehearsing in Betty's living room on Queen Street and began to rehearse in the basement of the "Green House." which the band loved because they didn't have to set up and tear down for every rehearsal-which they used to do at least two nights per week. Rick remembers John having access to a "work shop" in his basement. John's workshop became a place of constant creation and invention. John, now also had a place to work on U-control and RC airplanes, which is an amazing story in itself! (Later in life John would find himself on the cover of RC Modeler and an influential innovator and designer in the field of RC aircraft.) **Lyle Ernst**: "People were continuously hanging around the house, artists, other musicians, friends, girlfriends and girls in common. The house was a very hip place to hang out."

This was a highly creative period for the band

One of John's housemates, Jim, was an art major. The band asked him to design them a new poster and he gladly agreed. Jim came up with this iconic design, which we soon had to stop using because, the minute these posters were put up to advertise our gig, someone would take them down and decorate their house or dorm room with them. We've heard many stories of people's memories and love affair with this poster. (*In 2016 an original promotional poster like this sold for $50 on e-Bay!*)

86

The Hearse

"We could really haul ass!"

Lyle Ernst: "It was time for the band to find its own means of transportation and no longer rely on John's car or Betty and Ray's. "It was Doug's idea to get a hearse," says Rick. "He spotted one on the lot at Superior Coach in Hales Corners, Wi. It was a 1957 Cadillac with 10,000 miles on the odometer. We paid $500 for it. It came from a funeral home in the little town of Campbellsport, Wisconsin, located on Highway #67 south of Fond du Lac. **Doug**: "When we got the hearse to Betty and Ray's house, we found a blood stained sheet stuck under the casket area, and in the glove compartment we found a receipt for a body that was picked up. Under the casket area there was a lot of room accessible from either side. We stored the amplifiers in one side. There was a trap door in the back of the hearse where the crank for the caskets had been. It was the perfect size for a case of beer, and no one could tell that it was a trap door. We drove that old hearse hard. It would plow through deep snow with no problem, but after a while the engine would get so hot we had to turn it off. It had to cool down for several hours before it would start, usually about the length of time it took us to play a gig. Once we drove ten hours to the Upper Peninsula of Michigan in the snow at speeds of 85 to 90 miles per hour and never turned the engine off. Through the years we broke a lot of rims and blew out a lot of tires, and replaced a couple of transmissions."

    Rick: "Dad took amazing care of our hearse. He may have loved it more than we did! While working at Williams' Cities Service, he'd wash and wax it clean the windows (inside and out) and make sure it was running in tip top shape. Dad did this every week. We always pulled out of town looking like stars. One night while working at Hawthorn Melody, he weighed the hearse and trailer when they were full of equipment at 8,260 lbs."

    Rise: "One time Mourning Dayze came to pick me up after choir practice at church, and they brought the HEARSE. My mom got a phone call. My grandma got a phone call. My Dad heard from members of the church at the gas station where he worked. It wasn't good; the gist of it was: "How dare you let the band pick up your daughter at church with a HEARSE. Just sacrilege!" Needless to say, they only did it once. The next time they picked me up, they used a plain old car. Oh yes; everyone survived."

Steve: "The band was heading for a job using the interstate, I was driving and John was sleeping in the back. I had noticed that a family with kids in a mini-van had pulled up alongside the hearse, and then pulled back, which was not so unusual. (People were always pulling up to us when we were on the road, curious about what and who we were as well as what we looked like.) But then the mini-van repeated this three or four times. I woke John up, telling him what was going on. The hearse had original curtains on the side doors, which were pulled shut. John pulled the curtains open and made a face with mouth wide open as if screaming. As the mini-van approached us again, the kids saw John's face and they all began to scream...I could hear their screams as I was driving, and John and I couldn't stop laughing."

Steve: "On a trip to northern Wisconsin, while running without a spare, the rim split and we blew a tire. We stopped at a funeral home in Green Bay where the people were kind enough to sell us a used tire and rim from their own hearse so we could make it back home."

Doug: "I had "found" a red light, similar to those used by law enforcement officers. Occasionally, when we were running late getting to a gig, I would put it on the dashboard and other vehicles would pull off to the side of the road and let us go by. I wonder what people thought when we passed them and they saw the lettering "Mourning Dayze" on the trailer."

Doug: "Then there was the time a tire on the hearse had blown out on I-94. It was sunrise, and we were on our way back to Whitewater after an all-night party in Madison. Rick and I were changing the tire when a state trooper pulled up behind us. He watched us change the tire without saying a word. He didn't even answer when I said, "Do you believe the size of this tire, officer?"

Steve: "Doug was driving and we were all asleep in the back of the hearse. Suddenly, Doug slams on the brakes. I remember looking up and out through the windshield. All I saw was water. I said to Doug, "What happened?" He said, "The road just stopped." Somehow, he had gotten off the main highway and was somewhere close to the Wisconsin River. It appeared obvious that, instead of staying on the interstate he had drifted onto Highway 113 near Sauk City, Wisconsin, and had come to a point where there was a ferry crossing. There was only one problem. At two or three in the morning, there was no ferry to use. Another ten feet and we would have been under water."

More from Steve: "There was the time we were coming back from somewhere near Stevens Point, Wisconsin, on Highway 51, heading south. Once again, Doug was driving the hearse. All of a sudden, he slams on the brakes. Rick asked Doug what the problem was. Doug answered, "A deer ran in front of us."' Both Rick and I told him we didn't see any deer. He replied, "Look, there on the front of the hearse and you'll see deer feathers." We knew it was time for a different driver."

Doug: "We were coming home from some gigs in southwestern Minnesota and near Arnold's Park, in Iowa; a very long drive. I'm driving. Rick's dozing in the front with me. Steve's fast asleep in the back. We stopped in LaCrosse to listen to a band that was playing in a downtown bar. The interstate was not completed yet, so I was driving east on a two-lane road. It was very late at night (actually, early morning) but I could see cars driving east on the interstate. I got onto the interstate and I'm making good time.

There was no grass growing under our feet. Suddenly; "Ka-boom!" I drove off the end of the interstate. I thought I was going east, but actually, I was going west. Needless to say, that woke everyone up. Rick flew up in the air and hit his head on the hearse ceiling. Steve adds, "I was sound asleep, but when the road noise quit, I sat up. I couldn't see the road. It was gone." Luckily, a state trooper came along and told the guys how to get back on the interstate and continue in the right direction, east toward Whitewater."

Doug, like always... doing what must be done.

"In The Mix"

Mourning Dayze began to demonstrate greater interest in playing their own arrangements and writing their own music. There was no reason they shouldn't and preferable that they did. At a rehearsal, Rick told his bandmates that everyone needed to write a song, music or lyrics, and bring it to the next practice. The idea was simple; "I just wanted to see what we could come up with. We'd talked about it, but never really gave it a try as a band." Could any of us write anything? We got together the following week and everyone had brought a song, lyrics or an idea along and we began to work on them. John came up with the title "Man with the Thin Mind." Doug came up with the guitar part to "Are We Going to Say Good-Bye?" Steve wrote lyrics to "Rain Time," Rick attempted to see just how the Byrds did it with "Mourning Dayze" and "Moon that Gives no Sunlight." This is when Rick wrote "Fly My Paper Airplane." We began performing these songs to appreciative audiences. Pretty cool, eh?

Next, we had to see what we and our songs sounded like in the studio, we wanted to find out what kind of magic we could create in that environment. It was Doug and John that kept encouraging us to record; Steve and I were all for it. Our first recording was made at a small studio in Lake Geneva, which gave us first hand knowledge of how the process worked and how we needed to prepare to maximize our studio time. We were fully prepared for our next studio stop, at Leaf Studios, in a converted barn, in Janesville, Wi. *The tapes from this session in 2007 would be released on a CD from Gear Fab Records entitled: Mourning Dayze, The Lost Recordings.*

Used by permission of Roger Maglio/Gear Fab Records.

Lyle Ernst: *"In February, 2004, Rick, for the heck of it, because he'd never done it before, googles Mourning Dayze. He sees a CD listed from Gear Fab Records with Fly My Paper Airplane on it. He gets on the phone and calls Doug to tell him about it and then calls Steve. Doug promptly orders a copy because he doesn't believe it could be true. With the CD in his hand, Doug becomes a believer and immediately telephones Roger Maglio, the producer of the CD. Doug explained who he was and they chatted about 1960's music. The CD that Rick originally saw was titled Psychedelic States; Illinois. Maglio was producing CD's of 1960's bands state by state and because Fly My Paper Airplane was recorded in Chicago, it was included with Illinois songs. After talking to Doug, Roger said, "If I had known you were a member of the group, I would have sent complimentary CD's to you." Roger in fact then sent complimentary CD's to the guys. Maglio told Doug he was planning on producing a Wisconsin CD next and wanted to know if the Mourning Dayze had another song he could include on the Wisconsin compilation. Doug told him they didn't have another record but they had had an old reel to reel tape of original songs in the basement over 40 years that they recorded in a small recording studio in the 60's at Leaf Studios outside of Janesville, WI. Maglio told Doug to send it to him in Florida by registered FedEx. Maglio contacted Doug after some time and told him he was able to "steam" the tape and "salvage" most of it in its original form. He told Doug he had produced a complete exclusive Mourning Dayze CD from the 6 original songs on the tape plus the 45 record with "Fly My Paper Airplane" and "Sadman's Madness!" Never expecting an exclusive CD, the guys were overwhelmed and excited to have their original tunes come out on CD almost 40 years later! Thus, "The Lost Recordings" was born in 2007".*

The Mourning Dayze, a local band group, recently returned from are Rick Pfeiler, Whitewater; Doug Henery, Milwaukee; John Valen week'n tour of Canada. They have also recently played in time, Whitewater and Steve Ellman, Green Bay. The group i nomikee, Michigan, and St. Paul, Minnesota. At the present time booked with Ken Adamany, Ltd. Janesville. g are playing at Wisconsin Dells. From left to right in the picture

Rick   Doug   John   Steve

This photo was often used by newspapers

Exclusive Representation: KEN ADAMANY, LTD. . A.C. 608 - 255-7875 . Madison, Wisconsin

from bottom to top: John, Rick, Steve, Doug

This pic was always a fan "fave"

93

Searching for "that sound" – a couple of greats

While working with the Adamany agency, the band occasionally had the chance to play a job without everyone in the band being available to play. Instead of turning down the job, Ken would find a player to sit-in with us, so we could play the job. We had a date at the Country Aire in Appleton Wi., a club we'd played before, but this time John couldn't make it. Ken said he had a guitarist who was playing bass for the *Roemans* who could fill in for John. (For a while the *Roemans* were Tommy Roe's backup band.) The guitarist would be Berry Oakley, who would later be one of the founding members of the *Allman Brothers Band*. Berry came to Queen Street the day before the job and he and I went through the band's set list. **Rick-**"He was an amazing guy to talk with. I just loved it; he was completely immersed in music, the guitar and the blues. He was an incredibly kind man who didn't seem to mind my asking him countless questions about bands, music, amps, and guitars. (This I did for the entire two days he was with us!) Berry really opened my eyes when told me about Clapton's guitar and sound on the Blues Breakers album, which was a sunburst 1960 Les Paul Standard with two PAF humbucking pickups. (Berry also talked about "The Fretless Wonder", the Les Paul Custom guitar.) Barry said I should check these guitars out, saying they were no longer in production and currently a highly sought after guitar do to their great tone."

A few months after playing with Barry Oakley, Ken Adamany once again asked us to play a job for which he'd supply the guitarist because John was unable to play the job due to work commitments.

Doug: "Our agent, Ken Adamany, had asked us to stop at the high school in Wausau, Wisconsin, to check out a guitar player named Curley Cooke. Much to our surprise, he was playing drums in the band that was backing up the traveling Country Western Stars such as The Stoneman Family, Dave Dudley, Lynn Anderson and others including the headliner, Charlie Pride, whose record, "Kiss An Angel Good Morning," was a huge hit. We were backstage, talking to other musicians, while waiting for our chance to talk with Curley. I was talking to this black dude in a flashy cowboy outfit, not knowing who he was, when the PA announcer says, "And now, ladies and gentlemen, please welcome Mr. Charlie Pride!" The black dude next to me says, "Oh, I guess I'm on. See ya." It freaked me out. I didn't know Charlie Pride was black!"

We played with Curley at the Mount View near Rib Mountain, Wausau. Curley had just returned home for a break, after playing guitar with the Steve Miller Band. Much to my surprise and delight, he was playing a black Les Paul Custom through a, I think it was, a Fender Showman. He sounded fantastic, there was no holding back when he played the blues. I loved it! (I remember the club owner coming up to Curley and telling him to turn down, that his guitar was "too damn loud." I remember Curley looking at us, smiling and then turned his amp up all the way! I was in heaven; now this is rock 'n roll!)

Curley Cook would later play with drummer Rick Jagger and legendary guitarist/singer, Denny Geyer in a combo called "Cook County Jail." I knew Denny for his fine work with Knu Bluz and later A.B. Skhy. (We used to see Knu Bluz play whenever we could, seeing them many times at the Three Oaks in Oshkosh, where you could get a Chief Oshkosh on tap, as well as at Frank's bar in Whitewater.) Denny taught guitar at Tony Kipper's music store in Whitewater. (Denny also gassed his car up at Williams' Citgo where our dad worked. Dad and Denny always had a fun time talking about where each band was off to on the week-ends.) Tony would frequently comment that when Denny wasn't teaching, he was relentless in working to find a new idea or lick. Tony was a wonderful man and one heck of a guitarist. Tony loved the work of the great George Barnes. Tony also sold some of the coolest electric guitars on the planet, "National" guitars.

Tony Kipper

95

While playing a gig at the Rumpus Room in Belvidere, Illinois, I got talking with a guitarist who was sharing the bill with us. He happened to be playing a black Les Paul Custom and I asked him where he got it. He told me he bought it from Rick Neilson, of the then Grim Reapers, who later would be the guitarist with Cheap Trick. He'd mentioned that Rick had other Les Pauls for sale. I contacted Rick, through his dad's music store in Rockford, Illinois, and ended up buying a black Les Paul Custom from him. (The lesson learned; it's more about the player than it is about his guitar.) This guitar was stolen, and months later mysteriously dropped off at Betty's house.

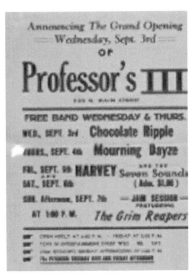

In 2015 a woman who had spent time in the Fox Valley area when we were saturating that area found this poster and then took the time to get it to us just because she loved that era and wanted to share the vibe.

Later in life, Doug would also have a guitar stolen. **Doug**: *"I had purchased a 2-pickup Gibson Sunburst Melody Maker guitar used from Ralph Well's music store in Whitewater when he was our bass player. It was probably an early sixties model that I paid about $100 for with my trade in of my 3-pickup Kay guitar. In 1980 I was working in Milwaukee and renting an apartment in a nice neighborhood, for about $265. I was always working and never home, so I decided to find a cheaper apartment. I found one for about $150 in a real bad neighborhood at 35th and Wells near downtown. [It was leveled a few years ago.] A lot of shooting and* *car chases could be heard in the wee hours of the morning. Eventually someone broke into my apartment and stole my Gibson while I was working late. I was without an electric guitar until about 1983. I was manager of the hotel in West Bend, Wisconsin. A band that had played there for a wedding left their guitar in the banquet room after their gig. I told the housekeeper, Shirley, to put it in the lost & found and she could claim it after 90 days if it was still there. I forgot all about it. Shirley came into my office several months later and said she really didn't have any use for a guitar and would I like to buy it. I said possibly. I had never heard of a Cortez but it did have a nice neck and the pick-ups looked decent. So, I said, "How much do you want?". She said, "Fifty bucks." I said , "I'll take it." It's the same guitar I play today. I think it has a pretty good sound for the stuff I do."*

An exciting photo shoot
top-left to right   John, Steve
bottom left to right   Doug, Rick

So much trouble, excitement, and creativity in the world.

On friday November 8, 1968, we saw The Doors perform live at the Dane County Colosseum. It was a stunning theatrical performance.

The Vietnam Tet Offensive, February 11-17, 1968, was the

deadliest week of the war for the US.

Tuesday, February 27, 1968, Doug, Steve, and Rick saw the *Jimi Hendrix Experience* perform at Ken Adamany's Factory in Madison Wisconsin. Rick's comment on the show was, "I had no idea what I just heard or saw."

Martin Luther King, Jr. was assassinated April 4, 1968, in Memphis Tennessee.

Robert Kennedy was shot by assassin Sirhan Sirhan, after midnight on June 5, 1968 and died June 6.

Mourning Dayze was headlining a show at Sturgeon Bay's Corpus Christi in late spring or early summer 1968. The opening band was "Grease," and they were phenomenal, playing very progressive, guitar based music that was remembered as a combination of blues and jazz with a rock "feel" and approach. Seeds were being planted. During their last year together, Doug, Steve and Rick were playing their own brand of progressive music that was a combination of blues and jazz, with a rock "feel" and attitude.

Steve, Doug and Rick parted ways with John during the summer of 1968 in pursuit of their "sound" and potential. The years with John would long be remembered as a highly productive, creative and fun period in the band's history.

Doug   Rick   Steve   John

A pic from our last photo shoot. Rick, was trying to get us to look like a blues band.

     Mourning Dayze composed of John, Steve, Doug, and Rick, had developed an enormous fan base throughout the state-all by way of their music. There was a sadness and uncertainty felt by many, regarding what the future would hold for Steve, Doug and Rick without John.

     Kathy Forkins, soon to become Mrs. Doug Henry, wrote the following poem in 1968 shortly after it was made public that Steve, Doug and Rick would be moving forward without John.

"Do Not Be Mourning in Your Dayze" Kathy Forkins

Intro

It seems funny now,

to think of each of you,

unique in your own ways,

but beautiful together.

It was the combination that made

that power, beat in your minds and blood.

The sincere smiles and faith grew

each time I saw those minds and fingers

lead their helpless instruments

into astounding accomplishment and glory.

Verse I: John

Joining the scene a little later, you were

still the one with the electrical and

wondrous mind.   It was you who invented,

discovered, and fixed the tools and

accessories that were so important to the whole.

You were the individualist of them all.

It was as though your moustache grew

with each separate mood that somehow thrust

itself at you. You were your own.

Though your mind was a wandering wonder,

you held final authority and respect.

Verse II: Rick

Right in the center of depression,

stood a little star.

The eternal smile of you can never end.

You were full of each bright ray

that sunlight casts on innocence, and is

proud of you. You, the youngest, were always

the leader in ability and enthusiasm.

You were the writer. Your full beard

may shield you awhile from the pain of

greatness, but the gift is yours, and will

someday present you proudly in its ranks.

It is there that you belong.

Verse III: Steve

Singing and swinging through the days, you

walked to the beat of a drum that would not

stop ringing in your ears. You were the man

behind the job, with a colored scarf around

your neck. You could talk your way around a

bush, or into a victory any time you chose.

You knew more about the entire experience

of the four-pillared enterprise and its strength

than you ever could have told.

Verse IV: Doug

During the darkness, there was a humor to
find comfort with. The silent and yet strong power
of your mind could never be known. You were an
electrical tower, but you were afraid. Only your mind
knew without fighting where it was, where it was going,
and when. You could give a smile only when your
thoughts and fingers were not entwined completely
in the beloved music of your guitar strings. Your
silent devotion to what you know will someday lead
you to your purpose. There will not be hindrance.
It was you I should have known best,
but I found I knew you least of all.

Ending Verse

It was an old and nearly forgotten tape that
brought all of you back so completely today.
It was you in your old and beginning glory
that I heard and it took me back to thoughts
I had written and left unfinished too long.
Since that time, three of you have chosen to
break one of your four pillars, and weaken
the strength of what you had strived so long
to build. I hope you will meet the challenge
of what you have done with the same power,
pride, and progress as before. My confidence
in you is great, but astonished.

Fly My Paper Airplane

Steve had been working as an agent for Ken Adamany out of his Madison office. As an agent, Steve found himself very much aware of which bands, state-wide as well as locally, that were breaking up, reforming or going through a personnel change as well as what musicians were looking to join or leave a working band. It was Steve who stumbled onto Chuck Amato, an organist from Beloit, WI., who was looking for work. Steve and Chuck had talked, and musically it seemed like Chuck could be a good fit for the band. Steve proposed the idea to Doug and Rick, and they were were all for it.

Chuck Amato

The band members have very little information on Chuck's musical or band backround. Many attempts were made to contact Chuck, with the hope he would contribute to this writing but to no avail.

With John no longer with us, we needed to find a rehearsal space; the "Green House" was no longer an option. Rick checked with Betty and

Ray to ask if we could practice in their garage, usually called "the barn."
This is when we really became a *Garage Band!* They, like always, without a second thought, said "yes." They would do whatever it took to support and promote the band. We could always depend on Betty and Ray. No matter what the circumstances or time of day, they'd be there for us.

Rise: *"One time while the band was practicing in the barn, the police stopped by to answer a complaint by the neighbors. A cop asked, "How long have you been doing this?" I answered, "About twenty-five years."*

The "Barn"

It wasn't long after Chuck joined us that we encouraged him to buy a Leslie speaker. This would expand our sound, giving us more "color" to work with. Chuck bought one from (where else!) West Allis Music-it was large, heavy, awkward to carry and sounded "fab"! We loved it!

With Chuck with us, we continued playing original music and our own arrangements. We continued to look for our "voice". Like most things in life, much of the creative fun is found in the "looking for." One of the first songs Rick wrote with Chuck in the group was "Sadman's Madness." This would be the B side of their 45 "Fly My Paper Airplane."

Author's note: At this time, the band was being handled by North Central Productions, Madison, Wi. Steve, was also a booking agent with NCP.

Fly My Paper Airplane; the beginning...

Lyle Ernst: "While opening up for the New Colony Six at The *Rumpus Room* in Belvidere, Illinois, Ray Peck of Kiderian Records heard Mourning Dayze play. He was impressed by what he heard and talked with the guys on their break, telling them if they performed any of their own material, he'd like to hear some. They played some of their original work during their second set, including "Fly My Paper Airplane." Ray Peck liked what he heard and set them up for a "big-time" recording session at Sound Studio on Michigan Avenue in downtown Chicago, in November 1968. David Suekoff, a disc jockey at radio station KSTT in Davenport, Iowa, was the producer. It took eight hours to record two songs on a 45rpm record. The "A" side was *Fly My Paper Airplane* (After they'd finished the session, and before they drove home, they made a stop at Chess Studios to see if a friend of Steve's was working because they hoped to catch the "vibe" of that legendary studio) In February, 1969, they had to make an additional trip to Chicago to finalize the mix before it went to press.

Doug and Rick made a third trip to pick up the records. This trip proved to be as adventurous as some of the road trips they made back and forth to gigs. Doug drove. This tells you something already, right? He drove because they took his '57 Ford. I remember those Fords. They were fast. Doug got stopped doing 85 in a 70 mph zone. This was in Illinois. The state trooper wanted cash for the *ticket*. The guys didn't have much cash with them, so Doug offered to write a check. The trooper wouldn't take a check, and let them go without a ticket."

To promote their 45, Kiderian Records set them up to play a show in Menlo Park, Il. with a number of other bands. Headlining was C.T.A. (later to be named "Chicago"). The band also pantomimed their 45 on Chicago television's Pandora Show. At the tv station the guys met radio

105

legends Joel Sebastian and Dick Biondi. *Betty, Ray and Rise,went to Ray's brother's house (Aunt Louise and Uncle Bob) in Chicago so they could see the show. Cool eh!*

"Fly My Paper Airplane" was played on WLS and WCFL in Chicago, but never really took off, although Suekoff told the guys that it reached #9 on the KSTT charts in Davenport Iowa.

The record became a great promo for getting into clubs. They would send one ahead before arriving for a gig. "It was exciting to hear our record playing on the jukebox when we walked in", said Doug. "It was great to walk into local bars in Whitewater and hear it," he added. Rick remembers hearing it on the car radio and feeling like it "had to be a dream!" The radio station in Fort Atkinson played the record on a regular basis, and the guys received royalty checks for the sales. Doug says it wasn't a lot of money, but he still has one of the check stubs."

The re-release of "Fly My Paper Airplane" in 2004 on Roger Maglio's, "GearFab Records," thanks to the internet, brought more airplay and attention to the song and band than it ever had during its first release!

Although "Fly My Paper Airplane" never made it to the national pop charts in the late 60's (it did make it to #9 in Davenport, Iowa in 1969); it will be forever embedded in the Psychedelic Archaeology Volume 9 on Track 5! The Psychedelic Archaeology History is a compilation-10 volumes of psychedelic tunes that were recorded in the 60's by groups, which were never released a second time. Mourning Dayze's "Fly My Paper Airplane" was an exception as it was released more than 35 years later by Gear Fab Records on the "Psychedelic States Illinois in the 60's Volume 1" album. Although Mourning Dayze is a Wisconsin band, they fell under the Illinois heading because they recorded in Chicago. It was again released in 2007 by Gear Fab Records on the album 'The Lost Recordings" by the Mourning Dayze which contains all original tunes. Both albums can be purchased today through Gear Fab Records and other prominent outlets.

Lyle Ernst: "After the release of the Psychedelic States: Illinois CD, Doug began searching online for radio stations that played "Fly My Paper Airplane." The first he found was WFMU, 91.1 FM (NYC/East Central NJ), and it was played on "Worldwide on the Internet." That was in May, 2004.

In June, 2006, KFAI, 90.3 FM in Minneapolis/ST. Paul played it, followed in September, 2007 by KOOP, 91.7 FM in Austin Texas. A Davis, California station, 90.3 FM, played "Are We Going To Say Goodbye?" on June, 2007 and "Fly My Paper Airplane" in September, 2007 and October, 2008. In 2010, 106.7 FM in St. Paul and KFAI in Georgia played "Fly My Paper Airplane". Obviously, it was played on the air many more times, but Doug had to keep his day job."

RADIO PLAY.............

Doug: "What a "high" it was to hear our record "Fly My Paper Airplane" on the local radio station in Fort Atkinson, WFAW, back in 1969! We were told it also was palyed on WCLO and WLS in Chicago. We would have our friends and relatives call the local station in Fort and request our record to be played and it was done! We could also go to the local pubs and hear our record on the jukebox. "Fly My Paper Airplane" was also sent to the clubs we played in Wisconsin and the surrounding states and placed on their jukeboxes prior to our arrival. Little did we know that it was going to be a short run at the time and would end sometime in 1970.

But little did we know that more than 35 years later "Fly My Paper Airplane" would begin to start appearing along with other songs from "The Lost Recordings" CD (i.e. "Are We Going To Say Goodbye?") coast to coast and north to south throughout the US and into Canada.

The first radio play of "Fly My Paper Airplane" actually came off the "Psychedelic States Illinois in the 60's" CD by Gear Fab Records on WFMU 90.1 FM in New York City on the "Cherry Blossom Clinic" show in May of 2004. Steve's daughter actually heard it when it was played! In May and June of 2007 KDVS 90.3 FM in Davis, California played "Are We Going To Say Goodbye" off "The Lost Recordings" CD produced by Gear Fab Records also. KDVS also played "Fly My Paper Airplane" in December of 2011.

In September 2007 KOOP 91.7 FM in Austin, Texas played "Fly My Paper Airplane" on the "Stronger Than Dirt" show hosted by Scott Gardner. His show was described as, "High energy showcase for underground rock and roll from the mid 60's to present day. "Stronger than Dirt" includes garage, psyche, glam, wave, power pop, and ot fun songs." In February of 2010 KFAI 90.3 FM Minneapolis and 106.7 FM

107

St. Paul, "Radio Without Boundaries," played "Fly My Paper Airplane" on the "Georgia" show.

In July of 2010 CIUT 89.5 FM, the University of Toronto Community Radio Station in Ontario, Canada, played "Fly My Paper Airplane" described as "Listen to Real Cool Time with Rocky and Deena." They used the promotion, "We play both kinds of music, rock and roll. Themes, knuckleheaded commentary, and old-tyme Boss Radio ads are often included."

In April of 2012 WMBR 88.1 FM from the campus of MIT in Cambridge, MA, played "Fly My Paper Airplane" from "The Lost Recordings" CD on the "Lost and Found" show hosted by Bob Dubrow, Their promotion read, "<u>LOST AND FOUND</u> explores music of the 60's to mid 70's. We cover all genres, and spotlight music you won't hear on commercial "Classic Hits/Classic Rock' stations. Hits that have been forgotten, or the "hits" that never were!" Other artists' material that was played on that day, April 19th, included "Frank Zappa & The Mothers of Invention," "The Byrds," and "Janis Joplin." We find it easy to understand why our "The Lost Recordings" CD made it on this program."

If you Google Mourning Dayze Band and go to page 10 or Google 50 Psychedelic '60's Bands to Hear Before You Die MP3 and go to the 2nd group listed under More Great Obscure Bands under Sod The Numbering you will find Mourning Dayze listed with bands such as The Byrds, Blues Magoos, Bubble Puppy, Music Machine, The Castaways and The Turtles.

108

CD Covers used with permission from Roger Maglio/Gear Fab Records.

Mourning Dayze

Posted by Joseph Tuesday on www.livinginatree.com

There's this band called **Mourning Dayze** and they are "A Rock and Roll band born in 1965 and still going strong. "

If you like 60s garage/psych and can track down any of their music I strongly recommend it. The thing is, the singer sounds so much like Thame Impala's singer. I like Tame Impala too, I am looking forward to when their CD is out.

Back to Mourning Dayze, I have only heard one song of theirs, it's called "Fly My Paper Airplane" Here is the only info I could find about it "(Kiderian 45115) 2:34 (196?) – B-side is "Sad Man's Madness." A decent psych/rock song with a driving organ throughout. Features a wild lengthy guitar lead in the middle. Maybe 67/68?" Anyway it's good, very much inline with that era, but looking on their site, they seem cool.

Plus their band logo is AWESOME! ☻

This entry was posted on Monday, April 19th, 2010 at 11:22.

Mourning Dayze Discography of CDs

★ ADD ARTIST TO MY WISH LIST

Click on price to add Mourning Dayze albums to cart

Mourning Dayze
Lost Recordings CD (2007)

Discog
raphy

●CD**$12.05**

Recorded in 1967, these psych-pop tracks represent the entire known output of this obscure Wisconsin psychedelic quartet, which layered airy harmony vocals over its fiery guitar solos in a manner reminiscent of the Jefferson Airplane. This collection includes an alternate version of the cult classic single "Fly My Paper Airplane," as well as five previously unreleased tracks. Contains 45s and unreleased material. This Whitewater, Wisconsin band appeared on our Psychedelic States: Illinois In The 60s compilation with their swirling psychedelic track "Fly My Paper Airplane." Now the band have discovered six other original track

Artist appears on
Psychedelic States: Illinois In The '60S, Vol. 1 CD (2004)

Mourning Dayze CD discography

●CD**$12.39** ♫

27 track collection contains many songs that have never been released before. Features a load of Illinois psychedelic groups including Poother, Ultd., Children Of Darkness, Nervous System, The Untamed, The Todds, Mourning Daze, Intruders, Lord & The Flie Gear Fab Records has continued to unearth some of the most obscure '60s psychedelic sides for their massive undertaking of issuing these records region by region, in this case, Illinois. It's a remarkable task, especially since so many relics from the psychedelic era have already been mined for the immensely popular Nuggets box sets, the Pebbles collections, and myriad other small-label collections, but even more of a feat is that the Psychedelic States: Illinois in the '60s, Vol. 1 collection is a truly enjoyable ...

Appear
s On Album

111

Two Responses to "Mourning Dayze"

1. *rick*

   May 3, 2010 at 12:01 pm

   thanks for the kind words. I'm the guy that's singing, playing the guitar and wrote the tune. I continue to gig regularly and keep in touch with the rest of the guys in the original band. It was a good band.
   We always played from our hearts, trying to connect with those who would listen, to share what we felt we had to give.
   rick

   #367

2. *Tuesday*

   May 5, 2010 at 10:42 pm

   Awesome! Thanks for leaving a comment Rick, if you are ever in Western Australia make sure you play a show!

   #386

As a band we had no idea until 2016 that our 45's B side, Sad Man's Madness would have some released with a different title Sad Man's Dayze.
That could be a real collectors item!

2-20-2016 Doug: *"We're on a roll , Fly My Paper Airplane just sold on e-bay for $222.69 in St. Louis!   There were 23 bids!*

Reviews of the Lost Recordings

Artist: Mourning Dayze **Title:** *The Lost Recordings*
Genre: Psych By: Beverly Paterson, the Lance Monthly
Label: Gear Fab Records   2007-07-20

Formed in 1965 in Whitewater, Wisconsin, The Coachmen eventually changed their name to Mourning Dayze, and became one of the most popular acts in and about the region. Curly Cook from The Steve Miller Band, and Berry Oakley of The Allman Brothers once held roles in the group, which actually still exist today. Mourning Dayze never really broke up, as they have continued to play local gigs on a steady basis over the years.

Aptly titled, The Lost Recordings certainly is dominated by material that has been locked away in the vaults since the sixties. The only official release presented on this disc is "Fly My Paper Airplane," which appeared as a single on the Kiderian label. And, what a great song it is, with its celestial Strawberry Alarm Clock styled harmonies, shimmering psychedelic textures, and exciting interaction between a ripping round of crushing drum fills and cutting guitar explosions.

Mourning Dayze also boasted a serious Byrds fixation, as evidenced by a couple of tracks on "The Lost Recordings," which are basically rewrites of "I'll Feel a Whole Lot Better," and "The Bells of Rhymney." Jingle jangle riffs set to brooding tones are regularly heard on the album. The quality of some of the tapes on "The Lost Recordings" tends to suffer at times, but nonetheless, it is a fine souvenir of a band that had their hearts and minds in the right places and a good grasp on the music they made.

A review from All-Music Guide

The Mourning Dayze were a Wisconsin garage band in the mid-'60s heavily influenced by the Beatles and the Byrds and this extremely brief (22 minutes) collection of the group's recordings from 1967 shows just how derivative they actually were.

Copping from the Beatles, the Byrds, the Rolling Stones, the Kinks, the Animals and the Yardbirds is what gives the whole garage band phenomenon of the '60s its signature feel and sound.

"Man with the Thin Mind," which is probably the best track here, bubbles along on a speeded up "Taxman" (via the Beatles) progression while "The Mourning Dayze" is clearly the Byrds' "I'll Feel a Whole Lot Better" with a different set of lyrics. Likewise "Moon That Gives No Sunlight" takes its melody and even the tone and feel of its lyrics from Bob Dylan's "Chimes of Freedom," and the arrangement is exactly the same as the Byrds' version of the Dylan song. All of this is a bit bothersome, but the Mourning Dayze weren't doing anything that a thousand other local bands weren't also doing at the time

Still, nothing here generates more than historical interest, and even the much lauded "Fly My Paper Airplane" (included here in two versions), which has been cited as a lost psychedelic classic, hardly lives up to its billing. Bands like this one were extremely valuable in their local communities, places where megastars like the Beatles weren't likely to visit, but translated to a larger stage, well, the world already had the Beatles and the Byrds, and while imitation is flattery, it's still imitation, however nicely configured it might be. ~ Steve Leggett, All Music Guide

 Mourning Dayze
Lost Recordings CD (2007)

Recorded in 1967, these psych-pop tracks represent the entire known output of this obscure Wisconsin psychedelic quartet, which layered airy harmony vocals over its fiery guitar solos in a manner reminiscent of the Jefferson Airplane. This collection includes an alternate version of the cult classic single "Fly My Paper Airplane," as well as five previously unreleased tracks. Contains 45s and unreleased material. This Whitewater, Wisconsin band appeared on our Psychedelic States: Illinois In The 60s compilation with their swirling psychedelic track "Fly My Paper Airplane." Now the band have discovered six other original tracks.

114

Man... there's bubblegum everywhere!

Lyle Ernst: The Dane County Fairgrounds in Madison was a favorite place for Mourning Dayze to play. One night, in the summer of '68, they shared the stage with the *Lemon Pipers,* yet another "bubblegum" band from the state of Ohio. Their big hit was *Green Tambourine.* Mourning Dayze opened for them and then alternated sets. After the gig, all the musicians got together. The guys from the *Lemon Pipers* said they didn't like the song *Green Tambourine,* saying they were a blues band, and played the blues most of the night.

Janesville: The Meadow was a teen club converted from the old Ace High Roller Rink near the "five points." While promoting their record, Mourning Dayze was on the bill with yet another "bubblegum" band, the Ohio Express. This was another band out of Ohio. Their big hit, which made it to #5 on the charts, was "Yummy, Yummy, Yummy." Doug: "They traveled in a Volkswagen bus that had a picture on the outside of them from on the back cover of Life Magazine. The musicians from the "bubblegum" band told Mourning Dayze that their equipment had been stolen. They asked if they could use our equipment. Later, it was disclosed that this was an "everyday" occurrence because the Ohio Express was one of the bands that was made up of musicians hired by a recording studio and did not have any instruments of their own."

The next day, the Janesville Gazette wrote a review that said Mourning Dayze outperformed the Ohio Express.

Fond du Lac: The Cow Palace at the Fond du Lac County Fairgounds is where Mourning Dayze opened for the "Music Explosion," a one-hit-wonder garage band out of...guess where?...ya, you bet 'cha...Ohio! Their song "Little Bit O'Soul" reached #2 on the charts in 1967. The "Music Explosion" was one of the so-called "bubblegum" bands of the late "60's. After the gig the band joined the "Music Explosion" for some burgers at a local truck stop on U.S. Highway #41 outside of Fond du Lac. As the long-haired musicians from both bands walked into the restaurant, truck drivers began whistling at them. The musicians pushed a couple of tables together, sat down and ordered their food. A few minutes later, the "Music Explosion" keyboard player, who wore really long hair, got up, walked over to the jukebox and played "Little Bit O'Soul." The truck drivers didn't share the irony, but the musicians enjoyed it.

Author's Note: "The Music Explosion traveled in an old
115

Greyhound bus. There was an outside marquee above the windshield that said "Music Explosion." Doug wanted the band to have a bus like that."

The band had often played the clubs in Green Bay and surrounding area, and developed a good following in "Titletown USA," home of the Green Bay Packers. There were plenty of clubs to play in Green Bay and we played our share of them. We were playing the "Prom Ballroom" in DePere for four nights, concluding with New Year's Eve. In 1969 we were staying in a motel five miles from the club. It had snowed so much on New Year's Eve that we couldn't drive our hearse to the job. That was something that just never had happened; our hearse always got us through, no matter what, except this time. Steve and Doug left the motel to make a phone call to touch base with home and to call the club to explain our situation. To get to the phone booth, which was outside the motel, they had to walk up and then slide down a snow drift that was twice as tall as they were! That night, the club owner sent snowmobilers to take us and our guitars, to the job.

In the year two thousand and something, Doug read the book, "When Pride Still Mattered: A life of Vince Lombardi" by David Maraniss. On page 386, he writes about Vince's daughter Susan: "Sometimes after a few beers at the Prom off highway 41 she lamented to friends that it was no fun being the daughter of a famous man. If she did not often break curfew, she loved to nip it." "I was nineteen and my friends could stay out till one and I had to be in by midnight, so I took it right down to the last minute. I had it timed from the moment I left that wherever I was I had to get home by twelve o'clock sharp."

While reading these lines, Doug began to wonder if Susan Lombardi could have been at the "Prom Ballroom" on a night that we were playing there. We don't know, but it's very possible and lots of fun to think about!

Eagle River, July/August of 1969, located in the heart of musky fishing, advertises itself as "The Snowmobile Capital of the World." Situated along Highway 32 and 45, it's about a half-hour from the Michigan border. The band had played Eagle River before as the opening act at the Tank-Teen Center for Chicagoland's "Mauds," who had a hit record in 1967 covering the "Sam and Dave" hit "Hold On." "We were playing at the Modernaire Bar, where we'd played before, and at the Eagle River Sports Arena/hockey stadium. (People came from all over the area to hear us play; they really loved our "West Coast" styled music and sound, especially music by the Doors which Steve just "nailed.") The terrific owner of the Modernaire, "Hop," on one occasion put us up at his beautiful lake home and threw a huge party for us the following day. This time, though, we were staying at an inexpensive motel (what's new!) which surprisingly was located on its own private lake. There was no development on this lake; it was pristine. The owner of the motel told us there was a row boat we could use if we wanted to. So Doug, Steve and I went down to the lake to check it out. Steve told us he was a very good swimmer and could easily swim across the lake. Doug and I made a bet with him that he couldn't. Doug and I hopped in the row boat, and Steve jumped in the water and swam across the lake. Steve won the bet, and that night played and sang as well as always. For the record, Doug and I also made it across the lake, nobody seems to remember that!

Chuck Doug Steve Rick

While gigging at the Modernaire, Hop had told me about a group called "Soup", which had just played his club. He'd stated over and over again what a great, ground-breaking band they were, a trio doing a lot of original material, with jazz, blues, rock and country influences, led by a phenomenal guitarist and singer. Hop, the owner, couldn't stress enough how important he felt it was for us to see them perform. One month later I heard "Soup" perform live in Whitewater at the University. I was blown away, like, what in the world is this! I'd never heard a live guitarist do what "Soup" guitarist Doug Yankus did. I wanted to learn as much as I could about how he played and where he was coming from musically. "Soup" would influence the band, in some form, for much of its life.

MOURNING DAYZE

Bookings: NORTH CENTRAL PRODUCTIONS
P. O. Box 1812
Madison, Wisconsin 53701
(608) 256-0588

IT WAS WILD!

Lyle Ernst: Madison, Wisconsin: The home of the University of Wisconsin was not just any college town. It was one of the leading campuses in the country, and turned out to be the home of one of Mourning Dayze's wildest gigs. October 12, 1969, was the Wisconsin Badgers' homecoming; the band was playing at Elroy Hirsch's former frat house. Elroy "Crazy Legs" Hirsch was a running back at the University of Wisconsin in 1942. The next year he joined the United States Marine Corps and transferred to the University of Michigan where he played football for the Chicago Rockets and the Los Angeles Rams. (It's interesting to note that Bob Burrows, while proofreading the first this segment of the book, commented in the margin that Elroy Hirsch briefly

118

was in the same USMC company as he was.) After retirement, he became Athletic Director at Wisconsin. This would be the day the football Badgers would end a 23-game losing streak by overcoming a 0-17 deficit to beat the Iowa Hawkeyes 23-17.

After the victory, Madison went wild! The streets were mobbed by delirious fans chanting, singing, dancing celebrating the win. The city had reached an all new party level, beer was flowin' and the good times were rollin'! The atmosphere was contagious...It was sooooo much fun! It took the band over 30 minutes to drive 10 blocks. Wisconsin cheerleaders were sitting on the fenders of the guys' hearse trying to clear the way for them. Nobody listened; everyone just cheered! After the band set up at the frat house they found out Elroy Hirsch was there. He was having a great time, pouring beers and getting beer poured on him! A lot of events get labeled great moments in time; this one didn't need a label, it was.

Mike Warner – Singer/Drummer

One of the former agents that had worked for Ken Adamany was drummer and singer Mike Warner. We'd first met Mike a couple of years ago at Ken's Janesville office. (Ken's receptionist was Mike's wife, Sue.) We'd never hung out or played together. We knew that Mike had played with Madison's "Marauders" who had recorded a cover of Bobby Comstocks' "I Wanna Do It" which was a tune, for a few years, every bar band in Wisconsin was expected to play. It was big, and the audiences ate that tune up. We knew Mike as an agent, someone who liked to talk and could tell a story. We also knew he could play drums. Rick remembers the first time he heard Mike play; it was at Ken's Janesville office in the jam room. **Rick**: "I heard someone playing the drum kit, and working on the intro to Led Zeppelin's "Good Times, Bad Times." Mike nailed it with one bass drum and one 'ole bass drum pedal. That was impressive. You can't play the drums with your mouth: or any other instrument for that matter." (unless you're Hendrix!)

Mike had heard Chuck was no longer with us and really wanted to join our group. (One day, Chuck simply vanished from the band and our lives; we never saw or heard from him again.) We hadn't done any business with Mike for over a year or two. Mike, quite unexpectedly, contacted us and asked us to consider having him join our group as our

119

lead singer and front man, not as our drummer. It was a funny thing: we'd never heard him sing. Mike had many contacts with clubs and club owners and was convinced he could get us as much work as we'd be able to handle; we all liked that. Steve, Doug and Rick discussed the idea. Steve liked the idea of having another lead singer in the group: this would give him a break from doing the majority of the vocal work and allow him to concentrate on his drumming. This would also allow Steve to get out front on a few tunes while Mike kicked tubs, like he had done in the band's first years. Having Mike to share the booking and club owner responsibilities with was also a plus for Steve. As long as a change would advance the band, Doug was for it. **Rick**: "I liked the idea; the band would be a trio with a singer out front. With Mike as our front man, that left Steve, Doug and me to handle the music. I really enjoyed us playing together as a trio. It was fun to keep us sounding full and interesting. I loved the challenge and freedom it allowed me as a guitarist. I was curious to see how and if Mike would expand and enrich the group's musical pallet." We agreed to add Mike to the group.

MOURNING DAYZE

204 N. Queen Street
Whitewater, Wisconsin
Phone (414) 473-3916

Rick, Doug, Mike, Steve

Steve   Rick   Mike   Doug

120

Mike brought new musical influences to the group with his love for "soul" music, which he had the ability to sing and perform at a high level, plus he liked the "jazzier" side of pop music-e.g. "Little Wing" and the "fab" New Orleans styled rumba, Albert King's "Crosscut Saw." Mike also listened to a lot of contemporary jazz. When the band was coming home from a gig, the radio (now this is before we had an eight track remember!) was often tuned to WHAM, Rochester NY, listening to Harry Abraham's very hip, iconic late nite jazz show, "The Best of all Possible Worlds," which was a heavenly ear opening, life changing experience.

Mike, as a performer, was very interested in stage presence, especially in how the band dressed and presented itself. Mike enjoyed putting on a show for people on and off stage! I think he really felt that was important. (Mike also introduced the band to "Hall's" cough drops!)

With Mike and Steve booking the band, we found ourselves having as much good work as we wanted. (We had to put a band phone in the "barn" to keep in constant contact with club owners, as well as ordering pizzas and making sure we had plenty of beer! Thanks Paul!) We continued to gig throughout the state, weekends and week nights, all while attending the university. For example we regularly play in Wausau on a Tuesday, Green Bay on a Wednesday and still make our morning classes. We weren't doing "A" classwork, but...we were there! We played a six-night gig in La Crosse, and shuttled back and forth from La Crosse to Whitewater every day and thought nothing of it, "just part of the gig."

Betty would often tell Mike, "I love you Mike and you're a sweet guy but you're such a crook!" Well, when Betty had found out that Mike had a debt of $500.00 which he owed Ken Adamany, Mike's former boss and our former agent, Betty told Mike that she "would not stand for Mike's ignoring the debt." Betty handled most of the band's secretarial needs, which included writing our checks. Betty told Mike she would take a percentage of his cut of the money out of every job we played and send it to Ken until the debt was paid. Betty did exactly that, until the debt was settled. When it was fully paid Ken was very gracious and thankful for Betty's efforts and told her that he owed her a favor. (We had hoped Ken would comment on our book to "return the favor" but demonstrated no interest in responding to our efforts to contact him.)

With all of the traveling we were doing, it was time to replace our hearse and trailer. We'd logged over 100,000 on it; it was a work horse; we loved it; but it had served its purpose. It was time for "new wheels."

121

We decided to purchase a brand new 1970 Ford, Econoline van from Ketterhagen Motors in Whitewater. We couldn't buy it on our own, but with Betty and Ray agreeing to co-sign for us, again, we could...smiles...thanks mom and dad! (We never missed a payment.)

Paul Hazard – Wonderful Friend

Rick: I first heard the name Paul Hazard in an 8:00 a.m. English class I had at UW-Whitewater in 1969. That class met three mornings a week. Every morning the professor would read the role, and every morning no one would answer to the name Paul Hazard. The professor would make jokes or comments every day about this mystery man-to a point, where the class would look forward to what the professor was going to say about the missing Paul Hazard. Paul may have attended class once that semester. Our drummer and lead singer, Steve Ellmann, took me to a lakeside apartment where his sister Carol was living. Paul Hazard, to my surprise, was visiting with Steve's sister Carol and a friend also named Steve; finally I met the mystery man.

Paul and I soon became good friends. Paul loved life, people, pop music, books, higher education, nature, playing poker, living in the moment and being spontaneous. Paul had a deep passion for history, particularly the history of Russia and Royal families throughout the world. Paul had an overwhelming drive to chart the family trees of royal families;

it was research and documentation he did constantly. Paul would attend funerals when he felt there may be royalty or their ancestors in attendance. He usually worked late into the night on his "trees" with enthusiasm, discipline and limitless energy. Paul's love for his work went unabated throughout his life.

Paul loved traveling with the band and always did his share of the work, hauling equipment and taking care of needs as they arose-such as, getting the band drinks and asking women if they'd like to meet the band! Paul was on the payroll for a while, yep, a paid roadie! Wow! Paul was a lot of fun to travel with; he loved life on the road as much as we did, if not more. He was someone we could trust, depend on and was always a great rep for the band .

Paul found himself without a place to live his Jr. year at UW-Whitewater. Betty had no problem letting him stay at Queen St. for a year for next to nothing, and thought nothing of it. It's just the way mom and dad were. It never seemed a burden or an issue, in fact, they really seemed to enjoy having more people around. Paul quickly became a member of the family.

Paul and I loved doing things together, I think he and I majored in pool our sophomore year in school! We spent our share of time at "Howie's Hilltop" watching sports, playing pinball, foosball, the jukebox, and, of course, the bowling machine. Paul, Tom Nelson, "Turtle" and I used to go to watch the Brewer's play ball on Sunday afternoons whenever we could. Those were some good times. Money at times would be so scarce we'd collect pop bottles then return them for deposit, put 50 cents' worth of gas in my '49 Chevy to drive to a bar that had a $2.00 all you can drink special. We always had fun and made our own fun no matter what the circumstances.

Paul loved his family dearly, doing whatever he could to be supportive and help them out. He was the first of his family to graduate from a University an achievement for which they were all very proud. While attending UW-Whitewater Paul participated, in a year's study at the University of Copenhagen, Denmark. Paul had very little, if any, money when in Copenhagen, the letters he wrote were written on toilet paper and the beer he had; was usually thanks to the courtesy of a Carlsberg or Tuborg brewery tour. Yet this was magical for Paul; he traveled throughout Europe and visited his beloved Russia, seeing first hand the world renowned libraries, museums and artifacts he'd only read about. It can be tough to get people to leave a bar or party when they're having a good time, right? With Paul, the problem often was getting him out of a museum or library...smiles. When history came to life, he really was in heaven. While in Denmark, Paul seemed to have found himself and began to live his life as he chose. After graduation, Paul went home to Milwaukee where he worked for a few years, then later moved to California to work in the then exploding, vibrant Silicone Valley. Once a year, Paul would return to Milwaukee to visit his family. He would always make a point of setting aside one night to come to Whitewater to catch up on all of our lives over dinner at a local restaurant. Paul would always insist on paying the tab, usually for a group of about 12.

Astrid and I visited Paul at his beautiful home among the giant redwoods in Boulder Creek, California. It was great to see him so happy and doing so well. He was enjoying life to the fullest and doing it his way. We all loved Paul. He was a wonderful person, loved life and was a great, great friend. Paul died way too soon. I miss him dearly.

Two Memorable Rides Home

Old Main

Lyle Ernst: "It was early morning on February 8, 1970. The

124

guys from Whitewater were heading home from a gig when they heard on WLS radio in Chicago that "Old Main" on the Whitewater State University campus was burning. The fire had been discovered around 10:30 on Saturday night. Someone ran into the Student Union yelling "Old Main is burning." Students rushed to the scene and formed a line to carry out books and other items from the burning building.

Despite the courageous battle by over 100 firemen from Whitewater, Fort Atkinson, Jefferson, La Grange and Palmyra, the 102 year-old four-story building, a campus landmark, was left in ruins. The fire marshal concluded that a fire had been set at three different locations inside the building. Investigators were never able to locate any person, or persons, connected to the tragic fire."

Mike Warner lived in Madison, Wisconsin, while a member of Mourning Dayze. Many of the band's gigs would have them driving through Madison to get to the job. Because of that, they'd naturally pick up Mike on their way through town. In early May, 1970, they were returning to Madison around 3:00 a.m. to drop Mike off at his home. The band was unable to enter the city on John Nolen Drive because the National Guard was halting incoming traffic to the downtown and campus area. A week of protests and violence took place on Madison's UW campus due to the killing of students at Kent State who were protesting the Vietnam War.

Mike was let go in May, 1970, after a gig at Jefferson's "Char-Bar."

Three on a Cycle

Lyle Ernst 2014: *"Doug and Steve each bought motorcycles in 1970. Having lost track of one another for over thirty years, Doug and Steve had no idea that each of them was involved in a motorcycle crash that almost cost them their lives.*

Steve and his fiance had returned to Fish Creek in Door County, Wisconsin, from Galveston, Texas in May, 1976. Steve spent a few years as captain of a charter boat owned by Tenneco Corporation in which he ran scuba charters, marine salvage and harbor tours out of Galveston harbor. (Is that what Doug meant when he would say, "look, there goes Galveston!"?)

125

He had purchased a charter boat in Door County, Wisconsin, with plans to conduct the same type of tours, etc, as he did in Texas. Steve kept his new boat docked at the picturesque little resort community of Egg Harbor, which is situated on the Door Peninsular between the waters of Green Bay and Lake Michigan. Steve's insurance that Tenneco supplied him had run out the day before and he had scheduled an appointment to meet with an insurance agent to purchase insurance. He got on his cycle and took Highway 42 to meet the agent.

Almost immediately, Steve noticed the front wheel of his bike was shivering. He tried slowing down, but it became worse, so he sped up, driving around 70 mph. Suddenly, without warning, the fairing came off, throwing the front wheel into the air. Steve catapulted off. The driver of a bread truck that was following Steve said that Steve slid on his head on the pavement for forty or fifty feet, after which the bike fell on him. Fortunately, Steve was wearing a helmet.

Injuries endured by Steve included part of his left kneecap torn off; collarbone broken in three places; his back was dislocated; a kidney and lung were punctured; there were rubber wheel marks on the back of his leather jacket, and all the teeth of the jacket zipper were gone. The agent passed the ambulance carrying Steve on his way to meet with him.

Doug was employed as a manager/trainee at the Hoffman House Restaurant in Madison, Wisconsin. He lived in Broadhead, Wisconsin, fifty miles from Madison. It was about 8:30 p.m. on August 7, 1977, and Doug was on his way home on his motorcycle after working a long weekend at the Hoffman House. Doug dozed off for an instant causing the front wheel of his bike to leave the road. Waking up he jerked the wheel back towards the road, but it didn't work. He zoomed through a field hitting fence posts and trees. Later on he was informed that two youngsters walking home from the nearby ball diamond spotted him and called for help. He was told that his right leg was wrapped around the back of his neck, which explained his right leg being broken, and his right hip totally wiped out.

Doug's injuries included two broken legs, two broken ankles, broken bones in his back, a broken pelvis, right hip wiped out, the fifth vertebra in his neck broken, as well as numerous hand, arm and finger cuts.

He was transported to the St. Claire Hospital in Monroe, Wisconsin. Doug said, "The first thing I remember after waking up was seeing my family standing around me, along with a priest." Later, he

126

learned that the priest was there to conduct last rites.

The second day the doctors explained his injuries and what they were going to do to repair them. It was at that time that Doug asked the doctors, "What about my neck?" He told them he couldn't turn his neck. Because he was alive, unbelievably, they hadn't given much thought to checking his neck. He was immediately transferred to the University of Wisconsin Hospital in Madison. This was a blessing in disguise, as that hospital has the necessary expert staff to repair the most serious injuries.

Dr. Thomas Lang, the head of the Orthopedic Department, was assigned to Doug. "I became Dr. Lang's "adopted" son during my stay," said Doug. Dr. Lang's support for Doug was immeasurable, considering that about three weeks into the ordeal his wife served divorce papers.

Rick and Rise picked Doug up the day he was released. Betty and Ray took Doug into their home. They gave him Rick's room downstairs and Rick moved upstairs.

Doug recalls that the day he got out of the hospital it took him three hours to put on his clothes."

__Author's Note__: "Four years previous at approximately 2:00 p.m. On November 11, 1972, __Berry Oakley__, a founding member of the Allman Brothers Band (who filled in for one gig with Mourning Dayze) was involved in a motorcycle accident in Macon, Georgia. Driving too fast to make a sharp curve, Oakley lost control of his motorcycle and slammed into a bus. Berry was thrown off his cycle and skidded across the street. His cycle landed on top of him. He was knocked unconscious, but soon came around a bit and refused to go to the hospital.

About one hour later, he became delirious. His friends rushed him to a hospital. At 3:40 that afternoon he was pronounced dead. He was twenty-four years old.

Doctors told his friends that even if he had gone to the hospital immediately after the accident, he would not have survived because he had a fractured skull and was hemorrhaging."

Doug sees Elvis

__Doug:__ *"As a Manager trainee at the Hoffman House Restaurant in the Midway Motor Lodge in 1977 in Madison, Wisconsin, I had an Elvis*

Presley encounter. Elvis had a gig in Madison. I remember the restaurant being extra busy that night very early in the evening so folks could get to the concert. The dining room also emptied early that night, but the entertainment lounge was very busy. w I was in charge of it.

At closing (about 1:30 a.m.) it was my responsibility to collect all the bar tills and count the monies in the back room as I checked out each bartender. As I was counting the money a bartender came running into the office yelling, "Elvis is across the street!" I said, "You're kidding." He replied, "No!" I quickly locked the office door with the money on the desk and ran outside to the parking lot. Actually, I should have put the money in the safe.

From the Midway Motor Lodge parking lot I saw Elvis across the street in the Standard Service Station parking lot. He was in the process of breaking up a fight between three people. Later, I was told the fight was between two customers and an employee. Elvis had exited his limousine. No fight took place. The individuals involved looked on in awe. Elvis got back in his limo and took off. By this time quite a crowd had gathered.

As was previously written, less than two months later, August 7, 1977, I was involved in a motorcycle accident on my way home from working at the Hoffman House. Having been incoherent for over two weeks, Doug was not aware that Elvis had died.

About a week after Elvis's death (August 16th 1977) the bar manager, Bruce Tacke, from the Hoffman House in Janesville where I had worked prior to Madison, visited me and gave me a book on Elvis's life. I asked, "What is this?" "Is Elvis dead?" He said, "Yeah, he died a week or two ago!" It was quite a surprise to me.

The dates are easy for me to remember: August 7th 1977, because of my accident and August 16th 1977 (Elvis's death) which is exactly one year to the date my mom died, August 16th 1976."

The Last Few Months

With Mike no longer in the group, working as a trio seemed like a natural move for Steve, Doug and Rick. After all, they'd been a trio for nearly a year with Mike fronting the band. They knew how to succeed, play, and live together, and really enjoyed the lifestyle. It was never work, they were doing what they loved, and they had their sound together. In their minds there was no doubt that this was the right move. And it was. As a trio they excelled.

Our first gig without Mike was a week at D.J.'s in Madison. As a band we knew we'd go over just fine in the clubs, but we weren't always sure how club owners would receive us because now we were a trio. Most of the venues we played used 4 piece groups and larger. *How many members there are in a band can at times be more important than how a band sounds to some venues. Drawing and holding a crowd will often negate those thoughts, especially when the cash box shows a strong profit.*

The gig went extremely well with fans and club owner. During our week at D.J.'s we began to discuss plans for our summer. It was already late May.

None of the band members were really sure "who" booked them into the "Grotto" in Dyckesville, just north of Green Bay on highway 57, but they were there for two weeks. The band used so many different means of booking themselves it occasionally was "unclear" just "who" booked them "where." Rick had thought Gary Van Zeeland had booked this gig, but when asking Steve commented: "Gary tried to get us to work with him forever. We might have taken a gig with him, but if we did, it was only through Phil Dutcher. We were the band that several agencies wanted because we always went in and pleased the venue, making the agent look good. (Believable in the eyes of the venue owner.) We opened the door for many other bands to follow us including Grand Island and NY."

This summer would be different, and we knew it, our band was soon coming to its end. Steve had been drafted into the military and needed to report for duty at the end of September and Doug, who had been married 2-22-69 at St. Mary's in South Milwaukee, would begin student teaching that same fall at Delavan High School and would later graduate from Milton College in December, 1970. (Doug and Kathy's reception was at Nino's Steak House, Milwaukee across the street from the airport. Steve and Rick left right after the meal for the gig...couldn't miss a free meal!) We made the decision to play as much as we could those last few months. Steve got us working with A.C.A.out of Milwaukee, an agency which had plenty of work for bands that were looking for full-time work and could travel. But not many were like ours! We were no "lounge act." **Steve**: "We weren't playing your "average material by any means; the people who came to see us found us to be refreshing and were often fascinated by the material we played and how we played it. Musician's enjoyed us, and came to see us as well, often wondering how we got away with playing the material we did. We could play high volume material at a lounge volume and easily adjust to the room as it evolved throughout a night." Steve's rapport with the club owners can not be overlooked as a key element to our success. We "hit the road," playing six nites a week.

Ogdensburg, New York:

Doug tells of their trip from Whitewater to upstate New York for a two-week gig, which ended up being a full month.

Doug: "We decided to take a shortcut through Canada to "save time and money by using the tunnel to cross the Detroit Windsor border." It was a big mistake with three "long-haired" musicians in a Ford van. As we got near the border, we could see vehicles going across at a relatively steady pace, but not us. We were pulled over and had to provide serial numbers for all of our musical instruments. And they made us pay a $50 deposit, which was just about all the money we had. After pooling all our money together, we were left with a total of $1.38. Not only did the border guards take all of our money, they delayed us for four hours. They assured us our $50 deposit would be mailed to us. It took quite some time, but about three months later a check for $50 arrived at Betty's house in Whitewater.

When we finally got on our way, we all were starving. There was a Holiday Inn on the Windsor side of the border and we pulled into it in a hurry. Steve checked to see if their restaurant would accept either the "Gulf" or "Skelly" credit card we were using to purchase our gas. (For years we used Ray's "Skelly" credit card to purchase our gas. We weren't sure how far from Wisconsin the "Skelly" card would be accepted, so we asked dad if we could "borrow" another card "just in case" we'd need one.) We were in luck, they accepted the 'Gulf' card, we ate well, then hit the highway.

We had seven hours of driving ahead of us before we'd reach the U.S. border which we crossed early Monday morning. When we reached Ogdensburg we stopped at the first restaurant we saw. With only $1.38 between the three of us, we had to ask a lot of questions of the waitress; questions like, "How much is a cup of coffee? How much is a piece of toast? How much is the tax?" As tired, broke and "grubby" as we were, we were still having fun and making the best of the situation. When we arrived at the hotel we were to perform, we told our story to Corky, the club owner, who was nice enough to give us a cash advance.

Rick: The hotel we performed at is also where we stayed. Rooms were included in the contract. This was by no means a five star hotel. There was one shower on each floor that everyone staying on that floor was to share. The shower on our floor was rusty. The floor mat was covered in thick, green, slimy moss. (It took us nearly a week of cleaning before we began using it.) My room had the only sink with running water. Every morning Doug would knock on my door and announce he was going to take sponge bath in my sink rather than use the funky shower on our floor. (Hmmm... I don't know how Steve ever cleaned up....Hey Steve, did you shower that first week we were there!!? This might explain the reason his drumming was so damn funky that week!) I was getting bored with the lack of color and art in my room and decided to do something about it. One of the things I did was to make an American flag with a peace symbol on it and put it in my window which was overlooking the street. Doug continued to knock on my door every morning so he could clean up, except one morning it wasn't Doug. I heard the knock on my door and a voice said this is the police. Hmm, I thought, Doug again eh? I told him "go away, I'm trying to sleep!" Again there was a knock on the door with a voice saying, "open up, it's the police". This time the voice didn't sound like Doug's. I opened up my door and sure 'nough, there were two policemen at my door! They told me I had to take my peace flag out of the window, "We don't allow things like that in this town son".

We really enjoyed our time in Ogdensburg due to all of the wonderful people we met. We played there a full month and were invited to home cooked meals and plenty of parties. On our day off one party was held on the banks of the St. Lawrence seaway. I can still see Doug in the middle of the seaway with huge tankers and barges passing by as Doug was sitting comfortably in a little rubber inner-tube with beer in hand. Steve and I did our best to get him to come back to the shore, but he'd have no part of it. Steve and I left him there and went back to town.

A memorable day off, Odgensburg to New York City, day/night trip.

Doug: I had talked to Rick so much about NY & NYC in the past that we just HAD to make the long trip (375 miles) to the City now that we were actually playing in NY. Rick had never been there and I don't think Steve was ever there. I had lived in Huntington Station which is next to Huntington, (The home and resting place of the great Harry

132

Chapin.) Long Island, until 2nd grade and returned several times to visit relatives and participate in the 1964 World's Fair in a concert band.

My dad was from Brooklyn so I knew the city somewhat and the famous Jones Beach and Fire Island where the big waves come to shore without any brake waters. We made it to all these places plus drove past Yankee Stadium. The Brewers were playing the Yanks that very same day and we listened to parts of it on our vans radio. I remember a corner bar downtown NYC that had wooden plank boards for a floor and served SCHLITZ! We did the Empire State Building. I felt somewhat bad that I didn't call my relatives but we were on a real tight schedule.

We had Mondays off in Ogdensburg. Right after the gig Sunday night we started driving to NYC. The three of us took turns driving and actually had to stop and rest, being so tired from the gig and all. It seems I remember getting to NYC about 9 or 10AM. I pointed out a parking ramp when Steve was driving where we should park and ended up on the top floor. Rick was leaning so far down his head was almost touching the floor to see the tall buildings. Rick was amazed at the size of the buildings and the amount of the buildings! It was so cool to share this with the guys. We never got a hotel and headed back to Ogdensburg. I believe we once again had to pull over and rest. We got back to Ogdensburg the middle of the morning Tuesday and got some "bed" sleep before going back to "work" Tuesday night!

Lyle Ernst: On another off day, Doug and Rick decided to go Ottawa, Canada, just to see what they could see. (You might begin to get the feeling that there wasn't much to do in Ogdensburg, other than listen and dance to Mourning Dayze, well, you're right!) When the three left for NYC the week before, they put an old hotel mattress in the back of the empty van. They wanted to be able to have the chance to get some decent sleep due to the long trip, there would be no planned stops for rest on that trip. Doug and Rick had no trouble crossing the boarder to get into Canada. They were stopped by the border patrol coming back into the United States, and thoroughly searched and questioned as to why they had a mattress in the back of their van. The border patrol had a hard time believing their story but eventually let them cross.

One more day off in Ogdensburg. The "Boone's Farm" story: Rick and Doug had spent an entire day drinking something new for them, "Boone's Farm Apple Wine." After a little wine, they decided to look up Steve and his dinner date. Yup, you guessed it. Doug drove, and a cop stopped them. He asked Doug for the vehicle registration. By now, the

"Boone's Farm" had taken hold of Doug. As he pulled the registration, which was taped to the visor, he accidentally tore it in half. So, he calmly handed the cop two pieces in stead of one. The cop drove off without saying another word.

The hotel drew some pretty rough people who worked on the St. Lawrence Seaway. The guys found out early on, that it was a good idea to make friends with a sea captain named Joe Marney. Joe may have had more to do with law and order in Ogdensburg than the "law". Everyone respected Joe. He had served some jail time, had been a professional boxer and was very opinionated. You could often find Doug "jawing" away with Joe while they sat on the front steps of the hotel.

Across the street from the hotel was the Windsor Bar. Not only did it have a "three drinks for a buck" happy hour, they also had, the now famous, "Windsor Light Show", which was a single string of Christmas tree lights, with most working, strung overlooking the front of the bar. Doug and Rick stopped in on occasion before gigging. Steve always remembered those nights.

Before leaving for Ogdensburg, Rick just barely caught up with his friend Tom Nelson, then living in Lake Geneva. Rick desperately asked if he could borrow the first album released by the Appleton based band "Soup". Rick: "I was completely "blown away" by this band, specially the guitarist, Doug Yankus. It seemed to me he and his band were miles ahead of everybody else and I didn't want the band or myself to be left behind. I "borrowed" as many licks and as much "attitude" as I could off of that album. We covered many of their tunes and our audiences always, always wanted to know more about those tunes we were covering. The point being, I listened to that album all summer long. It also inspired me to begin writing songs for the band again. I've been eternally grateful for Tom's kindness".

The band had always enjoyed playing pool. It was a great way to relax and clear the mind. When pulling into a new town amongst the first questions we'd ask was, "is there a pool hall in town?"

Doug and Rick loved to take an hour out of their day "shooting a little stick" playing straight pool. Fortunately, Ogdensburg did have a very old, dimly lit, pool hall with well maintained 10' tables. The owner was a woman in her 70's who would sit on an armed raised wooden chair which overlooked the entire length of the long hall and looked you over as well! It was a beautiful picture from a time gone by.

      The band often ate at Bar's Restaurant which was a few doors down from the hotel. (Unless they were eating rotisserie chicken from the hotel after the gig.) This place was great. It featured real home cooking with atmosphere "like you were in an old friends home." It was located right next to the fire station where firemen could often be heard playing horseshoes. One regular at Bar's was named "Springboard." He was an older man who often wore white bib overalls. We never knew why he was called "Springboard." Rick thought he was called "Springboard" because he had a "Gabby Hayes" air about him," 'cause when he talked it looked like he had no teeth and he flapped his jaws just like a springboard!"

      When we left Ogdensburg for good there were a lot of tearful goodbyes. Several of the locals who religiously came to see us play gathered around the van to say their goodbyes. We "hit the road" with many fond memories of Ogdensburg, New York.

      While flying to Germany Doug's wife Cheri was watching the in-flight movie and Doug was watching the GPS route provided by the airline. As we're flying north of New York and thru Canada, Ogdensburg shows up on the moving map! Doug, "I really want to go there and do a book signing when the book is finished."

Eau Claire, Pete's 5th Avenue Bar

The reader needs a little back round to fully appreciate this gig, so here goes. (A year and a half prior to the gig at Pete's 5th Avenue Bar.) **Lyle Ernst:** "Sitting snug in the Chippewa Valley, Eau Claire proved to be a favorite area for both the boys in the band and the girls who cheered and clapped for them. Chippewa Falls, Altoona and Menomonie, all are within easy driving distance of Eau Claire. Fans from those cities flocked to "Fanny Hill", "Pete's 5th Ave. Bar", and of course the fabulous "London

Inn" when the band came to town.

There was one group of fans in particular. **Ronny Larson**, who grew up in Eau Claire, and never missed a Mourning Dayze gig, says, "we always felt lost when Mourning Dayze wasn't playing. All of us would call each other and talk about them. They definitely were a conversation piece." Ronny remembers the London Inn was always packed when Mourning Dayze was playing and always a line to get in. When posters were put up at the bar telling us when Mourning Dayze was coming to town, there was always a buzz. Calendars would be marked and plans would be made. She says that some of the groupies she hung out with included Barb, Tom, Pat, and Linda. "All the girls had a crush on Doug," says Ronny, smiling. "The girls would say, he's so cute, but when we tried talking to the band he would walk away!"

Sandy Thomson and Ruth Anderson were two of the girls who rode in the hearse with the band. Ronny remembers going to Piason's Pizza Place to eat pizza with the Mourning Dayze guys. She recalls one of the band members said, "man cannot live on bread alone. He must have peanut butter."

Laughing, she said, "they never could decide who was going to pay the food bill!"

Now that you have a little back round, let's get back to our week at "Pete's". We pulled into town going directly to Pete's 5th Ave. to introduce ourselves, set up, and check out the club. We also had to find an inexpensive place to stay for the week. No rooms were included with this gig. When asking Pete where we should look for rooms, he just laughed saying we wouldn't find any vacancies in town this week due to a huge bowling tournament that was in town. Man, was he right. *In the mean time back at Pete's... Steve: "There was a very pretty woman with long dark hair sitting at the bar. Her name was Mary Stevens, an art student at the college. We talked for a few minutes, and then she left. She said she was coming back, but she didn't. Many years late, I was in Galveston, Texas, delivering a boat. I was tired, hungry and thirsty for a beer. I asked someone at the marina where was a good place to eat. They recommended a bar/restaurant called "Tuffy's". I walked in and sat down at a table. A waitress came to my table and handed me a menu. I looked up and was shocked to see Mary Stevens smiling from ear to ear. We reminisced about "Pete's" in Eau Claire. I asked her out on a date that night. We dated for awhile, after which we got married and moved to Fish Creek in Door County Wisconsin" Mary and I had a son we named Jon.*

He and I are partners in our company, "Door County Sound and Lights."

So...with no rooms available in Eau Claire or surrounding area due to a bowling tournament, we had to rethink how we'd handle our accommodations. We began playing our first set when who comes to see us play? Ronny and her friends! We got together during our break catching up with each other and began talking about how we were looking for a place in the area that would be able to put us up for the week. Ronny and her friends graciously invited us to stay with them for the week, which we did. Doug's wife, Kathy and our friend Paul, came up the last night and stayed at the house, too. It was a fun filled week topped off by an afternoon spent at "Big Falls". It was a great time.

Ronny Larson and her friends spending a day at the beach with the guys at "Big Falls" near Eau Claire, Wisconsin.

40 Years Go By...and this happens

Doug: "I enjoy going to "Bernie's Bar" (Now called "Steiny's Pub.") in Baraboo to watch football, basketball and baseball games. I had been chatting off and on with a tall blonde named Ronny. One night while talking, I mentioned to Ronny that I wouldn't be in to watch the game the next night because I had a gig at the "Ho Chunk Casino". She said, "I didn't know you played in a band." "Oh yeah," I replied. "I go way back." She said, "Really! I'm from Eau Claire and I used to go see a band called "Mourning Dayze" play at the "London Inn". I looked at her..... "You're Ronny, as in Ronny from the "London Inn" in Eau Claire," and she says, "Oh no! You're Doug from "Mourning Dayze." We had been watching sports and talking at Bernie's for seven or eight years and didn't make the connection until this night!

Doug invited Ronny to come to Whitewater to reminisce with Steve and Rick. The flood of memories was incredible! Ronny, you're as wonderful as ever, how could you not be?! Thanks so much for coming down, it was an fabulous night!

Rick, Steve, Ronny, Doug and Rise at Betty's house

138

Our next stop would be two weeks at the "Erin Pub" in Grand Island Nebraska.

It had been less than two months since we'd played "The Grotto," located a little bit north of Green Bay where we'd met and hung out with a guitar player who'd been playing Green Bay's "Tropicana". "And," says Rick, "like so many people you meet, we never thought we'd see him again." Traveling through Iowa in the middle of the night on I-80 heading for Grand Island we found ourselves approaching the unmistakeable van of the guitarist from "The Tropicana!" We got his attention and stopped and talked for a while. It was a one in a million possibility."

Lyle Ernst: "Steve recalls the two weeks as being a very enjoyable time because the three of them were as tight musically as they ever had been. He recalls that they had been playing at least six nights per week for quite some time. He remembers the three of them discussing this: If one missed a beat or forgot a cue, another would fill it in a way that was almost telepathic. We were locked in!"

The guys traveled to Columbus, Nebraska, on several occasions to take in the horse races. (Hey fellas, don't blow all your earnings! One week Doug and Rick had nothing to eat except liverwurst and white bread.) **Doug**: "Didn't we see a horse run right into a fence one day?" hmm... (*Doug: "On a recent flight from Denver to Wisconsin my wife and I flew over Grand Island and Columbus NE, and the Columbus horse track!")* Steve remembers students from Kearney State University in Kearney, Nebraska asking them to play at their school. He said they would have loved to, but our schedules wouldn't allow it.

Steve recalls that they were playing in a bar and dance area on the second floor of the hotel.

"There was a large glass dome like a bubble in the middle of the room that allowed you to see the pool below. This was my first experience at drinking beer with tomato juice. A "very friendly" waitress put me onto it."

It's worth reminding the reader that not only did these guys have lots of fun on the road, they also rehearsed nearly everyday. They were constantly working on new material and refining their craft even though their last gig was fast approaching. That's just the way they had always gone about their business.

Ft. Leonard Wood, Missouri

The next two weeks found us playing the *Top Hat Club* just outside perimeter of Fort Leonard Wood, in St. Roberts, Missouri. The club is remembered as being made out of cinder block or large concrete block, with us playing on the first floor. Nothing fancy but had everything you needed and served its purpose. Our first night there we realized it was not your usual nightclub. Most of the patrons appeared to be working girls and not really interested in small talk with the band. The motel we stayed at was similar in that respect. Cars and cabs kept coming and going all night long. What was very, very cool about our first night at the *Top Hat*, is that musicians from the U.S. 1st Army Band stationed at Ft. Leonard Wood came to check out the new band in town. Many of the guys in the Army Band had also played in rock'n roll bands or other working combos and really looked forward to talking "shop" with the groups that came through town. These guys not only genuinely dug our band, they also made us feel very welcome and filled us in on "the scene." These guys invited us to visit them at the base where they showed us around the music department. One fella who had his PhD. in music was very interested in hearing some of the current recordings we were excited about. He really enjoyed hearing A.B. Skhy's version of "You Upset Me," loved the horn arrangement and transcribed it after hearing the tune just twice. It blew me away! I have to go over and over and parts before I can nail 'em. (but I do get 'em!)

Steve informed the guys from the Army Band that he had been drafted and would soon be entering the U.S. Army. The Army musicians requested that Steve be stationed at Ft. Leonard Wood. Their request was granted and after Steve was inducted he joined a 9-piece rhythm & blues band that played in the area. In addition, Steve hooked up with a trio (piano, bass & drums) that played for a featured vocalist at the town of Osage Beach situated in the *Lake of the Ozarks*. The band called themselves *The Three Coins* and played at *The Fountain* which was a club/restaurant (500 seat cap.) and were billed as *The Three Coins at the Fountain*. Steve was offered a full-time job there, but shortly after he was transferred overseas.

The first Saturday they played Top Hat a woman came up to them on their break and asked if they would play at her club the coming weekend. Doug told her that our gig wasn't over until one o'clock in the morning. She said, "That's ok, honey, we have an "after hours" club. You wouldn't start playing until 2 a.m.!" So the guys talked it over for a minute then agreed to play her club. She said, "you'll start at 2 a.m. and play until 5 a.m. Friday and Saturday." The club they were going to wasn't very far from the Top Hat.

Doug: We decided we would not pack the equipment like we normally did after finishing a job to travel to the next job. It would take us about 20 minutes to travel to the "after hours" gig. Being a trio allowed us to get all the equipment in the Ford van without packing it tightly. The microphones stayed on the assembled mic stands with the cords rapped around them. Rick and I were "in charge" of hanging on to the equipment as Steve drove. Going around curves and making turns became very interesting hanging on to everything that moved! This worked out well Friday night so we did the same procedure Saturday night.

At 1:30am after the Saturday night gig and traveling to the "after hours" gig we spotted what appeared to be a male hitchhiking in our direction. With no room in the van there was "no way" we could stop and pick up a hitchhiker. As we passed this individual one of us shouted out, "that looks like Paul!" Steve hits the brakes almost injuring Rick and I with the loose equipment flying! This person comes running up to the van, it was Paul!

It's hard to capture moments of excitement but this was unbelievable. Not only were we pumped from just finishing a gig but we

141

were on our way to another gig! Paul never mentioned any intentions of coming all the way from Whitewater, Wisconsin, to Ft. Leonard Wood, Missouri, let alone hitchhiking! Obviously we "found" room for Paul in the van between the equipment and also found room for him in our hotel room! We had a great night (morning) talking with Paul and his surprise visit!

We all loved Paul. I had a question for Paul. "Paul, did you realize that you were hitchhiking in the opposite direction of where we were suppose to be?" "If we hadn't gotten the "after hours" gig you may have never found us until daylight!" Like old times Paul helped pack and load the equipment and like old times we downed a couple beers at the hotel before the sun became too bright in the early morning!

King Turkey Day Festival
Worthington, Minnesota

Steve: We drove all night to get to Worthington where we were headlining for the annual King Turkey Day Festival in their hockey stadium after playing a gig in LaCrosse, Wisconsin. It was around 5:00 or 6:00 o'clock in the morning and we began looking for a place to stay for the night. After asking around we were told that there was an old hotel that had some rooms available. Everything else was full because the town was celebrating "King Turkey Day," a day in which the good citizens of Worthington actually celebrated turkeys.

We found the hotel and booked our rooms. There was a single cot in each room, with a mattress that had a severe sagging problem. The light in the room was a bare light bulb hanging from a ten to twelve foot ceiling. There was an open box by the window that said, "Open In Case Of Fire." It had no glass cover on it. Inside the box was a rope with instructions, "Tie To The Bed And Climb Out The Window."

Sometime during the morning I woke up to a noise I could not identify. I looked out the window and all I could see were turkeys completely covering the street. I went back to sleep thinking I was dreaming. Latter that day I learned that there actually was a "turkey parade!" They herded turkeys down Main Street. Later I realized that when I had looked out I couldn't see any people because of an overhang that blocked my view of the sidewalk below."

Author's note: Turkey Day in Worthington began in 1939, and continues to be celebrated every second Saturday after Labor Day.

The White Hare, Middleton WI.

Our last two weeks together we played six nights a week for two weeks at Middleton's *White Hare*. We also played a Sunday afternoon farewell performance for friends, family and fans at the Armory in Whitewater.

Mourning Dayze Disbanding

The Mourning Dayze have just returned from a busy summer schedule which took them to New York, Nebraska, Missouri, and Eau Claire and Madison, Wisconsin.

They will be playing their farewell and final dance as the "Mourning Dayze" at the Recreation Dance in the Whitewater Armory this Sunday afternoon, September 20, from 1:30 p.m. to 4 p.m.

The group consists of Rick Pfeifer, Doug Henry and Steve Ellman. They have been together for five years, and will be disbanding as Steve Ellman will be leaving for the Armed Forces.

The group wishes to thank all of Whitewater for their continuing attendance and support, and expressed a special thanks to Chuck Coulthart, director of the Whitewater Recreation program.

Steve: Our last gig was at the *White Hare.* A club that featured topless dancers. When we arrived we were told to use a particular room for our dressing room. When I walked in there was a nude dancer standing next to her locker. She said, "welcome to the Hare," and added that there was no problem sharing the room with us.

The club owner was very skeptical about us playing there because we were a trio. He told me that he never had a group of less than six pieces. He was worried that we wouldn't sound "very full." I told him to listen to us first and then make up his mind. He was very pleased that the three of us could put out that much sound. *Steve: "This practice of showing club owners what we could do was why the booking agency used us often. We would be the first band booked into the club from our agency. Because we did such a good job, they would hire other bands from the agency."*

Our Last Night

Steve: That was a terrible night. I had to be at the draft center by 5:00 or 6:00 the next morning. We finished playing and tore down around 1:00 or 2:00 am. I packed my drums in my car and drove to Milwaukee. I got there around three in the morning. My mom gave me a "butch" haircut. She had always wanted to do that.

Next I went to the draft center where I was running around until about 2:00 p.m. That day I got on a plane, then a bus, then another plane, then another bus. Next thing I remember is getting off a bus in Ft. Campbell, Kentucky. That was a very, very strange night and day. I had gotten drafted that spring and thought I was going in right away, but they said I could sign up for a 120 day delay which I did. This allowed us to play together that summer.

Doug: I wasn't accepting it. By then I had a family which made it tougher. I finished school that year and started teaching Junior High English and History. I think the big story is how we stayed together for five years and how Rick was able to keep the band together for over fifty years.

Rick: It was an unbelievable night for me because I'll no longer be playing music and sharing life or hanging with my two best friends. We'd done everything together and now they'd be gone, just like that. How will

144

I manage musically without them? We worked so well together for such a long time. It took me nearly five years after this night to realize that I could not recreate or reconstruct that group or its vibe. To this day I look at the way Doug and Steve handled situations and the day to day business of playing in a band because it worked. There were no egos. We were open with each other and always talked things out and were far from perfect. We always found our way when it seemed there was no way.

Author's note: When the band broke up Doug got the hearse, Steve the trailer, and Rick the P.A. System. Steve still has the trailer and Rick still has the P.A. system. Doug wishes he had the hearse!

The Mourning Dayze
Doug, Steve, Rick

Places we Played
Lyle Ernst

Amery is a little town sitting alongside the Apple River in the heart of the St.Croix Valley. The bar *Mourning Dayze* played in was called the Woodly Country Dam. It was a large under one roof divided by a wall that featured an 18year old beer bar on one side and a 21 year old liquor club bar on the other side. Many of the most popular bands from the Twin Cities played there. *Mourning Dayze* played in the teen bar while *The Trashmen* played in the over-21 bar. Headquartered in Minneapolis *The Trashmen* was another rock and roll band that enjoyed the limelight for a brief period of time. Their biggest hit was "*Surfin' Bird*" that made the top ten nationwide early in 1964. The song was a combination of two songs, "*The Bird's the Word*," and "*Papa-oom-mow-mow*." The Trashmen toured around the world on the popularity of their hit record!

That same weekend the band took a trip to Minneapolis to check out the city and "B Sharp Music," which was a must stop for musicians.

Appleton: The Dar-boy club, (**Doug**: "At the Dar-Boy club, my fingers slipped on a three string cord while playing Neil Diamond's, "Thank the Lord for the Night Time." I turned to Rick and said, "tough cord.") The Quarry,Lawrence University and Country Aire where Berry Oakley, later on a member of the Allman Brothers Band sat in with the guys for a nite. Appleton is where Steve fell head over heels for a hot-looking girl at a club they were playing. The two hit it off until Steve found out she was only 14 years old. **Steve's response**: It's amazing how stories can change over time. There are variations of the girl at the teen bar in Neenah, Wisconsin. During the gig this girl kept coming up to me at the breaks and flirting. After the show, we were packing up and she began telling me that she didn't have a place to go and wanted to move to Milwaukee. I don't recall exactly what she said but it was something about having to move out of her place because of a problem with her roommate. I assumed she was a least eighteen because she was in an 18-year-old bar and they checked people close. So, being the nice guy that I was, I told her I lived in Milwaukee and I would take her there and help her get set up. I lived in Milwaukee where I was going to school at Spencerian Business College and driving cab on the nights when we weren't playing. She came with us to Whitewater and then I drove us to Milwaukee in my car. I let her stay with me and gave her some places to call and start

146

looking for a job and a place to live. Rumors aside, I did not sleep with her, nor was I in love with her. My sister came over and gave her some clothes and makeup for her to do interviews. After a couple of days I come home and find my brother Dave in my house. He asked me to come in the back with him as he had something private to tell me. He told me that the State Police had come to his apartment in Whitewater looking for me, and they had a warrant for my arrest for kidnapping an underage girl. It turned out that she was fourteen-years-old and had run away from home (not the first time). I told her I knew what was going on and told her to tell me where she lived. It was out in the country and I let her out at the end of the driveway. From then on I checked ID's!

Arnolds Park, Iowa: A city and amusement park-just south of Spirit Lake where Buddy Holly, the big Bopper, and Richie Valens crashed and died in a small plane.

Baraboo: *Mike's Teen Bar* and *Fischer's Teen Bar* were "The" place for teenagers in Baraboo in the '60's. But, the *Highway House* proved to be the most memorable for the boys from Whitewater. Traveling the highways and byways of Wisconsin under the banner of the *Coachmen,* the guys played one of their most memorable gigs in 1966. The occasion was the birthday of Dave Dembroski, owner of the liquor store in Baraboo. Betty and Ray drove all the way from Whitewater for this momentous occasion. Doug was out in the audience playing his guitar that was strung with a 35-foot bright red cord. Those were the days before cordless. The next day Jerry Walker, a friend of the band who lived in Baraboo, reported that 23 half-barrels of beer were drank the previous evening.

    Author's Note: Thirty-six years later, in 2002, Doug returned to the *Highway House* as a member of a Baraboo-based band called *Myrtle Moon Pickle & the Spastic Camel Hammers Featuring "Bil" with one "L."*

Beloit: Beloit College, The Pop House

Belvidere: The Rumpus Room.

Bloomington/Normal Illinois: A Huge Teen club. Betty traveled with us to visit with her long time friend Elaine.

Brookfield: In 1966 we played a week at *Papa Joes*. **Doug**: While playing there, Steve drove truck for Stewart's Sandwiches and I worked

147

for Gagliano's at the fruit market downtown Milwaukee. We got done playing at 1a.m., and I had to be at work at 5a.m.. That was my 3rd summer there. During this summer I quit in the middle and permanently moved to Whitewater.

Bryant: The *Polar Country Club*, located on Highway 64 is still in business, At the time the band played there it was a wooden hall out in ther middle of nowhere. The guys were surprised when they first saw it. With the name "country club" they expected something fancier. An all girl band named the *Mini Crystals* played there the same night Mourning Dayze did. The Mini Crystals parents were with them. And good they were. There was a bloody fight in the bar after the gig.

Burlington: The Youth Center and High School. Burlington is famous for the home of the National Liar's Club, Chocolate and Tony Romo, current Dallas Cowboy quarterback.

Cambridge: The *Coachmen's* first gig was at Nora's Store and teen bar.

Clearwater, Florida: Rudy's Surfside

Cottage Grove: The Gun Club and Fireman's Park.

Deerfield and DeForest: The City Festival

Delavan: The Clown Lounge

De Pere: A small town south of Green Bay. The guys were playing at an 18-year-old beer bar called *The Prom*. A terrible snowstorm came up and people came with snowmobiles to take the guys to the gig. Steve remembers a huge snowdrift that was higher than a phone booth. "The phone booth was our only contact with the outside world," said Steve. We slid down the snowdrift to get to the phone booth. But, the snowstorm didn't stop people from coming to see Mourning Dayze play. There were great crowds at the Prom. **Doug**: I think I still have a reel to reel recording from there if anyone has a tape recorder that works!" Doug isn't certain, but thinks there's a good chance that same evening Susan Lombardi, daughter of the Green Bay Packer's renowned coach Vince Lombardi, was in attendance.

Eau Claire: The London Inn, Pete's 5th Avenue Bar, Eau Claire University student union.

Elkhorn: Johnny Cash wasn't the only musician to perform at a prison. In 1968, Mourning Dayze played a gig at the Walworth County Pre-

Release Center in Elkhorn. (The job was offered to the band by their local musician's union, "Local 680," to provide a public service and to help them pay for their annual union dues to "Local 680.")

Granted, these were not hard-core convicts like those in Folsom Prison, but Doug recalls they were extremely appreciative. He says, "when we entered the hall through the back door there was thunderous applause." He says he remembers the prisoners clapping and cheering loudly after each song. The hall was packed full of prisoners that sat in tiered seats like a movie theater. Doug says his most vivid memory is how different it was playing in front of prisoners as opposed to teen bars and youth centers.

Walworth County Fairgrounds (Saturday Night Bandstand)

Fennimore: The Fennimore Hotel

Fond du Lac: High School, Cow Palace at the county fairgrounds.
Doug: This is where we played with the "Music Explosion." At the time they had the top ten hit "Little Bit of Soul." They later changed their name to "The Crazy Elephant" and had the top ten tune, "Give Me Give Me Good Lovin". We ate with them after the gig at the local truck stop. The truck drivers were whistling at us and I think that is the place I said, "that guy's got an education!" It was pretty neat when the keyboard player got up and played their top ten song on the juke box! I believe the keyboard player was 21 and had a Masters in Music. They had an old Greyhound Bus and had "Music Explosion" in the outside marquee above the windshield. I wanted one of those!

Fort Atkinson: The Municipal building, The Owl's Club, and in a dairy barn for post prom.

Freeport: Catholic Church teen dances

Gillet: The Oconto County Fair

Green Bay: Picadilly, Starlight, Riverside, the Teen Center, The Bow Wow Club, The Prom and

Houghton-Hancock, Mi.: Teen Center

Iron Mountain, Michigan: Iron Mountain High School

Janesville: The Meadow was a teen club converted from the old Ace High Roller Rink near the "Five Points." This is where the band shared the stage with the "bubblegum" band, the Ohio Express. The Left Guard,

Red Lion, Ken's Klub, and Isabell's Tropical Ballroom, where they auditioned for Ken Adamany.

Jefferson: Little Mac's, Shorecrest, and Char-Bar

Johnson Creek: The VFW hall. (Ron Wolfe played his drums while set up on table tops!) Their buddy Paul came to a gig played there several years later and while parking the hearse got pulled over by the police. He didn't have a driver's license!

Kenosha: The Fogcutter

Kaukauna: Club 55

Kewaunee: Birchwood Gardens. "Turn down or you won't get paid!" Once said the owner Lester. One night, Doug rode to the gig at Birchwood, in the trunk of Steve's sports car...and oh...he also had his bass!

Kincheloe Air Force Base, Michigan's Upper Peninsula: Rick: I had a final exam I had to take on Friday afternoon, that same night we were to play at Kincheloe in the UP. (nearly 400 miles away!) We did not have "plenty of time" to make this gig-far from it. To make this job "on time" every hour Doug would calculate, then tell the driver just how fast they needed to travel to make the hourly goal. We were movin...and made the gig...on time. We also drove 400 miles back to Whitewater after the job...the drive home took a little longer!

LaCrosse: The Varsity Club, The Bar

Lake Geneva: Majestic Hills, Lake Geneva Yacht Club , Hilton, The Lady Of The Lake. **Doug**: "This is a boat that we played for frat parties. At one party, John had a few drinks while unloading our equipment from the boat at the end of our gig. John walked out to the boat without using the dock! We also got his Comet and trailer stuck in the sand on the beach while trying to turn around and lost the car keys in the sand!"

Madison/Middleton: **Doug**: We played Elroy Hirsch's former frat house- he was at the party. This was the night WI beat Iowa in Madison and the town was going nuts. It took a half an hour to go 10 blocks. It was WI's 1st win in 23 games and it was Homecoming. We had the WI cheerleaders sitting on the fenders of the hearse as we crawled down the street. Countless parties at frat houses on Langdon Street, White Hare, D.J.'s, Dane County Fairgrounds- this is where we played with the "Lemon

Pipers" who had the top ten hit "Green Tambourine." We alternated sets after opening for them. They were doing heavy blues and really did not like the hit song they had. I believe the crowd was out applauding us over them. This was the summer of '68."

Manitowac: The Red Bird

Marinette: Mike's Resort and the Northern Inn. Mikes Resort: This was the first booking we got from Ken Adamany. Steve and I were having a party with some gals at his grandmother's house on a Thursday night while she was out of town. Ken gave Steve a call about 10p.m. that night wanting us to play in Marinette Friday night. We took it.

Marshfield: The Airway. Doug says, "It was a great bar with great crowds. The first time we played there we walked in around six o'clock to set up and a biker was lying on the pool table passed out. One night after playing there I remember Steve and I drinking beer with the owner until nine the next morning. At least I know I was drinking. It was free."

McFarland: Country Club

Menomonie: The Out of Sight (located on the lower level, all of the lights were ultraviolet)

Milton: Milton College's student union. (Doug finished his teaching degree here.)

Milwaukee: O'Brads, Papa Joe's

Monroe: The White Elephant

Mosinee: The Shindig

Neenah: The Ravino had Mourning Dayze '45 "Fly My Paper Airplane" on the juke box. This place was energized. It was a large teen bar that held 300-400 people. Once Mourning Dayze began playing the dance floor would fill up and stay that way all night long......."fab!" Deputy Sheriffs wearing white shirts and badges stood guard for every gig.

Nekoosa: New Year's Eve and 25 below zero!

Oconomowoc: Hight School

Oshkosh: Ralph Hotel, Twin Oaks, UW-Oshkosh

Palmyra: Played on a flat bed truck for a city wide event in 1966.

Pardeeville: High School (Home of Diane, of the famous Madison duo, "Barb and Diane") **Doug:** I believe we played there for their prom or Homecoming. Dick Steele, who is a music teacher in the Dodgeville schools that I met a few years ago remembered the Mourning Dayze and in fact, came to see my C. Monte band play at the West Side Club in Madison and Bonzo's in Baraboo. I believe he has seen the current incarnation of Mourning Dayze at the West Side Club as well."

Platteville: The Grotto

Portage: The Roost, a roller rink that doubled as a teen dance hall

Port Washington: The Old House, Weiler's Teen Bar... **Doug:** "This place employed about 20 Deputy Sheriffs per night. It was a rough crowd with a lot of "greasers/hoods" from Milwaukee. There was actually a chicken wire fence enclosing the stage to protect the band. We took breaks behind the stage in the beer room away from the crowd. One night two guys broke their beer bottles on the edge of the stage and went after each other. We kept on playing as we were instructed to when fights broke out and the cops cleared them out of there.

Prairie du Sac: The youth center

Racine: The Nitty Gritty, Ivanhoe, and Park High School.

Rhinelander: The youth center

Rio: The Country Bar

Ripon: The Brat Haus

Rockford/Loves Park, Illinois: Guilford High School, Loves Park Lanes. Paul Hazard played tambourine with the band because our contract required the band have five members.

Salem: The Pit

Shawano: City Park Pavilion

Sheboygan Falls: "Saved by sailors." The band was playing in the lower bar area of Harold's Club 23. A bunch of drunks got into a fight with the band. One of them blindsided John and cold-cocked him. A group of sailors in uniform jumped in and helped put an end to the fight. It took nearly 30 minutes before the band could begin playing again.

South Milwaukee: South Milwaukee Senior High School... **Doug:** My brother Brian booked us for his high school dance. It was great coming home with the hearse and trailer and the guys all together for the first time. At that time my sister Gayle and her friend Kathy were 11 years old and loved "Fly My Paper Airplane". Kathy is a teacher in Eau claire and they came to see my C. Monte Band a coulple of years ago when we played at HoChuck Casino."

Sparta: The old A&P

Springfield, Illinois: The Red Lion. A long trip on a two lane highway.

Stevens Point: Poor Henry's teen bar where everyone threw their empty beer cans on the floor; also played the University Student Union and a "Teen" club downtown which was for kids 18 and under.
On one of their trips to Stevens Point the heater in the van went out while it was below zero. (Band: we could hardly tell the difference!) The band often stayed at the Holidome in Stevens Point. The night crew regularly let us swim in the pool after hours. The Ink Spots played the Holidome quite often, we'd often run into them after hours at an all night truck stop. (This would be the same truck stop that long time Mourning Dayze bassist Bob Jenson would find himself early one morning sitting next to a man he thought was Johnny Cash. So...Bob, as only he can, asked if he was indeed Johnny Cash...and yip, he was. Bob and Johnny talked a while.)

Sturgeon Bay: Hassie's, Corpus Cristi **Doug:** "Oh yes!....Lots of good times here. Hassie's teen bar by the airport where John did a student pilot cross country flight to this town for one of our gigs. We had a great group of locals that we hung out with after gigs. One girls parents had a funeral home and she had a station wagon with a siren and red light to go with our hearse. Several of them went to college in Oshkosh and came to the Ralph Hotel when we played there. They had a great pool hall in town that Rick and I would go to. The guy running the place was hilarious with his rapid repetition of anything that was ordered from the counter, "orange, sure, sure......big one or little one?, sure, sure."

Thiensville: Teensville. Our Manager Wally Jones booked us here.

Two Rivers: The Library, a long narrow downtown bar.

Waukesha: The Attic at the YMCA where the guys had to carry their equipment up two flights of iron stairs used for the fire escape on the outside of the building.

Wausau: Jack's 23 Club, The Cotillion teen bar, the high school, The Chalet, a 21-year-old club located on Highway 29, and Mount View teen bar where Curley Cooke, noted blues guitarist, sat in with Mourning Dayze. Cooke was an original member of the Steve Miller Band. The guys stayed in a little motel across the street and ate at a restaurant kitty-corner from the Chalet on Highway 29. The first time the guys saw "Fly My Paper Airplane" on a a jukebox was at that restaurant. The restaurant still stands.

West Allis: State Fair Grounds

Whitewater: Hawk Bowl, UW-Whitewater's student union and frat houses, Main Street Freshmen Night, the High School, Riolo's, Baker Hall, girls dorm, The Huddle and Fogcutter. Rise never missed a gig, even before she joined the band!

Wisconsin Dells: Vans, Chula Vista, Del View, Purple Haze, youth center, and street dances. When they played at a beach house on the river, people in Portage, fifteen miles downriver, could hear them.

Wrightstown: The Grotto. We had a good following in that area.

Rick: There were more gigs in more towns than memory will allow.

Now You Know...

This band practiced two nights a week, every week, sometimes more.

During the bands first year, Doug's guitar playing of instrumental classics was heavily featured. Doug played with outstanding style and sound on a Kay guitar with three pickups, ('cause it was cool!) through a Gibson Invader amp. Most of what Doug played you'd recognize, but how 'bout: Moon Race, Let's,The McCoy, Lariet, or Tear Drop? Check those out you surfer wannabes!

During the summer of 2014 Doug and Rick heard Dick Dale play live and perform "Let's Go Trippin," a tune Doug played the first night we met in 1965. Great stuff!

Ever heard of Oconto Beer or Bond's Pickles? Well if not, just ask Steve

154

the next time you see him.

John loved U-control and R/C airplanes. Later in life he would find himself on the cover of R/C Modeler magazine several times for is designs and innovations.

Doug loved shooting basketballs at amusement parks. He thought it was a great attraction,

This band was never late for a gig.

Steve's mom made the cases for his drums.

We all miss the many great friends we had during these first five years.

John was learning to fly single engine airplanes and flew to a gig we played at Hassie's Tap in Sturgeon
Bay, WI. Door County Cherryland Airport was right across the street from Hassie's.

When on the road, Chuck, Steve, Doug and Rick would often stop at a wayside to play wiffle ball.

Flower Power! Doug's first wife had a car which she and her girlfriends hand painted with flowers!

Here's a little known fact......Doug likes Schlitz!

Steve was the bands leader.

One morning after sleeping in our motel long after check-out time the owner of the motel knocked on our door saying in a loud voice, "Dayze, it's morning!"

Rick's mom would deliver his 80 newspapers while he went to band practice.

Doug made sure that all of the equipment was packed up and in its place before and after gigs.

Steve was occasionally complimented for his British accent.

Campbellsport..We didn't play there, but this is where our hearse was from. When we bought it in Hales Corners (Milwaukee) there was a bloody sheet in it and a slip to pick up a dead body from the airport!

While taking some girls home after a gig, we asked them directions to their apartment. They said, "oh, turn right at the tracks." Somehow, we ended up turning right ON the tracks!

Steve took care of nearly all of the bands business needs.

There were very few all night gas stations in the mid-60's. You really had to think and plan ahead if you were planning any long-term traveling after nine o'clock p.m. The Pure Truck stop on Highway 41, Oshkosh, WI., was one of the few you could count on. Always an interesting stop.

The band purchased nearly all of it's equipment from West allis Music.

At gigs we'd tune our guitars to songs that being played on the clubs jukeboxes. It worked for us!

Everyone was welcome at Queen Street, regardless of circumstances or time of day.

Doug occasionally played in a jug band while attending UW-Whitewater.

This band never turned down a gig.

Steve was talking up his home town of Oconto telling us about it's famous Bond's Pickle factory, outstanding Oconto beer and it's local airport. Of course Doug would have a comment about that and asked Steve, "What do they fly at your airport, kites?" Doug, currently a small plane pilot, commented on his remark in 2016, "Little did I know then that any airport is a "big" airport!

Whitewater's Charlie Watson was the photographer for several publicity shots for the band during these early years. The cemetery pic at the beginning of this book was taken by Charlie. Thanks Charlie!

While traveling our stage cloths travelled in Leffingwells garment bags.

Betty not only fed the band and their friends. She also washed and ironed their clothes, gave them free use of her home (anytime time or day), acted as their secretary and promoter, and was also their biggest fan.

A gig we played at Ft. Atkinson's Municipal Building began with John firing up an electronic siren he'd made to start our show. It was realistic, loud and got people's attention. Panicked firefighters from the fire department right next door told us the siren couldn't be part of our show. People thought it was a real emergency!

Betty told a story of Hank William's tour bus stopping in Whitewater by Williams' Cities Service on the corner of Jefferson and Main streets. She recalls watching Hank get out of the bus, then change his cloths right on the street.

"Turn down or you won't get paid!"

The band loved shooting straight pool.

Steve swam the length of a lake in Eagle River, while Doug and Rick rowed the boat.

John's comet pulled a U-Haul trailer full of luggage, band equipment and band to Rudy's Surf Side in Clearwater, Florida. Look out mountain!

The band had a favorite place to make a late night "pit stop" between Hy.41 and Rosendale, WI. on highway 26!

We met the Rockford based group, "The Museum" at Corpus Christi in Sturgeon Bay and hung out with them off and on for two years.

MD played covers of four songs that were regional hits in Wisconsin: "Say Mama"/*The Legends*, "Peter Rabbit," "Stop and Listen"/ *The Shag* and *The Marauder's/Robin and the Three Hoods* cover of Bobby Comstoc's "I Wanna Do It." Former Mourning Dayze singer and drummer, Mike Warner, played with *The Marauders* and on *The Marauders* recording of this record.

After a gig we found ourselves in John's Delavan apartment and we were hungry. Steve called his friend and pizza joint manager (Red Lantern) Dave at 1:30 a.m., asking him if we could order pizza's and have them delivered 15 miles away! Dave delivered the pizzas himself.

With Chuck playing a Farfisa organ sometimes through a full sized Leslie speaker, it brought a whole new sound to the band. We loved playing music by the Doors. (and Steve could really sing it!) Our audiences couldn't get enough.

Chuck never really wanted to sing, but we begged him to sing the Beatles, "Bungalow Bill", which he reluctantly did.

The band shopped for "hip" clothing at Johnny Walker's in Milwaukee and loved looking for new music at Radio Doctors.

A local band, "The Suns," lived on the outskirts of Whitewater at the Puzzle Factory and loved performing the tune, "Don't let the Sun Catch You Crying."

A friend of John's created the first Mourning Dayze banner.   Later friend and artist Rick Cleminson would recreate that banner and design one of his own.

We absolutely loved the life we were living!

DOUG STEVE RALPH RICK
LEAD DRUMS BASS RHYTHM

INTRODUCING THE

Coachmen

"BEST SOUND IN MUSIC"

JOHN - Mgr.   204 N. QUEEN
CALL 473-4510   WHITEWATER, WIS.

PHIL DUTCHER TALENT   P. O. BOX 336   MADISON, WIS.
A C 608-256-5580

WHITEWATER, WI 53190   414-473-4510

Mourning Dayze

204 Queen Street   Phone
Whitewater, Wis. 53190   414 473-4510

160

Mourning Dayze

204 Queen Street
Whitewater, Wis. 53190

Phone
414-473-4510

SCREAM

MOURNING DAYZE
204 Queen St. Whitewater, WI 53190
414-473-4510 or 473-2082

MOURNING DAYZE

204 N. Queen Street
Whitewater, WI 53190

(414) 473-4510
(414) 473-2082

PART TWO:

MOURNING DAYZE:
1970-2016

Fall of 1970: Putting a New Band Together...

Rick: I needed to begin putting a new band together. Not only did I want to continue playing, I also had contracts to fulfill. I wanted to continue playing and keep building on what the original band had established.

Denny Ketterman, my very good friend through high school and college, was also a drummer. We had played together in the percussion section throughout high school. Music was a big part of our lives. We shared many hours of heartfelt soul searching and fun as we were pushing and challenging our limits through conversation while listening to music and playing chess. As long as we had known each other we had never played rock 'n roll together. That was going to change. Dennis and I seemed destined to play together. Denny had been playing in bands for quite a while and had just returned from Texas where a musical project he'd pursued fell through. Denny was currently looking for a new group to play with. Denny enthusiastically agreed to come on board with this rebuilding project. I was grateful to have someone who was familiar with the original group, its music, and me.

Dennis Ketterman - Drummer

Dennis: I first remember performing in front of an audience when I was about five. I went to a Christmas party with my brother's first grade class. The nun asked if anyone wanted to sing or do something to entertain the class. I don't remember what I sang, but I remember thinking that it was fun. This may have been the start of my desire to perform in front of others. When I began high school I met Rick Pfeifer in my band class. He was playing guitar in a band made up of college guys called *The Coachmen*. I believe this planted the seed in my mind that playing in a band would be really cool. I especially enjoyed performing in concerts, and I loved that other classes from school

165

and our parents would come to listen to us. With positive reinforcements, fun and good times, I was hooked on performing.

I began playing drums in a band called *Boiling Point*, and played with them off and on through 1972. I don't know what we would have done without my mom and dad, Betty and Larry. When I started with Boiling Point in high school, we needed a place to practice. Of course, mom and dad let us practice in our basement. I know the loud music was not their favorite thing, but they knew it was the only choice. Because they supported me, they let us play to our hearts content. While attending college I lived at home and mom and dad continued to let us practice. They also knew some of the band members did not have a lot of money, so, once a week or more they would make us spaghetti or some other dinner. Dad also co-signed for a loan for us when we needed some new equipment. How can you beat support like that?

Most of us were under 18 so we needed a chaperone. Thank goodness for Betty Pfeifer, Rick's mom. She was Rick's biggest supporter when he wanted to play in a band. One night she came to our rescue. She chaperoned us so we could play this job. Some other fraternity guys heard us and we began playing for frat parties in Whitewater three or four times a month. We signed with an agent and our playing nights increased as we played throughout the state well into our college years. My idol was the drummer, Ginger Baker. Gradually I got into double bass drums and all the drum solos.

I played with a number of other bands through the years and always dreamed of making it big. However, like a lot of musicians during this time, I joined groups when they first were formed. They would constantly change musicians and gradually they would fall apart, but those were good years.

I didn't make a lot of money but managed to play in some fun places with some talented musicians. There were long trips that got us home after 4:00 in the morning. But despite the long travels, nothing compared to performing for all those people and knowing how much fun we gave the audience, whether they were just listening or dancing their fool heads off. Around that time, the best times were playing at frat parties and when we became the regular band at the old Whitewater Lake Inn. People simply wanted to let their hair down after a long week of working and studying. After all, frat parties were planned to have a good time and, I suppose, to get laid. Who wouldn't like that?

Al Schmidt was one of my favorite characters. He traveled with a couple bands I played with. He was a very intelligent guy who loved listening to music, reading, and studying art. He wore his army jacket with his draft number on the back! Al developed a light show with tons of lights that he controlled during the performance. The lights were hooked up to flat pieces of metal that he would play like a piano to make the electrical connections. He co-ordinated the bright lights with the darker ones while playing them according to the type of song we were playing. I can still see him "freaking out" on his light keyboard as the band was playing an upbeat song. He would be bouncing around singing and being as much a part of the show as the lead singer. He was great fun and very instrumental in getting us gigs with fraternity parties that kept us busy playing locally and also helped us get "tighter" as a band. The more we played together the better we became. Tom Nelson was another favorite with our band. He was a groupie and an all-around good friend who drove the car pulling the trailer. Later on our booking agency put together a local "super band" called US Pure. The drummer's name was Ray Cyr. He was one of the best drummers I had seen up to that time. I learned so much from him. We would be together and he would play a little rhythm on whatever surface was available, and I would copy it. Then it was my turn to lead and he would copy me. The goal was to find a rhythm that the other could not copy right away. This was one of many learning experiences I had. I never really had formal drum lessons except for those I received in grade school and high school-they mostly dealt with playing one drum at a time. Most of my trap set learning came from listening to records and watching other drummers. I worked hard at my trade and I feel that I became a good drummer. All this time I maintained my friendship and music relationship with Rick. By now the name of his band was *Mourning Dayze*. I recall many days spent with Rick in the garage listening to music as we compared lead licks of the old blues musicians to those of the new ones and gazing at pictures of Connie Kreski, the 1969 Playmate of the Year, stapled to the garage walls. We had some interesting chess matches too!

Don't tell Betty, but I remember him not eating lunch at school because he had to save his lunch money for new strings and band equipment. He lives and dies with being able to play music. He was the first guy I knew with this kind of attitude towards something besides sports. Rick knew more about contemporary artists and their influences than I could ever know. He would sit in his garage where he practiced and listen to music and play those licks all day long. He was in heaven! Larry Black, a well-respected Hammond organist asked me to go to Texas and play with a band. So I took a chance and moved to Denton, Texas. When Larry and I arrived in Denton we went to visit the guys who lived above the garage of the house we moved into. We knocked on the door. When it opened all three of them were pointing rifles at our heads. It turned out they were big-time drug dealers. That scared the hell out of me.

Next we went to visit the friend of a new guy in the band who lived out in the country. As we drove up to the back door his friend rushed out and told us to get in the house NOW! One of the guys staying there had just busted out of jail and the police were after him. We left immediately. When we drove back into town, the police stopped us as we were letting our friend out of the van. The police pulled their weapons and told our friend to lie down on the ground and proceeded to search the van.

We located some other musicians but couldn't get anything going. I decided to go back home to Wisconsin. Rick and I had kept in touch, so when I returned and heard that Rick needed a drummer for *Mourning Dayze* I jumped on the opportunity. It was great to be a part of Rick's musical career. He was always a musical inspiration to me.

The Mourning Dayze had turned in their hearse for a van which we travelled in. We had Bob Jenson on bass. Patty Behl sang with us for a while and then Rise, Rick's sister, joined us. I really enjoyed those times as we played every week and Rise' added a great dimension with her enthusiasm, talent and ability to connect with the crowd. As always, there was Rick who was constantly looking for new ways to improve his music and you could tell he was in a different world when he played. This was my last stint with a garage band as I began to turn my life in a different direction. I often wonder what would have happened to me musically had I played with *Mourning Dayze* from the beginning of my musical adventures. I think I would have been a much better drummer and maybe even would have made it an even more important part of my life.

There were many parts of being in garage bands that were not always fun. The time we auditioned for a music contract and failed, the long nights and travel, traveling in all kinds of weather, setting up and taking down our equipment and sometimes not making very much money. But as a young kid that didn't know any better, all these things were part of the fun and excitement I had playing with all the different musicians and rockin' and rollin' to my heart's content. Not much more I really wanted at that time in my life. After all there was always the "dream!"
But, with a great wife, a great family and having had a great career as a special education teacher for over 35 years, life has been good to me.

Denny working out on his kit

Denny's band began as "Boiling Point" later changed to "Tuloma Blue"
left to right Bud Wellman-vocals, Bill Fisher, lead guitar, Dennis Ketterman –
drums, Dave Egnoski-organ, Ken Leszewski-bass (Ken would later play banjo
with the legendary "Piper Road Spring Band")

"Boom Boom" Bob Jenson - Bass

Denny was a critical piece in getting this project moving forward. Denny came with the original group many nights while playing our last two weeks at the White Hare to get a feel for our current material, how we interacted musically and where our vibe was at. During this same two week period our soon to be bass player and soon to be great friend for the next 45 years, Bob Jenson, would by chance on a night out stop by the White Hare catching our gig only days after being discharged from the Navy. None of us had a clue that in two weeks Denny, Bob and myself would be playing our first gig together as Mourning Dayze, nor that Bob's relationship with the band would last for over 45 years.

With help from my great friend, Paul Hazard, who traveled with the original group was like the fifth member of this new

170

group. For the following two weeks Denny and I auditioned a lot of bass players all of whom were from Milwaukee and Madison except for one.

My mom had been contacted by Bob Jenson's brother-in-law, Chuck Coulthart, who had been my seventh grade math teacher and Whitewater State College football standout. He washed is own car on Saturday's at Williams' Cities Service in Whitewater where my dad worked part-time. These were the days when your car entered the drive at a gas station and your wheels ran over a rubber hose that would sound a bell so that a gas station attendant would be aware that a car was on the drive and needed service. My dad with a smile on his face, skip in his step and a little whistle, would greet the driver of the car asking how much gas to put in your tank. He would check the oil for you, check the air pressure in your tires, and wash your windshield. Dad always made his customers feel wanted, welcome, and important. It was a fun and personal experience. Chuck told Betty that Bob had recently gotten out of the Navy and was looking to play with a band "that was serious about playing music."

I was looking for someone who would be familiar with our style and sound as well as being helpful with behind the scenes business. Even though Bob was unfamiliar with our style, he adjusted quickly to our style of playing. Bob was playing his Baldwin bass with nylon strings at that time. (He still has the bass, not sure about the strings.) Bob has a great natural feel for music and for the people he's playing with. He has a natural knack for being in touch with the flow of the moment and being ready to jump in without testing the water or asking why. Bob excells at the art of conversation and public relations.

"Boom Boom" Bob Jenson

Bob Jenson, bass player with Mourning Dayze for over 45 years, grew up and continues to reside in Edgerton, Wisconsin. **Bob Jenson**: "I first became interested in music, when, as a youngster I became a huge fan of a local band called The Ventrills, a group lead by Frank Ellison, a local boy. Following them got me interested in music, so one day I bought a bass guitar and an amp. My first real job as a musician began in 1965 as the bass player for a five-piece band called The Profiles, Edgerton's first rock 'n roll band. Playing with The Profiles was a blast as we were playing strip clubs in Madison. We told the owners we were college kids from Whitewater. They had no idea that our drummer was only 17 years old!

But my career as a musician was put on hold due to Vietnam, as was my career as a hair dresser which I was going to school for at that time.

I got out of the military in 1970 and came back home to Edgerton and went back to hair-dressing school. About that same time I heard that a garage band out of Whitewater had an opening for a bass player. I auditioned and got the job. I enjoyed my time with Mourning Dayze, but after a couple years they decided they wanted to go on the road. I couldn't abandon my hair business, so I left the band.

I was gone from Mourning Dayze for ten or twelve years during which time I played for Dan Riley's country band called "The Barn Swallows." Eventually I wound up back with Mourning Dayze. I've been with Rick and Rise now for over 35 years. It's been an enjoyable run. I've met a lot of nice people and a lot of crazy people. I get paid to drink free and watch pretty girls dance. There's nothing wrong with that kind of job.!

The Profiles!
Coming straight at you!

Howie Stiff, George Henry,
Bob Jenson, Tom Hoge, Vern
Culp

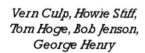

Vern Culp, Howie Stiff,
Tom Hoge, Bob Jenson,
George Henry

When Bob came to gig with Mourning Dayze, his good friend Wally Bartz would usually come with him. (I think Wally may really have been Bob's body guard! Wally is big enough to play defensive end for the Kansas City Chiefs!) Wally has been a great life long supporter and friend of the band. I wrote a song that the band played called "Big Wally." The chorus went, "hey, Big Wally's here, come to see the rock n roll band," it's the stuff legends are made of! In the early 80's the entire band and friends, were on the road, playing a room in Columbus Ohio across the street from Buckeye Stadium. Wally was a tobacco buyer for Mail Pouch tobacco and living in Wheeling, West Virginia. Wally had always told us we should visit him if we were in the area. Columbus wasn't far from Wheeling and we had a few days to fill before our next gig. We gave him a buzz and off we went. All of us stayed with Wally for a couple of days. He made us feel so welcome. Thanks "Big Wally!"

Wally Bartz

The first week Denny and I were together we rehearsed every day in preparation for our first gig which took place at the Lamda Chi Alpha frat house in Whitewater. *Local lore says this is where John Belushi, a Whitewater student, did a fair amount of partying. Rumor has it that the frat house in the movie, Animal House, was patterned after the one we played for.* The gig went well. It led to other gigs on the Whitewater campus and fraternity scene. We weren't the original group, but we were working hard to be our best.

I was doing all the singing with the new group. We had no one who could sing background. We also needed some stage presence. I had been thinking about adding a female singer to the group. It would give us many more options regarding material as well as give us some sparkle on stage. Female

174

singers were exploding on the pop scene at that time. Lots of great new material would be available to us. It seemed like the right move for the band. I placed ads in area newspapers and on billboards on the Whitewater campus with Paul's help. The response was good. We hired a woman who knew music, played keyboards, and sang. Her name was Pat Behl. She was a UW-Whitewater student who lived in Whitewater which made it easy for her to practice with us.

There was one slight problem. She was a bit shy in front of an audience. Our first gig with her was for an Eagle River Homecoming in Eagle River, Wisconsin. We took the stage. There was a buzz in the air. Ok I thought, stage presence; here we go. The crowd began gathering around the stage anxiously waiting for us to begin. All of the guys were gawking at Pat. She turned around, looked at me and said, "they're all staring at me, what do I do?" In my infinite wisdom, I told her to, "sing." She answered, "I know, but they're all looking at me." I said, 'SING!" She sang and the gig went well.

It's a long ride from Eagle River to Whitewater. Pat slept on the speakers all the way home. After two months Pat told us she had to leave the band because her boyfriend didn't like her traveling or hanging out with us. About two weeks later, we heard that Pat had left her boyfriend and had gone to work as a Bunny at Lake Geneva's *Playboy Club*. It was quite apparent that her stage presence with *Mourning Dayze* paid off.

For the remainder of the year Denny, Bob and I gigged as a trio. Bob didn't have a working amplifier of his own at this time. I'd asked Doug if Bob could use his black "tuck and roll" Kustom amp. Doug had no problem letting Bob use his beloved amp for almost three years. (Rise also used Doug's amp for a couple years.) Thanks Doug! (It was the strangest thing to see Doug's amp on stage and no Doug!)

Rise

Sister Rise Joins Mourning Dayze

We still needed a singer. I'm pretty good and was doing my best, but I'm no Steve Ellmann. My sister, Rise, had expressed interest in singing with a band. She came by and watched us play numerous times and knew how much time and work was involved and what was expected. I thought long and hard about hiring her. It was not an easy decision to make mainly due to the lifestyle. Finally I said to her, "if you're really interested in singing for a band, why don't you try out with us?"

Rise was interested. I gave her a song that she and I could sing together. (Believe it or not we had never sung together before this.) It was a pop tune; Neil Young's *Heart of Gold.* The moment we sang together we both knew it would work. Our singing together had that something extra. We both knew it sounded good.

Rise sat in with Bob, Denny, and I a few times just to see how it would go and how it would work in real time. We all knew she could sing and wanted to sing, but how would she handle being on stage as well as "the scene." Rise was just out of high school and bussing tables on Friday and Saturday nights at Riolo's, now Randy's, in Whitewater. Rise began to sit in with us a few times after she had finished work. She'd show up while we were into our third or last set. Imagine her finishing work at Riolo's, cleaning up as fast as she could, getting picked up by our dad, and then rushing to the first gig she would play with us! Denny, Bob and I were playing at the Lamda Chi fraternity house in Whitewater which was a great party house with plenty to drink and lots of heat on the dance floor. Rise arrived dressed to rock and ready to sing. (ya Rise, your hair looked good too, all frizzed, wasn't it?!) The crowd loved her. She was fantastic.

Rise didn't know it then, but soon she would be singing and playing with Mourning Dayze for most of her life.

My great friend Denny had other interests in life other than playing music in a garage band. Things like a wife, utilizing his university career, and considering having a family. Can you believe that?! For me those thoughts just weren't part of my world. All I wanted to do was learn, play, sing and create in a world that was musical. That's how I'd lived before the original group broke up. I saw no reason not to continue. I thought that life was music and that music was life. (Don't tell anyone but I still believe that! "smiles") Denny and I parted friends as our life's journey took us in different directions.

It was time to look for a new drummer that Bob and I could gig with. Rise was not yet a regular member, but, she'd sing with us when she could. Nels Christiansen was a student at UW-Whiteater, had played with a couple successful local groups, was familiar with Mourning Dayze, and was looking for a band. We brought Nels over to the barn to rehearse. He was very surprised how hard we worked on our material commenting, "you guys really rehearse! I thought we would just get together, play some tunes, and have some laughs." We played one memorable gig with Nels on drums. We just weren't what either was looking for. It was a frat party. We were set up on a flatbed truck in the middle of a cornfield. The beer was flowing freely, people were dancing for all they were worth, and when it came time to pee there was only the woods! Fun times were had by all. Nels has always been very supportive of the Mourning Dayze project, Thanks Nels!

The band could not sustain itself and I needed to earn a living. I needed to find work. I still wanted to pursue the thought of making a living playing music. I wasn't ready for a regular job and couldn't even conceive of it, really. I regularly read through the classifieds in a national musician's publication looking for opportunities and networking possibilities for the band as well as my own curiosity and options. I had often seen an ad which was seeking solo artists who could travel and work full time. I had done some solo work in coffee houses and bars and always enjoyed it. I put a promo-pack together, got enough material together to make a four hour six nite a week gig interesting, found an agent to take care of bookings and hit the road. After three months I was rethinking my position and found myself considering putting another band together.

Here Comes Robert E. Lee!

Robert E. Lee

I was at Howie's Hilltop having a beer. It was late winter or early spring and I was talking with my friend Tom Egnoski. Tom's older brother Dave and I were high school and college classmates. Dave and Denny Ketterman were band mates in the group "Boiling Point" later to be called "Tuloma Blue." Tom always had some interest in Mourning Dayze. Our conversations often turned to music. I had mentioned to him that I was considering putting the band back together again with Rise on vocals, Bob Jenson, on bass and myself-and that I would be needing a drummer. I was hoping to find someone local to make rehearsing easier. Tom asked if I knew Whitewater native Bob

178

Lee, a drummer, who had led his own band "Robert E. Lee and the Rebels." He was looking for someone to play with. I didn't know Bob was a drummer. I sure knew the family and of course knew Bob's dad, "Cousin Otto," the world famous circus clown.

ROBERT E. LEE
AND THE REBELS

A Regiment of Rhythm

WHITEWATER, WISCONSIN

I gave Bob a call to see if he would be interested in auditioning. Bob seemed excited about the opportunity and agreed to give it a try. I gave Bob some tunes that we would play at the audition and told him to learn them. At the audition I could tell Bob had listened to the tunes but did not learn them as a bass player or keyboard player would learn theirs. He sure seemed to enjoy playing. The band needed a drummer who was a complete musician able to understand the tune, lay down the groove, play musically, be able to learn his parts just like the other members did, and rehearse regularly. I told Bob this is what was expected of him if he wanted the job. At the next rehearsal it was clear Bob's awareness had shifted. He began playing with an equal desire to learn, work, and have fun. Bob was on his way to becoming a musician and life long friend.

Rick   Bob Jenson   Robert E. Lee

179

With Bob on bass and Bob on drums we soon started calling Bob Jenson B.J. or Boom Boom so we would know who was who. It just made things easier. Soon Rise became a full time member bringing her great voice, sparkle and showmanship to the group along with the female song book. With Rise we also had the opportunity to sing duets and add some very welcome background vocals. It was a win, win, win situation, Yea Rise!

Rise: "All I wanted to do was sing."

Rise: "The first time I remember wanting to be a singer was in the fourth grade. That's all I ever wanted to do. I didn't sing the way most girls did back then. I was not real sweet and pretty but loud and soulful. A bunch of us would get together. Someone would bring their record player and all of us would bring our favorite 45's and hang out and dance. That was a big deal. Later on I was allowed to sing solo in the church choir. Not because I had the best voice but because I had the loudest. Every Thursday, Mom or Dad would drive Rick and I to Waukesha for music lessons. I played the organ and Rick played the guitar. Looking back I don't know how my father did it. He worked two jobs. The nights he took us for music lessons he spent two hours driving us back and forth as well as waiting a half an hour during lessons. As soon as we got home he went to work on his second job.

Some years later Rick joined a rock and roll band. Needless to say I thought that was the coolest thing ever. Never did I dream that someday I would be a member of his band. I would listen to them practice in my parent's living room. They were so loud you couldn't talk or hear yourself think and yet my little sister, Renee, who wasn't quite one-year-old would sleep right through it.

It was a different time and there weren't many girls in bands. While I was still in high school there were a couple college girls in a band. It was 1971. I was just out of high school and getting prepared to attend the university in Whitewater. I wanted to sing in the band, but even though Rick knew I could sing I had to audition. I sang "Heart of God," a Neil Young hit. I

only sang harmony on the chorus. It took about five minutes and after I was done they sent me out of the barn where they were practicing so they could talk it over.
I became part of the band. So here I am all those years later, and I sing!"

Rise

Rise and Bob Lee's first gig as regular members of Mourning Dayze was at The Lamp on Blackhawk Island, Ft. Atkinson, Wi. The owner told us we needed to play a few country tunes if we were going to get the job at his club. We wanted the job so we learned a few which were notably the Tennessee Waltz and Honky Tonk Angels. Rise and I still play those from time to time.
    The Lamp's door checker/bouncer, Frankie, really enjoyed what we were doing and suggested we try to get work at Gensler's Roadhouse in Janesville. We got an audition and got the job. For three consecutive summers we played Gensler's 5-6 nights a week. We loved the regular work. The band was getting tight and sounding good. We were living a musicians dream. Except maybe for B.J. who was working his full time job as a hairdresser at Bev's next to Len's Plumbing and was married. How'd you do all that back then Boom Boom? oh...I know, I just forgot...Sailors Do It Better! (Maybe that's his secret!, or, was the

back of his bass his real motivator? hmmmmm) It was a great club to play. We played whatever we wanted to, had plenty of dancers, and always had a good time. Frankie still comes to see us play when we are in the Ft. Atkinson area. It's always good to see him, and he's still pulling for us!

Unknown neighborhood kids who often came to the band's practices with Rise, Rick, B.J., Bob

Whitewater

Whitewater and the surrounding area during the 60's and early 70's was buzzing with great live music. You never had to go looking for it. It was always there. The Matadors from neighboring Palmyra were the hottest band in the area. They looked cool and sounded great. The local college brought in national and local headliners to perform at Hyer auditorium and other sites on campus. There was a very active folk scene on campus and off with plenty of places to play. Whitewater had its own folk club, the "Fertile Turtle" below the "Busy Bee." John often played there. Doug played in a jug band every now and

182

then while he attended Whitewater. The college's old heating plant used to be the site for musical "happenings,"or "freak outs" during the late 60's. These would involve teachers, students and locals-everyone was welcome. It was "anything goes" performance art! You could find Clayton Bailey riding his Harley and wearing a large rubber neck tie, Boyd Mefferd playing with light, and Rick Jagger wearing strange looking earmuffs. People would bring instruments they would play alone or with a group, others would dance or move to the music. Artists would create as they were inspired. There was a light art show to experience and individuals reading aloud. People had the chance to express themselves freely. It was fun while it lasted. Don Crawford was a folksinger who played the UW "coffee house" circuit and was like a star on the Whitewater campus. In many ways he was the voice for many on campus. Whitewater's "Hawk Bowl" ran some of the finest live music Wisconsin had to offer. Bands always played to a packed dance floor. Commercial Bank president, Jon Kachel, will remind you if you didn't know already, that his father, Dave, once booked "Bill Haley & His Comets" at the Hawk Bowl! Tony Kipper's music store in Whitewater was a magnet for guitarists. Tony was a kind and gentle man who loved the stylings of the great George Barnes, sold National guitars, and spent many a day listening to the great guitarist Denny Geyer playing in his store. Tony would say, "Denny's always looking for some new lick or idea to play." Denny's band, "New Blues/Knu Bluz," would often play at "Frank's" bar in Whitewater. That band had an all-star lineup. Sam McCue was on guitar, Terry Anderson on drums, Jim Marcotte on bass, Denny Geyer on guitar and Jim Liban on harmonica. "Frank's" was located across the street from Williams' Cities Service, where our dad worked. Denny often gassed up there and loved talking to dad about a life in music. The fabulous bluesman Paul Filipowicz could be heard at Mitchel's bar every now and then pulling out his harp and playing the blues with passion,love, energy and style. Live bluegrass was available, long before it was "hip" on Thursday nights at RB's bar by the now legendary, Whitewater born "Piper Road Spring Band." and the great Jerry Hartman and The legendary polka kings, Verne Meisner and his son Steve, who

183

lived just across the street from our parents home and the barn. Steve was young at this time and Rise would often baby sit for him. There was always music just pouring out of their house with a young Steve working on his chops, Verne's rehearsals, or a great gathering and party. It just seemed to me that that's what life was all about when you had music inside of you. Many nights we'd see Verne and his trailer pulling out of the drive about the same time as us going to a gig. We'd often see him returning home in the early hours of the morning. We'd wave to each other and that was enough said. Our bands played different styles of music but each had a lot of respect for what each other did in getting gigs, packing up, traveling to the job, setting up, tearing down and driving home.

A very special thanks for your life long support to Randy's, Johnny C's, Rick's Eastsider, Frawley Oil Company, The Whitewater Register, Alan Luckett and Whitewater Community Television, Pastor Jerry Wendt, First Citizens State Bank, Commercial Bank, and UW-Whitewater.

Thank you Whitewater for all of your support from 1965 on. You're amazing!

Twenty-eight Years at Alpine Valley
1972-2000

Author's note: "Every year for twenty-eight years Rick met with Alpine Valley management to request another year as their lounge band. There were dozens of bands who asked for that gig, but every year *Mourning Dayze* was hired for one more year!"

In the summer of 1972 Betty received a telephone call from Corinne Keith who worked at Alpine Valley Resort in East Troy, Wisconsin. Corrine told Betty that management was looking for a band to play for the grand opening of their new Rathskeller and wondered if Mourning Dayze would be interested in auditioning for the job. Corinne felt they would be a perfect fit. Rick was certainly interested. The band auditioned and got the job.

Rick vividly recalls how the audition went. "First off, we had to bring our equipment into the second floor lounge and set up. To do this, we were told to use the freight elevator, then bring all of our stuff through their huge maze like kitchen, squeeze through and around the bar, then finally to the stage. Whew! Fred Cimeno was Alpine Valley's fine manager and told us to play five songs for himself, his bar manager, and his head waitress. You could tell from the first look Fred gave us that he was taken by Rise's charm and appearance and seemed to understand that she was just being herself and not putting on airs. Fred recognized that was a quality that would be successful at Alpine as well as projecting his vision of what Alpine represented. Rise was only singing at this time and was always fronting the band. She was, and still is, a very animated performer always adding something visual to each song using hand gestures, dance, and body movements. We played a wide variety of tunes for our audition. We were tight and well rehearsed. Fred loved us not just because we were a good band, but because I believe he saw we all were genuine, everyday people, and a band that would work with the resort in providing for their entertainment needs and have fun doing it.

Alpine Valley was everything you could want in a resort. It had all of the right magical ingredients. It was the perfect resort to get away from the world. There were so many fantastic and memorable people managing and employed there. They were the ones who day in and day out made Alpine a world class resort. Alpine was one of those special places you'd consider paying management to allow you to work there 'cause it was so much fun! The service in all departments was extraordinary which made people feel genuinely welcome and well taken care of just as if you were being invited into your best friend's home. Like it or not tension and stress from the world would vanish the minute you passed under the welcoming Alpine Valley arch. It was amazing! The resort was bursting with life during the winter months with skiers and partiers, people detoxing from city life flocked to this winter heaven. The energy and vibe were infectious with the sounds of skiers dressed in bright colors shushing down the slopes. People excitedly talking in anticipation their first run or their first time on skis. You could often hear them talking about the adventures they had on the slopes at Alpine, in the U.S.,or somewhere else in the world! Much of the snow that was skied on was man made with giant machines blowing snow onto the slopes (what a sound they made!) while anxious skiers waited in long lines to hop on ski lift. I can clearly see Earl in his brown coveralls riding the Cushman around the resort. When real snow would fall, it was an unbelievably gorgeous sight. It could be a real zen moment making you stop and take it all in just like a picture from a travel brochure trying to seduce you in to taking a ski vacation to some exotic destination. Alpine Valley during the winter had all the magic you could wish for. The bar and lounge were fully charged with positive energy and excitement. Let the good times roll! (It was difficult to explain to our grandmother that not everyone came to the resort just to see the band!) Everyone felt welcomed and at home at Alpine. You'd hate to leave and couldn't wait to come back!

Rick and Rise often worked as a duo for special occasions at Alpine.

Lyle Ernst: In 1977 a 37,000 seat amphitheater was built at Alpine. Until 1993, when the San Manuel Amphitheater was built in California, it was the largest amphitheater in the United States.

Alpine Valley is two hours north of Chicago, one hour from Madison, Wisconsin and only thirty minutes from Milwaukee. On your way to Alpine Valley you will see cows, lots of corn cribs, and maybe a pig farm. You'll see fields and fields of corn as well as horse stables, and the smell of "Wisconsin's fresh dairy air," or as some farmers say, "The smell of money."

If you paid attention to your directions and made all the correct turns, you'd come upon this sign, "Welcome to Alpine Valley." You continue driving under the sign and down into the valley where you'll come upon a beautiful chalet just like you would see on a postcard. In the winter you'll see skiers and snowboarders flying down the snow covered hills.

With the new amphitheater and short distance to Madison, Milwaukee, and Chicago, Alpine Valley became a major stop on the national tour for rock, pop and contemporary styles of music. During the summer months *Mourning Dayze* was in the perfect setting to meet, jam, and listen backstage to national touring acts every weekend. The band had opportunities to meet and party with band members of 'top-drawing' bands such as *Chicago, The Climax Blues Band, George Benson, Doobie Brothers, Jeff Healey, The Harry Chapin Band, Bob Seger Band, Hank Williams Jr. band, Cher, Los Crusados, The Outlaws, Freddy Fender, Sha Na Na* and *R.E.O.Speedwagon to name a few.* Rick points out that numerous times members of big-time bands would tell them how lucky they (*Mourning Dayze*) were. **Rick**: We heard time and time again how many of the national acts on the main stage missed playing the bars and clubs where they began. So many wished for audiences they could actually see instead of banks of bright stage lighting in front of them, and a dance floor packed with people dancing their butts off, getting into the music and feeling that heat. It was as though some of those bands felt obliged to talk with us, wanting to tell us that life on the big stage was not where all of a musician's hopes and dreams would be realized. It was not the final destination but just part of the ride. That we, Mourning Dayze, had a vital part to play. We were part of their roots as well as brothers. They clearly let us know, so there was no doubt that our gig bore fruit that their's could not produce. They were reminding us that we are to be playing our butts off, loving our gig, and sharing our musical gift to the highest level with anyone who would listen. It was always heartfelt and deeply appreciated. (The wisdom of Steve Dougherty, "A gig's a gig"... says it all Steve!)

This was exemplified by Graham Nash of CSN who sat 10ft. away from us and watched our entire set. When we went on break, he talked with me for our entire break. (Those of you who've seen us know our breaks are way too long!) Graham talked about how much he liked our band and how fortunate it is to live life as a musician. Graham taking the time to talk with me about our band is a reminder I often think about: "the truth is, we are all part of one human family."

Doug Henry, original Mourning Dayze bassist, recalls a story he has told many times. "When I was recovering from by bike accident in '77/'78 I was living at Queen Street still using crutches and would go to Alpine with the band once in a while.

My "special" night was when I met Kansas at the bar while Mourning Dayze was playing and had drinks with Robby Steinhardt, the violinist. I even remember what he was drinking, Smith'N Kearns!"

We'll never forget the night that Sonny and Cher performed at the amphitheater. (This is also the night I first met my future wife, Astrid.) Cher came into the resort after their show and danced to our music. While Cher was dancing to us she couldn't stop looking at Rise who was singing her butt off as usual. You might wonder what Cher had been thinking when she made eye contact with Rise. We didn't talk with her, but I think I know...yip, Cher knew, yes she did. When she looked at Rise she thought...man, that singer is the real deal. (Go get'em Rise!)

So many of the big time musicians loved the talent and performance Rise brought to the stage. Rise: "One nite while performing I looked up and there was Freddy Fender staring at me from behind the juke box. Then there was Jeff Baxter of the Doobie Brothers sitting and watching me sing while I was playing electric piano and keyboard bass, (My keyboard bass was the same keyboard as the Doors used and was extremely well maintained and made easy to play by Rick and Bob Lee.) Jeff Baxter was quite impressed with my bass playing. The guys with Sha na na said, "Go to California. You'll make it there." Stanley Banks, bass player for George Benson, really seemed to enjoy my singing and bass playing."

Rick: *Speaking of Stanley Banks, like most musicians in the early '70's, we were blown away by guitarist George Benson. Rise, Bob and I first saw him and his great band perform live at Teddy's in Milwaukee. His playing and interpretation took music and the audience to a whole new level. I'm not sure but maybe a year later we saw his band again. This time he was playing Milwaukee's prestigious PAC. Opening up for George was John Klemmer, a sax player on tour, promoting his new album "Touch." All three of us loved John's playing, writing and feel. So much so that I remember us trying to do a cover of the song "Touch." I was unable to capture the vibe regarding what I loved about that tune, when I tried to arrange it for guitar. We did give it a good try! Years later Robert E. Lee would find himself playing drums with John Klemmer. Now*

190

how cool it that!?

Big-time musician's really loved Rise. She not only looks like a star, she has the talent to back it up as well. She has all the stuff to be a major performer-the whole package. You've been validated sis. 'Nuff said.

Tragedy: None of us will ever forget performing in the lounge the night before Stevie Ray Vaughn and four others were killed when their helicopter crashed into a fog shrouded ski hill at the resort in the early morning of August 27, 1990. Skip Zehms, our drummer, had been talking with Stevie Ray's bassist and drummer the night before in Alpine's Fairview lounge which is where we played. Skip thought nothing of it. It was just like talking to the guys who played in the band next door talking about band life in the same way we would talk to each other, personable, honest and real. Stevie's death that night shook the music world. The echos, vibes and impact from this event will never end. We all made it home from our gig-our brothers didn't.

Rick: I have one piece of unfinished business regarding *Alpine Valley.* I've always wanted to place a bench with a plaque commemorating Stevie Ray Vaughn's life overlooking the area where his chopper went down so those who loved him or are simply curious would have a place to share a moment of silence and celebrate his life. I hope someday to get off my butt and pursue this idea. If I don't, I hope there is someone out there who will."

Playing Alpine Valley for 28 years was so much more than the music theater. Sure it was part of our experience but it was our gigging in the resort that was heaven for us. Everything else was really secondary. We were so fortunate as a band to have worked for such top shelf managers as Fred, Glenn and Connie. They made us feel more like part of a family rather than employees.

Rise has many fond memories of her days performing at *Alpine Valley.* She recalls there was a time or two when they got snowed in at Alpine. The name, *Alpine Valley*, means exactly that. (According to our dad, Alpine Valley wasn't always called Alpine Valley, it used to be commonly known as "skunk hollow," thanks dad!) It's situated in a valley, so when the snow got too high or when ice covered the roads there was no way to motor up the steep hill and out of the valley. When that happened, the band slept on the floor in the manager's plush office. In the morning Rise and Bobby Lee helped serve breakfast to hundreds of stranded guests who slept anywhere they could find a spot.

After being snowed in at Alpine and on our way home,
Bob Lee tackles a huge snow drift that stopped us dead
in our tracks. Lucky for Bob, a snowplow is coming in the distance.

In the "heyday" of *Alpine Valley* we would perform Wednesday, Thursday, and Friday nights as well as Sunday afternoons we would take all of our equipment home after Sunday's gig so we could work on new material Tuesday nights in the barn keeping us fresh and current. Wednesday night, back at Alpine, we would set it all up again which involved a long walk and two flights of stairs. Nothing dulls a bands edge quicker than constantly playing the same material...right guys?! Right! Hmmm...

A typical week-end at Alpine...really: The dance floor would be packed with people. To get to the stage you had to continuously say, "excuse me, excuse me." And they would be standing five or six deep at the bar. (Bar manager, John Lutz, used to tell us they were "10 deep at the bar" which was really more for affect than fact. I'm sure he would challenge that observation!) We had to clean up the stage before we could set up. There were beer bottles and pop bottles all over the stage and our equipment. It's not that the people were messy. It's that there was no place else to put the stuff. The place was that packed and a real challenge to keep up with.

Many people who frequented Alpine had their favorite or "own" song and the band always looked forward to us playing it for them. Many people came back year after year to listen to *Mourning Dayze* often planning their winter holiday around the band's schedule. Rise recalls that some people who were not regulars would say, "you are a LOT better than the group that was here last year," or "man, you guys have been here a long time, I remember seeing you here two years ago!" Rise said, "we would simply smile and say "thank you." During bitter cold weather the slopes would be closed. Even if they did stay open no girls would dare to ski in such weather and ruin their skin. So, of course, that meant more people to hang out in the lounge and enjoy the music.

The band would play at Alpine every New Year's Eve. Rise thinks back with a smile, "that was a special time at the Chalet. At 11:00 o'clock that evening after the slopes had closed the ski patrol would partake in a torchlight parade. The band would stop playing and all the lights inside and out were turned off. Then everyone would go to the windows and look up the main ski hill to watch the ski patrol come racing down the hill with what looked like flames shooting from the bottom of their ski poles. When they got to the bottom of the hill they would take a bow and extinguish their fires. The Chalet would explode with yelling and screaming and applause and the band would crank up their instruments and keep the moment alive."

The Alpine Valley Ski School Entertainment Committee, Sue, Pam, and Mary Jo

Alpine had its own ski school and ski patrol which was a big part of the resort's vibe. They also had their own song, "Tell Me," and when the band played it they packed the dance floor sometimes as many as twenty or more.

Mary Jo Loomans was a ski regular at Alpine Valley during the time *Mourning Dayze* was the house band. Mary Jo, along with Sue and Pam, taught skiing and were in charge of the Alpine Valley Ski School Entertainment Committee. For a ten-year period those gals made sure that some type of entertainment was planned for the weekends. Sunday afternoon cookouts on the lounge balcony were a big favorite.

Mary Jo recalls that the regulars were always the first couples to hit the dance floor on Friday and Saturday nights and Sunday afternoons. Lucky would be out there too just itchin' to dance. He would occasionally perform with the band by singing or playing his banjo to a crowd that absolutely loved him. "And," she adds, "We couldn't leave 'till the last song was played, even if we had to be at work by 8:00 a.m. the next morning."

Rick: Mary Jo and friends made Alpine what we all wished it would be. They embodied the ideal and always generated those "good vibrations! We are so lucky to have been part of their family.

During the 1970's and into the 1980's John Barnes was a bartender at Alpine Valley. John is now Group Sales Manager for the Marcus Center of the Performing Arts in Milwaukee, Wisconsin.

The Following are some thoughts and memories of John's days at Alpine Valley.

"In 1972 the state liquor law changed the drinking age to 18. That same year Alpine Valley opened The Rathskeller, a bar designed specifically for the 18 to 21 year old crowd. *Mourning Dayze* was the house band there. After a while the novelty of the new bar wore off and *Mourning Dayze* moved "upstairs" to the Valley View bar where they were the main attraction summer and winter.

During the same time period management tried to make the Rathskeller and Valley View into discos, but both failed as the

194

Alpine Valley audience wanted and demanded the live music of *Mourning Dayze*. However, the strobe lights and lighted dance floor survived and became part of the entertainment when the band was playing. The bar could have been a scene from "Cocktail," "Coyote Ugly," "Saturday Night Fever," and "54." It was an unparalleled combination of all of them with plenty of dancing, music and beverages.

Weekends during the winter were amazing. You could not move in the bar as it was so crowded. Skiers loved to party and during the 70's and 80's the place was rocking. On occasion the bar's closing time was "extended" to accommodate the customers who were having such a great time dancing and singing with the band plus spending more money at the bar. During those simpler times friendly gendarmes looked the other way.

Songs I remember best from my time was Savoy Brown's "Tell Mama," and Vicki Sue Robinson's "Turn the Beat Around," both got the crowd going. The cover of "Blue Moon" was also a winner, but my favorite was Rick Pfeifer's solo of a cover of Harry Chapin's "Mail Order Annie" where he got to play his guitar and share his vocal. That is the song I remember best.

Believe it or not all of those songs are on my I-Pod; not the *Mourning Dayze* versions of course. However, the *Mourning Dayze* memories are lasting."

Back Row: Tom, ?, Niles, Erv & Tiger. Middle: Sue & Pam. Sitting: Ron, Mary Jo, Judy, Don & Phil. Spyder Man: JJ

A book could easily be written about our 28 years at Alpine Valley. It's the people who worked, partied and vacationed at Alpine that made the magic. Here are some of the faces that made Alpine a wonderland. To all we've shared life with, Thank You!

WGN's Bob Collins, Alpine and us.

Rick, Rise and Bob Lee were long time WGN listeners. The band itself had a long history of listening to WGN. During the 60's WGN was one of the few clear channel all night radio stations we could count on not fading in and out on us as we made our way home from a gig. We'd usually listen to Franklin McCormick's "All Night Meister Brau Showcase". During the summer of '67 and '68 the band was extremely popular in the Wis. Dells area. One night after a gig about 4:00 a.m. Doug and Rick stopped in to see Franklin broadcast live from Lake Delton near the Wis. Dells just wanting to say hi and thanks, It was a memorable moment, Franklin with Meister Brau in hand! The WGN host Roy Leonard, who embodies the term "class act," came to WGN in 1967 and worked there for 31 years. Listening to Roy

196

daily introduced Rick to many national and local artists' ideas. Bob Lee, Rise and Rick will long remember traveling to see Orion Samuelson of WGN's farm show with "Lino Frigo and the Musical Wheels, " perform a live *Noon Show* broadcast for the annual Corn Festival in Walworth, Wisconsin. WGN was also home of the great Chicago Cubs!

WGN radio sponsored a "Ski Spree" weekend at Alpine for about 5 years. The event was hosted by WGN's Bob Collins who previously worked in Milwaukee at WOKY and WRIT. He took the afternoon slot at WGN in 1974. In 1986 Bob took over for the legendary morning show host, Wally Phillips. Bob was the top morning show DJ in Chicago until his unfortunate death in a light plane crash in 2000. The WGN "Ski Spree" weekend at Alpine Valley was always filled with a bit more electricity than usual- which was a hard thing to do. Alpine rocked! If you were a regular at Alpine, you could feel the added excitement. It was a lot of fun to talk with "Uncle Bobby" when he was in the lounge. In fact, he would often come and talk with us demonstrating genuine interest in our band. We always looked forward to playing tunes for Bob which he would play or introduce us to on his WGN radio show, especially because we felt he would never expect us to play those tunes. One notable tune was "The Moon's a Harsh Mistress," the great Jimmy Webb tune.

Bob seemed to really enjoy the work that Rise and I did together as well as how the entire band presented itself. Bob would often talk about the band on his morning show, specially when he was talking with his E.A.A. buddy (winner of the Preston Little Award of Excellence in 2004) and Alpine legend Jim Brady. Bob thought so much of us he asked us if we'd be interested in playing for a Chicago Cubs opening day WGN radio pre-game show at Wrigley Field and a Bears home game. Bob asked if we had a video tape of the band he could use to show those in charge at the station who were in charge of bookings. We didn't have one but we would get him one! Bob needed the tape quickly, in two days! My great friend Bob Schneider and good friend of the band was currently managing the local university cable TV station. On a long shot I asked Bob if we could use the studio for a live shoot, Bob agreed to produce us but it would have to be done at 7:00 a.m. (We're forever grateful Bob!) "Uncle Bobby" liked the demo but the gig never came through. The following year Bob requested a demo of Rise and I. He said he really wanted to help us out and give us a "break" if he could. Bob gave our demo to a producer who really liked our work but just couldn't use us. He was looking for groups that were doing their own material. I was not writing tunes at that time. We were grateful for the chance Bob gave us. Bob's wit, thoughtfulness, kindness and laugh will not be forgotten.

A few highlights from Alpine Valley...

In the twenty-eight years that *Mourning Dayze* performed as the house band at Alpine Valley, thousands of memories were collected. The following are just a few:

Cher dancing to the music of Mourning Dayze. Rise was very excited because Cher looked right at her while she was singing her butt off...wonder what Cher was thinking...ah...she knew..."That girl's the real deal."

Bob Lee, Rick and Rise, for years, would spend Christmas Eve at Alpine, to be together and to decorate the stage for the holidays.

Everyone loved the floor burners, Debbie Landry and Linda Prout. They always got the place rockin'. And, Sue Enright "always" made Rick laugh. Or, was it the other way around?

Jerry Thayer was always there when we needed him, and made getting paid a real adventure. Jerry was Rick's school bus driver!

The band got three "free" drink tickets at the beginning of their night.

ALPINE VALLEY
RESORT

198

Alpine's ski school and ski patrol were the heart and soul of Alpine's great vibe.

Everyone loved Mary Jo's "fuzzy boots."

Alpine's bartenders let the good times roll!

The Barnswallows played Alpine and the crowd love'd em! The Prez put a smile on everyone's face.

The "Gong Show" holds auditions at AV. The Prez refuses to give it a try and avoids stardom.

Alpine's manager, Fred Cimeno, tries to have Mourning Dayze open up for Boz Scaggs. Mourning Dayze gets bumped by South Side Johnny. (Boz Scaggs shared the same agency with the "60's Mourning Dayze)

From 1972 to the spring of 2000, a period of 28 years, we played a portion of every year at Alpine Valley Resort. Each and every year Rick would meet with management to renew a one-year contract.

Rusty, great AV bartender, gets MD to audition at Sterlingworth. MD would get the job and work there for nearly five years. During the summer of 2016 Rusty surprised the band by catching one of their gigs. We hadn't seen Rusty since the summer of 1978. It was a fabulous reunion!

Bar managers, Gail and Lisa, take good care of the band!

John Lutz, AV's bar manager, is still waiting for Rick to pay him for his slot cars. John has not told him how much he wants for them!

The game room was a big attraction.

Pizza was served in the Rathskeller

REO promises to pay for any equipment they might damage while jamming on our equipment. The drummer breaks Bob's drum pedal and REO does not compensate Bob for his loss. The following year REO asks to jam on our equipment, Rick tell's them no...

Alice Cooper, musician and golfer, comes into the bar looking for a foursome to play with in the morning.

After hours were unbelievable!

Rick at Miller Park with two of the finest people you could ever know. Glenn Kurylo, former manager of Alpine Valley, then working for the Milwaukee Brewers and legendary Alpine Valley bartender, John Barnes, then long time Milwaukee Brewers ticket manager.

Usually I could go back stage to the main stage of the amphitheater with no problem. One night when *Eric Clapton* was headlining my usual contact wouldn't let me in, saying, "Sorry, everybody wants to see God." I tried to explain to him that it wasn't Clapton I wanted to see, it was *Ziggy Marley*, the opening act. He looked at me as if I was lying through my teeth. It was the truth!

John Barnes, great AV bartender, gives Rich Little some tips on how to play Space Invaders.

Elvin Bishop asks Rick where the girls are. Then he asks him if he'd watch his guitar for him while he goes to pee!

For years the band met at Queen St. and travelled together in the van to gig at Alpine.

Junior Brantly of Milwaukee's Short Stuff plays keyboards at AV with the Fabulous Thunderbirds.

While jamming Rick asks Jeff Healey's drummer if he's familiar with "Road House Blues."

For Grateful Dead concerts we saw this many times and thought it was so funny. Many people would come in their high end automobiles with the women wearing a nice dress and the men a fine suit. Then they would change into their tie dies and jeans while in their cars. There we allso many well dressed patrons carrying gym bags around the resort looking for the Johns'. When they emerged from the restrooms, they would be wearing jeans and t-shirts.

The kitchen and salad girls at AV were the best in the world! Bet you didn't know that did you?

Steve Ellmann's dad occasionally played drums with his own group in Alpine's Rathskeller.

Getting the band together after a break could be a challenge, damn game rooms!

You've never had tunafish salad until you've had it at Alpine! (Did that stuff come with Andes Candies on the side?)

Heidi said she heard a song where she sounded "just like the singer", and wanted to sing it with the band. The song was "Sultan's of Swing."

Lucky loves his dancing, and he really has hopes that the banjo will make a comeback!

Glenn Kurylo, AV manager...you've always been a class act, absolutely the best! We thank you!

Who could forget the unforgettable sounds of people wearing their ski boots around the resort and especially going up and down the stairs?

One night after we got done gigging and ready to go home the bartenders and staff asked if we could give them a private performance. They felt they had never really gotten a chance to actually hear us. We were flattered and had a ball.

Driving up the steep hill to get out of the Valley when it was snowing could be an adventure!

Ever try going down a ski slope on a cafeteria tray?

Although band members and their families were able to ski for free, no band members ever did. One year Rise and Jerry's Cleveland family came for the week-end. Alpine gave us 12 free passes, boots, skis and lift tickets. Several band members did enjoy the free golf Alpine offered us.

At 11p.m. when the slopes closed, the lounge would be wall to wall people. Let the good times roll!

When Bob Lee drove his car he loved to hand drum on the steering wheel while playing along with tunes on the radio or the music in his head. Rise had a hard time handling all of this

202

creative energy while riding along with Bob. It's interesting to note that later in life, Bob, a highly skilled and creative drummer/percussionist, would be demonstrating to world renown ground breaking guitarist Michael Hedges some of his hand drumming techniques. (It's unclear whether or not Bob was demonstrating his grooves to Michael on his car's steering wheel!)

Playing AV was a dream come true. We've been so fortunate.

On the Road

1973: On the road with Vaughn Monogue...

During our 28 years at Alpine there were many personnel changes within the band. Each personnel change brought something new and exciting to the band. The most significant group was that of Rise, Bob Lee, Vaughn, and Rick. Bob Jenson had left the group of his own accord. We needed a bass player. Rise, Bob Lee and I wanted to play full time and would do whatever it took to achieve that goal. We auditioned many bass players many were from Milwaukee and Madison, but no one met the criteria. We needed someone who could play full time and most important of all would be a good fit musically and personally. I don't remember how we first met Vaughn Monogue who had played bass with the legendary "Ben Franklin and the Kites" out of Ft. Atkinson, Wisconsin, but he sure was the right guy at the time!

Ben Franklin and the Kites
Standing L to R: Ted Anderson, Jim Haag, Terry Woods Sitting w/o hat: Tom Belzer
Sitting w/hat: Vaughn Monogue

Vaughn's audition went well. He had a great personality and a huge love for music, playing, and writing. Everyone in the band liked him right away. Vaughn was very willing to work hard on the music we were playing even though much of what we were doing was not stylistically in his bag. This would prove to be a lot of work. Vaughn loved, loved to travel, especially in the Western part of the country and Alaska. I really doubt we would have played in the Western United States as much as we did without Vaughn's great love of that part of the world and turning us on to it. This was a time in our band's life that we all loved. Vaughn would play with us for the next five years.

Rise fronts the band in Alpine Vally's Fairview Lounge.
Vaughn, Rise, Bob Lee, Rick

Dressed for the road. Rick, Vaughn, Rise, Bob

Vaughn   Rise   Rick   Bob

Mourning Dayze with the Gary VanZeeland Agency

Sterlingworth
Vaughn   Rise   Bob   Rick

The winter season at Alpine would usually end for us after the first weekend in March. It was around 1974 when for the next six years we would travel out west until our summer season began again at Alpine Valley and Sterlingworth. We mainly played in Minnesota, Iowa, the Dakota's, Montana, Wyoming and Alberta and British Columbia, Canada. *This was a great era for full-time working bands. There were venues all across the country to play six nights a week. This kind of gigging was often referred to as to playing the "Holiday Inn" circuit. I was a great way to learn the business and get your chops together. Most of these venues have long disappeared which makes it very difficult for younger players to find full-time work.* All of us really loved traveling. We had the opportunity to see many of our national parks, monuments and historic sights in addition to experiencing a huge range in lifestyles and meeting many wonderful people. And don't forget we got to share our music too! I can still us sitting around a campfire we had made while spending the night in Yellowstone, a real slice of heaven...and yes Rise, those wolves howling are the real thing!

Yellowstone

(Rise, Rick and Bob Lee, after hearing John Denver's "Colorado Rocky Mountain High", took a week's vacation to camp and experience the mountains of Colorado. It was Fantastic!)

We were usually able to save money on lodging as the

clubs we played often provided us a place to stay which had most often two or more rooms attached to the motel or hotel we played at. Sometimes they provided us with a house or a trailer. Once in a while we would have to find our own lodging. That was always an adventure. We always made a home out of what we had, regardless. Which does remind me of a weekend gig we played at a hotel. The owner said that we could have a free room to stay in we all liked that idea. When we went to our room, we found the room to be completely empty! Yip, no beds, or furniture but we did have a working light fixture! That night we slept in our amp covers!

The Good Music Agency
2010 South Avenue West, Missoula, Montana 59801
Phone (406) 728-5520

We used GMA for five years to book our gigs out west.

How many times have we all heard someone say, "it's a small world." No truer words were ever spoken than the time we were playing a gig at Wild Bill's Saloon just outside of Missoula, Montana, a real cowboy bar. (Our agent somehow thought the music of Harry Chapin and Roberta Flack would be perfect for guys wearing 10gallon hats and chaps. Agents understand things about our potential, that we never will!)

We were working an afternoon matinee. The crowd was small and we were doing a lot of talking over the mic with the people that were there trying to win them over. We were playing a few "country" tunes. The song, "Tennessee Waltz" was introduced as a song that was a favorite of our Uncle Herman who lived in Lake Mills, Wisconsin. On our break a man comes up to Rise telling her that he's on vacation and that he just happens to be Uncle Herman's neighbor! Wow, eh? Small world indeed.

When we played in Canada and before we were allowed to cross the boarder, we had to take EVERYTHING out of the van to be inspected by the border patrol. That was a real pain. We were never sure we could fit everything back in! We were so packed.

Very similar to our experience years before when the original band traveled from Wisconsin to upstate New York taking the Canadian route through Windsor. On our way back into the U.S. good fortune smiled. At the border crossing to our surprise was a border guard who knew us. He had seen us play almost every night during the two weeks we were in Lethbridge, hung-out with us and showed us around the area. As our turn for inspection and interrogation came our Canadian friend said something to his co-workers and pretty much just waved us on through. We were so grateful not to have to take everything out of our van again. Thank you!

When on the road, Bob Lee and I would room together while Rise and Vaughn shared a room.
Vaughn had a love for sardines. Rise couldn't stand the smell of them. Rise would always make Vaughn eat his sardines outside the room no matter what the conditions. Vaughn has been seen eating a tin of sardines outside a cheap motel room in -15degree temps in the blowing snow. Is that real love or what?! Rise, I'm not talking about you I'm talking about the sardines. One of the cool things Vaughn turned us all on to was Taco John's. No matter where we went we would try to find a Taco John's. Bob remembers one night in Des Moines, Iowa, having a contest about who could eat the most tacos. Vaughn ate the most, but had to go outside into an alley and throw up after it was over.

On our days off we'd often be traveling to our next gig. If we were in town, we would usually check out other bands playing in the area and see what was happening locally. We would have diner together at the finest restaurant in town, practice and work on music, hang out together, or simply find a quite place to be alone.

Rise takes a pic of the boys in action
Vaughn, Bob, Rick

Glacier National Park, Montana.   Vaughn

Heading home.   Rick, Vaughn, Bob
(ya Doug, it's Coors)

In the spring of 1977 we were traveling to Montana hoping to reach our destination in time to watch the NCAA finals, Marquette was playing. It was a 22 hour drive which ended up taking about 30 hrs. as we ran into a huge spring blizzard. The driving was slow and visibility horrible. (It should be noted that at times like these Rise would always offer to drive.) With 150 miles to go we hit a long lonely stretch of road with one foot of unplowed snow on the road, high winds, cold temps, ice covering our van, no radio stations, (that was the worst part cause we couldn't hear the ball game) and everyone in the van was pretty quiet. We really were in the middle of nowhere and not sure what lie ahead. We had never taken a motel on the way to a gig, never! We all wished for one now, but there was nothing out there, no cars or trucks, no buildings, and no idea how much longer we would be in the storm. Like everything else we did we just kept at it and drove slow.going slowly. We had been on this desolate stretch of road for about about three hours when an eighteen wheeler approached us. It was such a welcome sight. Over the CB he told us we would be in the clear in 25 miles. We could not give him the same welcome news. We missed the ballgame.

Sterlingworth

At this time we were making our living as full-time musicians. In the summer months for five years we played five nights a week at Sterlingworth, a beautiful nightclub and vacation resort located on Lauderdale Lakes in Walworth County between LaGrange and Elkhorn, as well as every weekend at Alpine Valley. While at Sterlingworth Charlie and Trudy treated us like royalty. Trudy made the finest after hours roast beef sandwich you could imagine! We've never had any better anywhere. Herman, who worked third shift, always did his best to keep a fire lit under the band. John, the head chef, always made his presence known and supported our work with every opportunity he had. Can't forget the bartenders, Mike and Dick! These guys were the best. They put a smile on everyone's face and made you feel "right at home." It should be mentioned that we got this job thanks to Alpine Valley's legendary bartender, "Rusty", (Greg Rusteberg), who

212

also tended bar at Sterlingworth. As soon as Rusty heard that Dan might be interested in more live entertainment for the summer months he contacted me right away. I went out and spoke with owner operator Dan Seymour. We auditioned for him and his staff and got the gig. Playing at Sterlingworth was like playing for family. Sterlingworth was a top shelf club with a "home like atmosphere." We often found ourselves playing for the kids of the families that vacationed at Sterlingworth. Because of that we thought it would be fun to do some material specially for the kids. We incorporated some simple magic tricks and flash paper as well as wrote a couple of routines. But nothing entertained them more than when Robert E. Lee, who never sang or even had a mic, would be introduced as "Mr. E-Gads" and sang "Winchester Cathedral." Then while the band played, he would recite the middle sections in his big extremely deep bass voice to the Diamonds, "Little Darlin'" and "Zip Zip." The place would go wild with cheers and applause. The kids just loved him, and so did their parents. He was truly a showstopper, and a real "star" in their eyes. (Bob never got quite as excited about doing this as the rest of us did, but he did it!) When the summer season ended, we had to hit the road to get steady work. We traveled throughout the Midwest playing gigs in Illinois, Indiana, Iowa, Minnesota, Nebraska, Ohio and Wisconsin. Sometimes we would go on the road for a few weeks and then come home and gig locally doing whatever it took to get work.

Vaughn Monogue - Bass

Vaughn:I played in bands for over twenty-eight years. The first group I played in was Ben Franklin & the Kites based in my home town of Ft. Atkinson, Wisconsin. In those days Ft. Atkinson was a great place to be if you loved music. Every weekend there were jam sessions on Main Street and in the Municipal Building commonly referred to by teenagers as "the monkey house." No one really knows why it was called that, but most think it was because kids hung out there and "monkeyed around."

Before joining Mourning Dayze songwriting and recording were my main interests. I enjoyed writing songs and spent a lot of my down time doing just that. I thoroughly enjoyed playing music with Rick and

Rise. They are artistic and have great stage presence. During my time with them we played quality songs. I have many great memories of my time with Mourning Dayze. They were like family to me.

My most distinct memory is of the night we were playing a gig at The Dome in Marinette, Wisconsin. It was a cold and windy night and there were gale warnings on the Great Lakes. Not many people turned out that night and the next morning they said the Edmund Fitzgerald had gone down taking its entire crew with it!

Some random memories...

This was a hard working group that never quit and lived their lives to share what they loved with each other and their audiences.

Vaughn's prior experience driving to Alaska and traveling out West made the band's Western travels just a little richer.

We needed to buy a new van. It was Vaughn's knowledge and experience that helped us to buy the perfect vehicle, a brand new one-ton Dodge van. It was the perfect choice. (This one had a heater that really worked too!) Thanks again Vaughn!

Rise

Rise buys a 5-string banjo in Great Falls Montana and begins to learn Scrugg's style. Sounding good Rise!

During one trip home from a Western tour we bought as much Coors beer as we could carry back to Wisconsin.

While on Spring break in Florida Rise loved to bring the latest hits from Miami back to Whitewater.

A club we were playing in Jamestown, ND, didn't allow women to dance with each other.

Robert E. Lee loved to play the jukebox, he would even sing along to "The Night They Drove Old Dixie Down!"

Rise never drove the band's vehicles. For the record she would always offer in the middle of a blizzard or thunderstorm.

We were fortunate, we loved to travel and there was plenty of work available on the "Holiday Inn" circuit if you did. The "Holiday Inn" circuit was a generic name for motor inns throughout the country that provided lounge entertainment six nights a week.

When Bob drove he loved to tap out rhythms on the steering wheel. Years later this skill would prove useful as Bob found himself demonstrating hand drumming rhythms and techniques to world renown guitarist Michael Hedges.

In Glendive Montanta, our stage was surrounded by chicken wire, yip, just like in the movies. The best dancer on the dance floor was a woman dancing with her dog.

The first night in our motel in Des Moines Rise found the the cockroaches to be so bad that she spent the night sitting in a chair. Before breakfast the next day we found a new motel.

In Miles City, Montana, the owner of the club asked us if we knew the song "Lucille." I told her we didn't do any Little Richard...You picked a fine time to leave me!

Rise loved seeing real cowboys on horse back herding cattle. It was quite a site. She said something about looking for Rowdy Yates.

When Vaughn drove he would usually drive with the radio turned off. Rick picked up that habit from him and loves it to this day.

Waiting for Rise to fix her hair and get "lookin' pretty" was something we had to get used to.

We'd all get together at Vaughn's house to exchange gifts on Christmas Eve.

Vaughn's mom was fab. When she would take food off of the stove or out of the oven Vaughn would usually take a bite of it as fast as he could and always emphatically stated as though he'd just burned his mouth by surprise, "man, that stuff's hot" to which his mother would reply, "what did you expect, I told you it just came out of the oven!" This scenario repeated itself again and again always giving us plenty of grins.

After five years of being together, it was time for a change. The four of us were like family in so many ways but musically Rise, Bob and I were taking a different direction from our good friend Vaughn. It was time to say a difficult good-bye and wish Vaughn good luck with his pursuits. We went off once again looking for a

216

bass player.

Doug Matz - Bass

We once again placed ads in the classifieds of both
Milwaukee and Madison newspapers. We received a good
response from the ads and began the audition process. We had a
clear concept of what we needed from the bass section. Musical
chops were advancing and expanding rapidly. Our band was
part of this growth. Our bassist needed to be up to the task. We
auditioned Doug Matz from Concord, Wisconsin and gave him a
chance at the job. Doug was with us for about three months.
During that short time with Doug we rehearsed five times a week
from 7:00 a.m., until 11:00 a.m., in Doug's basement. (On the way
to these early morning rehearsals Bob would sing-a-long with
"Been drivin' all night my hands wet on the wheel" when it
played on the radio. This must have been due to Bob's budding
career as a singer. I'm really not sure though. One thing I am
certain of was Bob's vocal charm and talent didn't go to waste!)
(Oh voh de oh doh!) Doug's wife Ethel treated us like members
of the family. She was fantastic. She always made us feel
welcome and encouraged our rehearsing. We made a demo
tape at a studio in Watertown. It was a friend of Doug's who would
produce the session. This was the first time I had heard Rise's
recorded voice. I was struck by just how wonderful she sounded.
She was singing "Scotch and Soda" and a Paul Simon tune on
which we sang harmony, "Sunny Day." The picture we have of
Doug playing bass was taken at practice in "the barn." The pic
was taken by Dale Reich, our neighbor and writer for our local
paper, The Whitewater Register, for which he was doing a story
on our band. Doug played one weekend with us. Then we had to
let him go. It wasn't working. We needed to feel free to "go
where the music was taking us" and never letting chops or
instrumentation stand in our way of playing or being our best.
Doug was struggling to play our tunes. We needed to look for a
bass player again.

217

Doug Matz   *Robert E. Lee*

1977 - Rise plays Piano and Keyboard Bass

Our search for a bass player took a different direction this time. My thought was to approach Rise to see if she would be interested in playing bass. And yea, Rise was willing to give it a try. Rise has always done whatever she could do for the good of the band. I gave her some bass parts to work on. While practicing her parts she busted the nut on either Doug or Boom Boom's bass. Wow! I tell ya, it seemed a clear sign that the traditional electric bass wasn't going to be the direction we would take! I'm sure Rise would agree. We as a group never felt confined by what others expected or thought about us. We felt as though we would find our own solutions. Was there a way we could gig without a traditional electric bassist and still get gigs as a band? Rise had been playing electric piano with the band for several years. Piano players play bass parts all of the time. Was there a keyboard available that would allow us to play the notes used by an electric bass and amplify it through a bass amp? I didn't know but I was going to find out. My first call was to our good friends at West Allis Music and sure 'nuff Fender made a bass keyboard just for that purpose. It was the same keyboard the Doors had been using to cover their bass parts during their live performances. I proposed the idea of using a keyboard bass to Rise and Bob Lee. They were all for it. Well, at least they agreed to give it a fair try. Rise had been spending most of her performance time seated at her piano rather than fronting the band. So...having Rise play the bass parts seemed like a very natural opportunity for growth and development. Rise was willing to see how it would work. Yea Rise!

It would be more work for her, but quality work, which would include learning and fun. I would figure out the bass parts and keyboard parts for Rise. Then she would write them down on her note cards. Rise developed a brand new musical language! I think Rise is the only person on the entire planet who can interpret those cards! Here........YOU TRY!!!!!!!

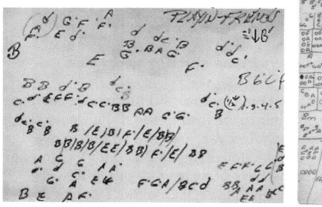 

RISE: "I have always been thankful that I had a chance to play bass in the band. Yes I complained. I am a singer first but I am so grateful to have the knowledge of what it's like to be the bass player. Even though singing and playing bass wasn't easy while laying down the groove and keeping good time it had its rewards. I laid down some classic bass lines during that era Boogie Oogie Oogie, Color My World, Hot Stuff, Bad Girls and on and on...Great bass lines for all time. People loved it.

Jeff Baxter of the Doobie Brothers whispered in my ear, "great left hand!" Screamer from Sha Na Na told me, "you should go to California!" And hey, the Doors, used the same bass machine that I used. Although I didn't know that at that time, it was pretty cool. The secret to the bass keyboards success was graphite. It made the keyboard much easier to play. I learned from Rick and Bob how to take the machine apart to maintain it and to give it its fix of graphite. I was pretty proud of that. Girls just didn't do those things back then!"

The bass machine worked very well for us. It sounded very good and Rise busted her butt singing, playing piano and bass. This move did not limit us as a band musically or gig wise. Our audiences were often quite surprised as well as impressed by how full we sounded. I was able to develop arrangements that not only sounded good but brought out the best in all of us. Rise, Bob Lee, and I continued to work together as full time musicians while playing Alpine Valley and Sterlingworth as we continued to travel in the Spring and Fall. We rehearsed regularly and gigged constantly. This group was playing at a high level during this period. Living and breathing music was all we did. It was a great time for us. It was also when Rise met Jerry, or should I say when Jerry met Rise!

Rise meets Jerry

Rise: "The year was 1978. I was on vacation in Miami Florida enjoying the beaches and warm sunshine when I received a call from Rick about a gig in Indy. Our agent in Montana needed a back up band for an Elvis impersonator who was booked for a solid month in Indianapolis. OK. I flew home. Our band practiced with Rick Newkirk from Seattle and off we went. One night at the Best Western there is this man at my feet crawling around by my piano asking me "Where is the door?" I told him to go away. Again he said, "OK, where is the door?" I said, "do you want a country song?" He said "where is the door?" He said I kicked him. No, I don't kick. Love struck me. It was love at first sight! Oh ya, and the Elvis impersonator never did his shtick but Bob Jenson and family stopped in to say hi on their way to Florida! Whew."

Jerry: "I was a Yellow Freight truck driver with my route being Cleveland to Indianapolis, 325 miles. By law you can only drive 500 miles in a day. The company would send us to the

Quality Inn for 8 hours rest. Of course driving 325 miles, I wasn't tired. I decided to have a beer. After 8 hours of drinking beer I couldn't walk, I needed help. I found myself crawling around the baseboard of the lounge where the band was playing trying to find the door out. I inadvertently landed on stage under Rise's keyboard. Being prudish she used a black cloth draped from the bottom of the keyboard to the floor so no one could stare at her legs. Rise discovered me and said, "get out of there, you can't be under my piano!" I looked up at her and said, "show me the door, I'd be glad to leave," our first meeting."

Jerry: "When talking to people in the audience I admit that I just happen to know the band. Rick & Rise are brother and sister and have been playing together for 44 years. Oh, by the way, she is also my wife! Bob is the bass player and has been in and out of the band for over 45 years. And Wayne? He's the new guy. He joined the band 25 years ago. People always smile."

Jerry has been hauling equipment and helping the the band set up and tear down since 1982. A thankless part of the job, Thanks Jerry!

Them Changes...

Bob Lee faithfully worked not only on our new material but also on a pedagogical approach to his drum kit and music as a whole. Bob worked on his discipline everyday which was essential and necessary. Bob would practice all of the time, I think Bob may have been trying to secretly drive Rise mad with his hand

221

drumming on the steering wheel! What do you think Rise? When on the road, Bob was encouraged to seek "the best drummer in town" to get lessons and learn whenever there was something to be learned. It was a slow beginning but a critical, necessary step. Bob took this challenging step. This brought him into personal, one on one contact with more experienced players. Bob took full advantage of the opportunity to learn from others.

MOURNING DAYZE BAND

Bob Lee   *Rise*   *Rick*

As a trio travelled for two years with Rise playing keyboard bass and piano.

After two years playing as a trio, Bob let us know that he was going to leave the band. This didn't come as a shock, but rather was the end of a wonderful time of playing and being together. In many ways we were like family. Bob had a love for jazz that kept growing. It was really in his bones. Bob fell in love, got married, studied music at the local university and did further studies at the great jazz school, North Texas State. He became a very successful jazz musician and outstanding national and international salesman for world renowned music conglomerates, KMC Music Inc. He is currently with Samick Music Corporation, the largest manufacturer of guitars and pianos in the world!

Rick and Rise's dad, Ray, and Bob Lee putting in a new floor in "the barn."

Bob, whose birth name is Robert E. Lee, just loved that name and had fun with it all of the time. Remember, Bob's own band before Mourning Dayze was called, "Robert E. Lee and the Rebels!" You've got to love that! Bob came from a wonderful, loving and supportive family. Bob's dad, Gene Lee, is a famous professional clown presenting himself as "Cousin Otto," "America's Favorite Relative," who had worked with Cole Bros.- Clyde Beatty and Ringling Bros. circuses as well as ad manager for the local newspaper, "The Whitewater Register." Bob's mom has a great love of music regularly playing the piano at home. Bob's sister Elle worked at the local University and had a great love of Mozart during the years we worked together (now it's either Cold Play or Green Day) and invited the band to her home for a wonderful diner on several occasions. Bob's brother Dick has always had a wonderful way of seeing the world with always seeming to find something to smile or laugh about no matter how grim the circumstances. Dick, who was also a "Randy's" alum, was doing some cartooning during the time Bob was with us and did a caricature of the band which we put on t-shirts, cool, eh?! Dick was also very supportive of Bob and the band's efforts. The

223

support and kindness we received from Bob's family is as appreciated now as it was then. It is not easy on a family when their kids at such a critical time in their lives decide to "give up everything" to play in a band or join the circus. It takes great love to support those who choose the road less traveled. Thank you!

Robert E. Lee's brother Dick, drew this caricature of the band.

Rise and I occasionally see Bob when he returns to Whitewater and stay in contact via e-mail. The friendships that grow out of working, playing, and living together are honest, strong, and lasting. Something you can count on. We're all fortunate for the experiences we've shared.

Robert E. Lee - Drummer

Bob: Growing up in a small community like Whitewater, Wisconsin, during the rise of rock music it was not difficult to figure out who had a band and who was in it. I played in a number of rehearsal bands in junior high and the early years of high school, but they never really got beyond meeting at someone's house once a week and trying to mimic the tunes off the latest release of whatever band had the number one song out that

224

week. We played very few gigs because none of us had a driver's license.

Towards the end of this early period I began hanging around musicians who were a few years older than me because they could play better, and I thought they were cool. But most of all I was hoping to get a gig or two out of it. Eventually I got "the call" from a local band named The Chocolate Ripple. These guys were all in college while I was still in high school. True to the name the band was half black, half white. They could play. They had gigs, and people came to see them, I was in heaven. Unfortunately this run only lasted a few months for me because I was underage and they played a lot of bar gigs. At least I had gotten a taste.

The one local band that always seemed to be working and had a big following was Mourning Dayze. They were by far the best band in the area but they already had a drummer and I was a few years younger than they were, I didn't pin any hopes on being part of their group.

It has been a few too many years to remember all the particulars, but one day I got a phone call from Rick Pfeifer asking if I would be interested in coming over to where the band rehearsed and audition a gig. My audition went fine. I became a member of Mourning Dayze and toured with them for five years or so. During that time we covered a lot of miles and played a lot of gigs, some good, some not so good. Most of all I was doing what I had always wanted to do, play music for a living.

At the time I thought playing music for a living would never end. Granted, it was not lucrative living, but none the less it was a living.

There were so many memories including some of the "not so great" places we stayed in while traveling. One that comes to mind was in Bemidji, Minnesota. I have never been colder. Then there was the "lovely" trailer behind the club that the owner put us up in while we worked the club. (one star does not begin to describe it.)

And there was the guy at the bar. As we were packing up our gear after the last night of the gig we kept walking past a guy with his forehead resting on the edge of the bar. After about the fourth or fifth trip to the van I realized the guy was passed out and had thrown up in his lap. It made me wonder; was this a statement on our music, or his life?

There were a lot of fun times like seeing Devils Tower, after-hours sandwiches at The Sterlingworth, Rusty, the bartender at Alpine Valley, Rick's cassette adventures played on the way to a gig, Paul "Hap" Hazard, and of course Betty always the band cheerleader.

After I left Mourning Dayze I traveled to the San Francisco bay area for a few years playing an occasional gig here and there. All of the musicians I ran into in that area were into jazz. So if I was going to get work as a musician, I would need to develop some pretty good jazz chops. So I listened, jammed, and studied and eventually got to be a pretty good player. After a few years of this, I decided that jazz was the type of music that spoke to me. If I wanted to play it on a regular basis, I needed to get serious about it.

After a lot of research on jazz schools the one that stood out was North Texas State located in Denton, Texas. So off I went to spend several eye-opening years playing, learning, and living jazz. (**Author's note**: In1990 the band's original bassist, Doug Henry would be at a hotel in Denton Texas, "Mean Joe Green's School," the night Stevie Ray Vaughn was killed.) During this part of my life I got to meet and play with some incredibly talented musicians. Many of whom are still actively playing in the music industry.

In the early 80's I moved back to San Francisco to play jazz in "the city by the bay." I was fortunate to hook up with some good musicians right away and we began gigging in the area. But it didn't take long to remember how expensive living in that area was, and that I would need a day job if I was going to survive. I took a job as a salesman in a local music store and did reasonably well right from the start. After about six months on the job I was promoted to general manager. This was a great store in a great area in the heart of Silicon Valley in Palo Alto and just down the road from Stanford University. This was supposed to be a short-term job until I got on my feet, but it lasted quite a

226

bit longer than expected.

Fourteen years later I left that business in search of the next challenge. I found a great opportunity in the wholesale music business at KMC Music, a division of Fender Musical Instruments. I started as a road salesman in Florida and I am now Vice President of Sales for the U.S. and work out of the corporate offices in Connecticut. Although I travel way too much to actively play on a regular basis, it's nice to still be in the music industry and be able to do something I love.

Howie's Hilltop
"Howie's Hilltop" bar just outside of Whitewater.

"Howie's" became a part of our lives during this period. "Howie's" is where we had band meetings and discussed business. It became this band's "Betty's." Doug Henry was doing some part-time bartending for Howie. When I turned 21 Doug told me to be sure to stop at "Howie's" in celebration of my birthday and I did. I tell ya, I really didn't understand what the attraction was. But as time went by Paul and I began to go to "Howie's" to watch the Bucks, Packers and Brewers play ball. Howie loved sports and was always very "into" the games, very animated and got people involved if they demonstrated any interest at all in the games. He made it fun and got his customers involved. "Howie's" was a fab place for conversation with a wide range of people including local farmers, hard working people, grave diggers, students and professors from the University. There were also lawyers and doctors and everything in between!

It was a fantastic mix of people. It was a fun relaxing place to hang out and worlds away from our band life. "Howie's" was always buzzing with life. Doug and I played at the Hilltop one New Year's Eve, Rise, Bob Lee and I also preformed there, musically that is! I'm really not sure of what you would call it, jug band music or bluegrass, but it was fun! Howie was an amazing man. He could always remember peoples' names no matter how many years it had been since he had last seen them. He remembered where they lived, what they were doing, and what they were drinking. Howie was always dealing or selling something. He had an answer for you if you had a question, any question. He would give you an accurate weather forecast, keep you updated on the sports scene, and the local, state, and national news. Howie liked to know where you stood on events of the day and didn't hold back when it came to letting you know what he thought or where he stood on a subject. Howie was a great friend. He and the "Hilltop" have always been part of our extended family. Our roots go deep and wide.

1978 - Mike Harmon - Drums

With Robert E. Lee no longer with us Rise and I began the search for a new drummer. We auditioned players from Madison and Milwaukee hoping that the larger markets would give us what we were looking for. We really needed a very multi-talented player. We needed someone who could play a wide variety of styles, moods, volumes and appreciate our established strengths and feel they had the freedom to contribute and be themselves. We didn't want someone to "be like Bob," but we wanted someone who could step in where we had left off and advance ourselves from that point. Rise and I very much wanted to go forward and not rest on our past. We were very lucky to have found Mike Harmon through the audition process. Mike, a great drummer out of Milwaukee, was a full time professional musician regularly working as an "on call" or jobbing musician with some of the best players in Milwaukee while playing in a wide variety of styles of music. Mike had worked with some great local players that we were familiar with namely the

228

legendary Milwaukee guitarist, George Pritchett, who owned his own jazz club and played guitar with Buddy Riches big band for a year. Rise, Bob, Vaughn and I would often go to Milwaukee and listen to George play with his trio, as a single and sometimes a duo with another great Milwaukee guitarist, Don Momblo. I had studied with Don a bit while he was teaching at UW-Whitewater. I remember being a bit shy telling Don I was a big Chet Atkins fan because I felt like I should have been sighting heavy jazzers instead. Don sensed that right away and told me what a great player Chet was and that I would do well by studying his style. I really enjoyed playing with Don and remember him as being a wonderful man. Our neighbor and legendary accordionist, Vern Meisner, asked me who was doing the drumming now that Bob was gone. When I told him it was Mike it was so funny. Vern gave me this big smile and said, "you'll like him." Mike had jobbed with Vern as well!

When we auditioned Mike, it was all business or should I say all about the business of playing music. Rise and I both loved that. Mike was the real deal, had a great sound, played musically in a variety of styles, and played very physically when that edge was needed. Mike's comment regarding the expectations of the people he was working with that stuck with me was this, "When we are playing cover tunes, I don't want to skip or gloss over rhythmic nuances or parts." I loved that and it was right up our alley. That's the way we approached our tunes and rehearsals. Later, as we'd played them out, we would make tunes our own after really learning them and learning from them.

Mike didn't mind Rise kicking keyboard bass. In fact he really appreciated her talent, dedication and hard work, playing keys, keyboard bass and singing. We were a powerful trio that played hard giving all we had for the love of the gig and the tune. Mike's drum solos were full of energy and depth. Without fail the people in the bar and lounge would stop what they were doing to listen and watch Mike when he soloed on his drums. He was always giving it all he had while sharing what he loved with those he played with and with those listening.

Mike Harmon

Mike and I never had a real close personal relationship. We just didn't. Mike and Rise seemed to have a good working relationship which was very helpful in moving us forward. That was a bit strange for me. I usually felt very close to the people I had played with. I was used to hanging out with my bandmates as a way of getting to know each other personally and musically. Mike and I did communicate with each other when we played- that's was really mattered. As I was getting older it was Mike who had made a lifelong impression on me regarding taking good care of one's physical health to maintain stamina and the physical and mental edge needed to perform at a high level from first song till the last. Mike took very good care of himself staying in very good physical condition, taking vitamins, eating well, and working out. I had thought I could just push my way through life with my thinking and desire. Mike may have felt me getting a little tired at the end of the night and commented that taking good care of oneself would allow a person to play at their best for the entire night especially if one played very physically. Mike lent me a book by Linus Pauling called "Cancer and Vitamin C." Reading this book changed my approach to life. I began to become aware in a very real sense that I needed to take care of my body as well as my mind and strive to live a balanced life in all spheres regardless of profession. I am eternally grateful to Mike. It has made me a better musician and a better person. Thanks Mike!

With this trio we all had the feeling we were good and we knew it. There was a burning desire for musical freedom personally and as a band. Our repertoire was just begging to expand into new territory. As a trio were playing very physically and were emotionally tuned in. We knew we could be better than we were. It wasn't just wishful thinking. We really were ready for the next step. We hungered for it. This had grown quite naturally out of our working together.

Rise was tired of playing keyboard bass that she played brilliantly. Her spirit needed to be free. We were all anxious to work with a player devoted to and "in to" playing bass and becoming an integral part of the rhythm section. Both Mike and I appreciated the fact that Rise had done more than her part playing bass, keys, and singing and needed to fully feel free to express herself. We needed a bass player.

Rise loved playing keyboard bass soooooo much, she even played it on her wedding day, 10-14-'79!

1979 - John Stull - Bass

Once again we turned to the Milwaukee and Madison newspapers with hopes of finding a bass player with broad musical interests, a life agenda that would work with ours, gigging experience, big chops, and a personality that would work with what we had established. In the early 80's it was once again through the Milwaukee classifieds we found bassist John Stull. John was a Californian, fashion conscious, loved classic and pop literature, and domestic and foreign films as well as fine art.

231

John's wife, I think her name was Susan, traveled throughout the country working with major art galleries and museums. We never met Susan.

It's interesting to note that due to the circumstances we were facing at that time, I hired John from a pay-phone from hotel lobby in Indianapolis. It was sight unseen with never hearing him play a lick. John did have an edge. He was able to chart all of his parts to the music we were playing. Our songbook was large and most of what we played was not the usual stuff bands played. John's charts were fantastic, spot on, and perfect for our next bassist, Tom McGirr, who read them with ease. John had a real love for the type of blues they played in Chicago and the blues in general. I hadn't played the blues for years. I really credit John with sparking my interest in playing the blues again...I've been playing them ever since. Thank you John! One memorable gig Rise, Mike, John and I played was in Huntington, West Virginia, where we worked a 5 star restaurant. (not our bag but sometimes you do what you have to do to pay the bills) We must have played John Denver's Country Roads at least four, sometimes more a night! All the travelers and tourists who stopped in the restaurant wanted to hear that tune while they were in West Virginia. (I finally learned the words.....smiles)

Rick   Rise   John Stull   Mike Harmon
Updated banner done by our great friend and
author/illustrator, Rick Cleminson-Keep

Mike   Rick   Rise   John
Huntington, West Virginia

1980 - Tom McGirr - Bass

In the fall of 1980 John was replaced by Tom McGirr, a friend of Mike's, and someone Mike had always hoped to work with on a regular gig. And that time had come. Tom was an extraordinary bassist...and wonderful man. Tom's playing made everything fit together and groove so well. It was amazing! We were playing at a very high level much of it thanks to what Tom brought to the group which was a rock solid foundation, breathing room, support for the essence of our material this provided unmatched freedom for everyone. Just what we'd been looking for! Tom and Mike's work as the rhythm section was extraordinary, always musical, played with soul and fun yet dangerous. They were always takin' care of business laying that stuff down. Playing with Tom made us all better. It was a wonderful time. So often the songs just seemed to play themselves. Our audiences loved it too. You could always tell, they just loved it. So did we! To the regret of us all we were not able to keep this group together. Both Tom and Mike were full time musicians and did not have an interest in traveling in order to make a living and nor did they have to. They had plenty of quality work in Milwaukee. We could not get enough work to keep this group together. This group was short lived but boy, it left Rise and I with many wonderful memories and many magical musical moments. We knew we were able to stand tall next to anyone, not talking trash here, it's just the way it was.

This version of the band played its last gig at Sterlingworth at Lauderdale Lakes for Dan Seymour, the owner, who had purchased uniforms for the Chicago Bear's cheerleaders, the "Honey Bears." The cheerleaders were going to perform at Sterlingworth as a "thank you" to Dan and needed a band to back them up for their group and solo performances. Dan asked us if we could do the job. We of course said yes. Dan had the cheerleaders manager call me to discuss what musical backing they would need. Their manager provided a sketchy idea of their needs and would give us more specific information as the performance date drew near. We never did get any concrete info as to what tunes the "Honey Bears" were going to need for their show. We rehearsed with them the afternoon before the evening's show. The "Honey Bears" had their routines down. We worked with them to find and perform music that would work well for them. The show was well received by an overflow house. I don't think there was a person in the room who knew how instrumental we were in making those girls comfortable and that night a success! It may have looked like we were in a supportive role, just doing our job, but we really were making it happen and much of it on the fly. It was just all in a night's work for us, and we were happy to be helpful in making it a grand night for the Sterlingworth.

Sterlingworth: Tom McGirr   Rise   Mike   Rick

Sterlingworth: Dan Seymour, Sterlingworths owner, had purchased uniforms for the Chicago Bears cheerleaders "The Honey Bears". As a thank you they preformed at Sterlingwoth backed by Mourning Dayze. Bass player, Tom McGirr, is seen in the background right behind Rise.

Rise and I found ourselves without a bass player and drummer and we needed to work. (There seems to be a recurring theme here!) For the past seven years we had hit the road in the spring so we could keep playing full time. Things would be a little different this year.

While playing at Alpine Valley a talent agent heard our band and offered Rise the opportunity to lead her own group. He would provide her with rehearsal space. He would get musicians for which she could hand pick as to personality, musical taste, interest, and chops. Rise left Mourning Dayze to pursue this musical course and see how far her musical wings would take her. Her husband, Jerry, was also 100% behind the idea. I wished her all the good fortune in the world.

Since the band broke up I found myself without a band and began to look for work with an established band. I had no interest in starting a group from scratch at this time. I did have

236

some interesting auditions. One was in St. Petersburg Florida with "Joe Trippi and Fantasy," a full time touring group working its way to New York City. Then on to Saudi Arabia for six months followed by a month in Scandinavia. It was the month in Scandinavia that really attracted me to this gig. I had no way to get to the audition. My very good friend Rick Cleminson had just bought his first new car. I had met Rick who became a great friend of the family, while attending UW-Whitewater. Rick is a highly creative artist who was always using his imagination and great fun to be around. Rick would gladly use his artistic skills to help the band whenever he was asked in doing photo shoots, designing band cards, and posters as well as updating the banner we used when we would gig. Rick would never let us give him any money for his work. *Rick is currently a highly acclaimed author and illustrator of children's books and often works with his wife Linda Lowery. Rick's book, Clatter Bash! A Day of the Dead Celebration, provided Rick with recognition and critical acclaim which put him in the spotlight. (He really wanted to be a rock star!) Clem's creativity and desire to teach and inspire just keep on growin'. We're glad you're out there!* I asked Rick if I could borrow his car to get to the audition. Rise and Jerry would come with me and drive the car home. Clem kindly agreed. I didn't get the gig. It was not because I didn't have the chops, but because I couldn't dance and play at the same time! The guys in the band tried to convince the leader to keep me. They liked what I brought to the table. The leader would have no part of it. He wanted a dancer. We went back to Wisconsin. Just so you know that group never did make it to Saudi Arabia.

An audition that would later pay off was with a group playing full time and working a club in northern Minnesota. I packed up everything I owned and left town hoping this new group would give me some steady work for a while. I turned down the offer to play with this group because the rhythm section was lacking and went back home to keep looking for work. I did however enjoy the groups bassist, Leroy Dehny. Leroy was a personable guy with a strong desire to play bass and succeed in the music business. Further on down the road Leroy and I teamed up playing in the "Rise" band.

1981 - The Rise Band

Rise: In 1981 while we were playing a gig at Alpine Valley an agent approached me asked if I had contacts. I replied, "yes I have contacts in New York and California, and I know a producer from London." He said, "No. I mean for your eyes." My heart dropped. I didn't want to be a trophy girl. I wanted to be a musician, a keyboard player. The agent said, "Just do this for a little while." So I formed my own band and called it "The Rise Band." I hired musicians that my agent knew and recommended. He was from Manitowoc, Wisconsin and a very nice man. My husband, Jerry, and I and the band members lived in Manitowoc above a strip club. The boys in the band loved living there, but it was not my cup of tea. When we left the building we had to walk through the club. I wouldn't look. The first few weeks were a little rocky. I fired my guitar player and after one week my drummer fell head over heels in love with a local girl and ran off with her. I called Rick. Thank goodness he came up to Manitowoc and we hit the road from there. I was so happy he decided to help out.

We were playing a gig in the lounge at a motel in Thief River Falls, Minnesota. About 3:00 the following morning the phone in our room rang. It was the front desk calling to tell me the bass player was in the pool naked with five or six underage girls. I told Jerry to take care of it. I wasn't interested in seeing my bass player naked. People asked me why I didn't fire him. I told them, "he plays a great bass!" In fact, he was so good that he left my band to play for the Neville Brothers and later Prince. Rick told me that underage girls were constantly knocking on his door. They all were "star struck!"

The "Rise Band" in uniform

Leroy Dehny, Rise, Herman Sarduey, and Rick

The "Rise Band"
Herman, Rick, Rise and Leroy

239

'Twas not meant to be...

Rise: "Jerry had bought an old Volkswagen bus for about $700. It looked like crap but had a Porsche engine in it. It was about four months later and we were on the highway near Kemmerer, Wyoming. Jerry was driving the bus. A car was coming straight at us sliding head on. It missed the bus and we both breathed a big sigh of relief. But suddenly we saw the trailer behind it. It whipped around and hit us head on. Thank God for the Stanley thermos that wedged between the floorboard and the gas pedal. The doctor at the hospital said it saved Jerry's foot. After all those years I can still see the band equipment flying by my head. Thank goodness none of it hit Jerry or me, but it busted out the windshield. I don't remember much after that. Rick had been driving right behind us. Later he loaded up our equipment and drove back to Whitewater.

The ambulance took us to the hospital in Jackson Hole, Wyoming. I remember the ambulance stopping for cattle that were crossing the road. We were allowed to share a hospital room which was against the rules but because it was our wedding anniversary they made an exception. Our physician was the doctor for the Olympic ski team. He was a wonderful man and we felt very blessed to have him. One thing that Jerry and I both remember vividly is looking out our hospital room window and seeing elk roaming about.

The doctor whose trailer hit us was very nice. He visited us in the hospital and paid all our bills. We flew back to Whitewater where mom and dad took us in. Jerry and I didn't have much money so while recuperating we would go to a bar and play the pinball machine together. We only had one or two quarters. I would play the machine on one side and Jerry would play on the other side each with a leg in a cast.

A doctor in Wisconsin removed our casts. Apparently, since that doctor did not put the casts on he misjudged while taking mine off and cut my leg. And to make things worse my Achilles tendon was cut in the accident and I couldn't tap dance for years!"

Authors note: "The wreck proved to be the end of The Rise Band."

240

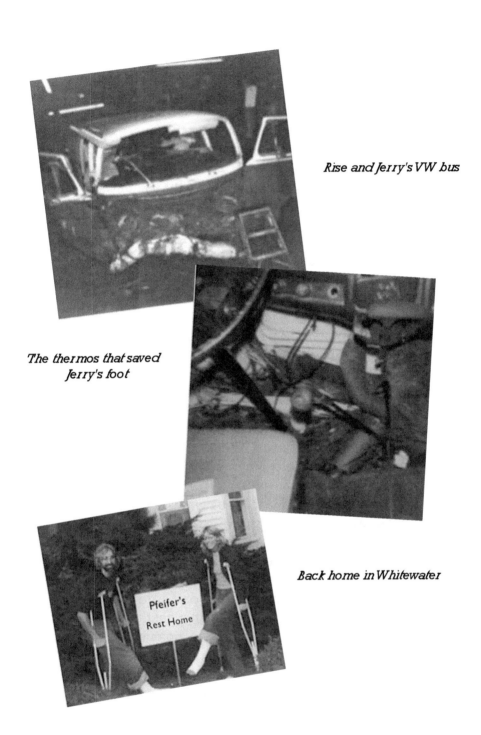

Rise and Jerry's VW bus

The thermos that saved Jerry's foot

Back home in Whitewater

Pfeifer's
Rest Home

While the "Rise" band played in Pocatello, Idaho, for what would prove to be the bands final two weeks a man introduced himself to us. He was the brother of Sandy and Linda Braun who were twins I had gone to grade school and high school with. Their father was the high school guidance counselor and was a regular customer at Williams' Cities Service, the station where our dad worked. We caught up on our past and then he mentioned if we were ever in Jackson Hole, Wyoming, we should look him up. He would be glad to put us all up if we needed a place to stay. He gave us his card left the club and we didn't think anything more about it. Two days later heading to our next gig Rise and Jerry were involved in a "Rise" band ending accident. Leroy, Herman, and I watched as their van was struck head on by a trailer after the car that was pulling it had spun out of control in the foothills of the Rockies. Rise and Jerry were taken to Jackson Hole, Wyoming to receive emergency medical treatment. Leroy, Herman, and I found ourselves in Jackson Hole needing a place to stay while pursuing options to see how we would get everyone and our equipment home. I gave Sandy and Linda's brother a call. He was more than happy to put us up for as long as we needed a place to stay. He let the three of us stay in his beautiful condo which was right at the base of Jackson Hole's world famous ski slopes. He gave us the keys and said, "call me if you need anything." These were real ski slopes! He was the owner of a restaurant just outside the city and was throwing a party for his employees the first night we were there. He invited all of us to join in the fun. We went and had a wonderful time. We were treated like kings and weren't allowed to pay for a thing! A beautiful act of human kindness I will never forget. We spent three nights in his condo and enjoyed being in Jackson Hole. I loved being in the mountains and hiking along the Tetons. Soon we found out Rise and Jerry needed to fly home due to their injuries. We put we everything that was salvageable from Rise and Jerry's van into my van and prepared to go home. We were packed. Every space available was used. We were horribly cramped yet none of my bandmates complained. Like everything else we just did it. Fortunately, Herman's home was in Ames, Iowa, which was right on our way back to Wisconsin.

Leroy and I wished Herman good-luck as we helped him unpack his luggage and drums. I drove Leroy home to Manitowoc. Then I went back to Whitewater. We never heard from Herman or Leroy again. As unlikely that it was that we would find ourselves playing together, it was an equally unlikely end.

Regrouping at Queen Street

Back in Whitewater Rise and Jerry were living at Queen
Street until they were able to make plans for their future, so was I.
Our parents as always made us feel wanted and welcome. I went
looking for work. I needed to gig.

The restaurant and bar my mom waitressed at, (and by the
way, you'd never find a better waitress!) The Blackhawk Hotel,
located in Fort Atkinson, Wisconsin was owned and operated by
her long time friend Rio Achilli and his wife, Fran, one of Betty's
long time friends. Rio had been running live music Friday and
Saturday nights for the past couple years. Betty told him I was
looking for work as a single, and hired me on the spot. I worked
as a single, December, 1981 through February, Friday and
Saturday nites. I played one weekend at the Blackhawk as a
single and quickly realized Rio's crowd really wanted dance
tunes as well as background music. I gave long time friend and
former Mourning Dayze bass player, Bob Jenson, a call to see if
he'd be interested in playing bass with me. It had been about
ten years since Bob left the band. He and I did occasionally play
together with the legendary "Dan Reilly and the Barn Swallows."
We were good friends and kept in touch with each other. Bob
agreed to work the weekends through the winter. It gave the gig
the flexibility it needed to keep our crowds. We could easily play
dance tunes. The first week-end Bob and I gigged together a
young woman from the bar started to shout out repeated requests
which we didn't know as a duo. They were jazz standards. She
was relentless. I went to talk with her on our break to discover
she was a professional jazz singer having travelled the country as
a singer, lived in Ft. Atkinson and had relation in Whitewater. Her
name was Sally Egeleson. I'm not sure of the spelling of her last
name or of a lot of other things now that I think about it! Sal,
"that's what ya get for being one of the guys!" We found some
tunes all three of us knew and had her come up and sing with us.

She was a jazz/lounge singer and very, very good, top-shelf. People enjoyed her work. Sally was not shy and asked if she could join our duo. Sal pointed out that most of the material she could bring to the group was already charted out. This made backing up Sal easy for Bob and I as well as allowing Sal to quickly and easily make an impact. Sal would join the group. We played together for about two months and had lots of grins. The jazz standards Sal brought to the group were a ball to play and Sal was a blast to be with. Sally tried to convince me to go to England with her where she had contacts and could make a living as a duo. I've always enjoyed listening and dabbling in the world of jazz, but it was not in my blood. It was nothing I'd wanted to do full time. My roots grew a different direction. I passed on that opportunity and was flattered to be asked by such a fine singer and wonderful person. Sal sang at our wedding when Astrid and I got married.

ROCK
COUNTY
GUITAR STUDIO
Home of The Pickers Preference

LESSONS FOR ALL AGES
A COMPLETE LEARNING
AND BUYING CENTER FOR
THE GUITAR ENTHUSIAST
33 SOUTH MAIN STREET
JANESVILLE, WI 53545   756-4404

During the spring of 1982 I began to teach guitar at Rock County Guitar in Janesville, Wisconsin thanks to Randy Holmberg, store owner at that time. I taught there for one year. Then Rock County Guitar closed. Randy went to work at Music-Mart, another local music store, and encouraged me to teach there as well which I did for about 1 1/2 years. Randy was a great human being and lots of fun to work for. One summer Randy invited me to go with him to the NAMM (National Association of Music Merchants) show in Chicago which I gladly agreed to. At the NAMM show I was truly a kid in a candy store who could not get enough. It was musician's heaven! What I vividly remember about this day was this: as we were walking around seeing what different vendors had on display and listening to some of the finest players in the world demonstrating their wares, I heard a

245

guitarist that really stood out. I thought I knew who it was. In fact I was sure I knew. It had to be the great jazz guitarist and instructor Ted Greene. No one else sounded like him. We walked over to where he was playing so we could see him. There was no one listening to this guy. He was playing solo. When I saw him I couldn't believe my eyes much less my ears! It was who Chet Atkins considered to be the world's greatest guitar player, Lenny Breau. He was stunning. I'll never forget how he looked at me and smiled while he was playing. He was doing just what he should. It was a moment I'll never forget. It's also worth noting when I got married and needed to get a regular job it was Randy's kind recommendation that landed me my first social work job after being out of the field for 11 years. Thank you Randy!

I soon left Music-Mart to begin my regular job. I never saw Randy again. He was a great friend. How did I ever end up teaching at Rock County anyway? The beginnings for my teaching experience happened years prior beginning with Doug's (Doug Henry) association with Dick Zastrow, a fine guitar player, and at one time owner of Rock County Guitar. Doug and Dick had played in a band together. **Doug**: The thing I remember most about Dick was how laid back he was and his guitorgan. He loved that thing. Our name was the TJ Trio derived from Marv Janes, our drummer. I believe Marv knew Dick from the store and I'm not sure how I met Marv. I believe we played in '73 and into '74. We played at the Anchor Inn, Owl's Nest, the bowling alley in Fort and other places I don't remember. Rick came to see us by a lake we played at. The place we had our pictures taken. We use to practice at the store and at Marv's house on Lake Koshkonong. Believe it or not, I was doing a lot of vocals! Dick never sang. Oh, we played at some bar in Beloit also. I would switch over to guitar and he would play bass on the old standard r&r tunes. At the end of practice Dick's parting word for good-bye was always, "Practice!"

TJ Trio: Doug Henry, Marv Janes & Dick Zastrow with his guitorgan

1976 U.S. Band Bob Paulson, John Paulson, Rick Lakin, Doug Henry

I was still hanging out at Howie's Hilltop during this time. It was always such a fun place with a great mix of people. A bass player, Tim Walters, lived in Whitewater and stopped in now and then. We had always end up talking about music and band life. Tim was playing with a highly successful group from Janesville, Wisconsin, called "Sleeper." "Sleeper" was about to lose one of its guitar players and was currently looking for someone to replace him. Tim asked if I would be interested in coming to a gig to check out the band and sit in on a few tunes to give his band mates a chance to meet me and hear my stuff. I agreed and went to their show. I had never heard them before, only about them. They played original tunes, modern southern rock, R & B,

247

and blues-doing it all with soul. I got the job. I worked with them for about two weeks and then was replaced by outstanding guitarist Freddy Dobbs of "Heartsfield." It was a good experience for me. I really loved playing with "Sleeper's" guitarist Matt Goodwin, a nice guy and great player and singer just dripping with emotion and soul. We were a very natural fit that would get down, dig in and play. I'd also met Dick Armstrong who played harp, guitar, and sang. Dick had a terrific feel for music, I always loved his "never overstated" "just enough" approach to the harp. Dick was very helpful to me while I was learning their material on stage. He was very aware and someone I counted on to make sure I was playing the right tune and not about to lead the charge straight off a cliff! With "Sleeper" behind me I found myself looking for a group to work with.

1982 - Grand Slam

In the spring of 1982 a week after my last gig with "Sleeper" I received a call asking if I was looking for a gig and could I audition that afternoon with a newly forming group. Dick Armstrong of "Sleeper" had given my name to the leader and thought my style might be a good fit. I threw my gear in the van and headed to Janesville to audition with the group "Grand Slam."

One never knows what a band is really about until you hear them for yourself. Even then you have to be very careful regarding your assessment. Walking up to the house where the audition was being held I could hear the band rehearsing in the basement. They were great players, playing good tunes, with a touch of R&B, urban funk and soul. What got my attention as I listened to them before I introduced myself was the drummer. Man, oh man, was he good! I loved his professional sound, balance and feel. He was playing at a very high level. Playing the songs first and his kit second. He was comfortable with his chops and didn't have to prove a thing to anyone. The rest of the band sounded real good as well. It seemed like they had something to say and I liked that. I jammed with them, was asked

248

to join, and signed on. Gigging was in their immediate plans which was important to me. I did not want to be with a group that never got out of the basement. The groups leader was Michael Atkinson or Cooper or Sax. I was never quite sure! Mike was a fantastic Hammond player with great chops and played with a lot of soul and energy. Mike also did some of the singing. Aaron Story, in whose basement we practiced, played sax and sang. Aaron was the rookie in the group but in many ways was the heart and soul of this band giving it direction and focus. Aaron sang and played with style, had a great sound, and was always fun to be with. There was no shortage of grins with Aaron around. Bob Vance played bass and sang. Bob had a laid back, dig in when you need to, highly articulate style of playing, and had a fabulous soulful voice. Bob was always very kind and concerned about everyone in the group. Bob turned me on to "Boxe's," a rib joint in Rockford. He and I would go there whenever we could and get the best shoulder sandwich on the planet! The strings on our instruments were coated in "secret sauce" which made our playing greasy and extra funky. (Later on I had to take Doug to "Boxes." I had to share the treasure!) Bob left the group early on and was replaced by the fine bassist and singer Jerry Lehr. Jerry was a highly skilled bassist with a strong jazz background which adapted well to the music "Grand Slam" was playing. I really enjoyed working with Jerry. He had a great sound, understood the language of music, and enjoyed being part of the rhythm section. Oh, and Steve, the bands fantastic drummer, could sing too! The first time I played with Steve I felt like we locked right in, riding that groove wave, and letting the music play itself. We shared many fun musical moments. Steve was always tuned into what was being played and very aware of where the action was. Steve would lay back, encourage, push, support and live in the music that was being played. He was always focused and ready to go to work, ya, really!

"Grand Slam" played together from about May of 1982 until November of 1982. There were some wonderful musical moments with this group but the best part, was meeting the great people in the band.

Grand Slam

Steve Dougherty, Arron Story, Jerry Lehr, Rick Pfeifer, Michael Atkinson

Jerry Lehr, Rick Pfeifer, Steve Dougherty, Aaron Story, Michael Atkinson

I left "Grand Slam" to play with some friends from Edgerton that included Gene Jenson, Earl Quigley and Wendy Halvorson and someone new to me who was the leader of this group, Ernie Martin. This was to be a very traditional country band which would stay close to country's roots. I was attracted to the group because it had two lead singers. I would sing a little, but I would really be able to focus just on my guitar playing. Country music offered me lots of room to play in a supportive role as well as a lead role. It seemed like a fun challenge. The band played one or two gigs, then dissolved. It was a fun group, but like so many it didn't have the staying power. Musicians are never finished paying their dues, never. It's just part of the gig and keeps those who are hungry on stage.

At this same time the legendary "Dan Reilly and the Barn Swallows" were gigging almost every weekend somewhere around Edgerton or Indianford. The "Barn Swallows" were not a regular membered band. Anyone who wanted to sit in and play or perform was more than welcome. It was Bob Jenson who invited me to sit in with the "Swallows." I enjoyed it. We played nothing but good time music in almost any style. It was music that made people dance, laugh and have a good time.

(Dan has an abundance of energy, loves to entertain, and is great at it. His audiences just love him and consequently has a huge following as a single entertainer. More on "Dan Reilly and the Barn Swallows" later.)

L to R: "The Prez" Tom Jenson, on the floor, Sandy Quam, Jeff "Elvis" Bartz, Dan Reilly. Top row: Wayne Skau, "Boom Boom Bobby!" Jenson, Rick Pfeifer, Gene Jenson

It was through a "Barn Swallow" gig I first got to work with singer/guitarist Wayne Skau. I had heard Wayne sing years ago with his legendary group "Stoned Hinge" at a bar in Milton, WI. I distinctly remember Wayne singing "Steeley Dan's" classic, "Reelin' in the Years," and thinking to myself, "this guys the real deal." Never did I even consider that he and I would be in the same band for 25 years and counting. The first song I heard Wayne sing with the "Barn Swallows" was Del Shannon's "Runaway." He sounded great and proved himself to possess a truly world class voice. It was a "what are you doing here!?" moment. Wayne and I tried to see what we could do as a duo.

251

We rehearsed regularly at Wayne's parent's house. We played one party together but that was it. We went our separate musical ways and seeing each other off and on when we would gig together as "Barn Swallows."

Wayne Skau - Singer/Guitarist

Wayne on slide guitar

(Member of Mourning Dayze for over 25years) Grew up and continues to reside in Edgerton, Wisconsin.

Wayne: My first guitar was a Stella acoustic, a hand-me-down from my uncle Jimmy Patton, who was a jazz and blues guitarist in Chicago. However, I didn't have it very long because my three brothers and two sisters enjoyed playing with it like it was a toy. They would dress it in clothes, pour sand into it and use it as a baseball bat! I didn't get another guitar for a long time. Later on I bought a Kay solid body single pick-up with an amplifier. From then on I was on my way.

In 1970 some buddies and I put together a band we named "The Stoned Hinge Band." This was the same year I recorded my first single. One side was "Janice," written by Maynard McIntyre, The Stoned Hinge guitarist. I wrote the song on the flip side called "Violet Lady."

The Stoned Hinge Band traveled nine states mostly in the Midwest for seven years. For two of those years I ran a bar in Ft. Atkinson, Wisconsin, called the Shorecrest Ballroom. During that time we backed up performers as diverse as REO Speedwagon and Frank Sinatra, Jr.

When the band broke up I took a job with my wife's family in Milwaukee. In 1980 I received a phone call from Paul Accurso, my former bass player with Stoned Hinge, who was forming a band in Chicago. This band ended up being Public Enemy, a power-pop band managed by the owners of the Headliners Bar in Madison, Wisconsin. During this time the band backed up some big-time bands including The Ramones and The Romantics. After about two years the band broke up because some of the guys wanted to go punk rock. I left because I did not consider myself a punk rock singer.

During the next ten years I played a lot with Rollin' Rock, a band put together by my former Stoned Hinge guitarist, Maynard McIntyre. Rollin' Rock was a fun band. We even backed up Cheap Trick at a benefit concert in Rockford, Illinois.

During this same time period I played with The Barn Swallows along with Rick Pfeifer, his sister Rise, Bob Jenson and myself. The band was a backup group for Dan Reilly. The Barn Swallows recorded a lot with Reilly on his original songs. We also backed up other artists including Highway 101, Sweethearts of the Rodeo, The Platters and The Cryan' Shames. And, we played Summer Fest and the Wisconsin State Fair. I was playing with Mourning Dayze during this same period. It has been Mourning Dayze that has been more satisfying and challenging musically.

253

Beach boys not "The Beach Boys"

Wayne Skau, givin' it all's he's got...

255

Putting Mourning Dayze together again...
Bill Johnson - Drums. Rick Niez - Bass.

Rick: In November of 1982 I found myself having the
opportunity to play the coming winter season at Alpine Valley but
didn't have a band, I needed to put one together and quickly.
Rise was ready to get back to playing and singing after
recovering from the car accident. That was good news! Rise and
I got together to discuss the coming winter season. Rise had a
long time fan, Bill Johnson a professional drummer, who came to
Alpine Valley to listen to her sing and deliver it. Bill had often
said that if we ever needed a drummer we should look him up.
Bill always seemed like one of the real good guys in the world.
We had never heard him play but he had a great track record
which included great venues, recordings and working with an
extremely popular band out of Milwaukee, "Bad Boy." I gave Bill a
call to see if he was available and interested in auditioning for
us. Bill was thrilled. It was something he really had long wanted
to do. When Bill asked who was playing bass, I told him we
needed a bass man as well and had been looking to see who was
available. As good fortune would have it Bill happened to have a
very good friend, Rick Niez, who played bass and was among the
elite in Milwaukee. The two of them had always wanted to gig
together. This would be the opportunity they each were looking
for. The audition went extremely well. These two were the kind
of big time players we had been used to. They were great. We
sounded good, real good. The time just seemed right to load our
musical guns with all we had and see where our wings would
take us. It was this thought that got me to give Wayne a call to see
if he'd like to join the group. Wayne's voice and presence would
add a whole new dimension to the group and expand our
repertoire and set list. The opportunity would also allow Wayne
to perform with a group working at a high level. Wayne agreed to
come on board. The group was set. Now to rehearse and see
what we had, and to see where our strengths lie. The group had a
good vibe. Everyone held their own contributed and opened
doors to new musical territory and direction. It was a group
whose heart lie in soul, heartfelt pop, rock 'n roll and filling the

dance floor. The group gigged around Whitewater and Edgerton for about six weeks before our Alpine Valley debut. We had "many a good nite," our audiences enjoyed us, and club owners wanted us back. It was a long drive for our drummer and bass player coming from Milwaukee to rehearsal and gig. A drive that would discourage many musicians from even considering playing with us. Rick and Bill didn't seem to mind at all. They enjoyed the band and felt it had a chance to go far.

Mourning Dayze at Edgerton High School   Bill Johnson   Ricky Niez

The gig at Alpine went well. Everyone in management loved us and our regulars were all smiles. It was a very special night when a large group of fans from Edgerton rented a bus and came to Alpine spend the night with us. Rise and Wayne were sounding great. Our crowds couldn't get enough of them. Rise was glad to be back performing after being almost a year away. It was so nice to have her back. It was a good winter season.

This group was not meant to last, Rick and Bill would leave us shortly after the winter season to gig with a newly forming Milwaukee group with recording prospects, "Floppy Disk." We had made plans of doing a demo to promote our group. Rick and Bill agreed to record with us even though both would be leaving us which was great of them because it was this band we wanted a

257

document of. I always laugh at this. We went to a great recording studio with a great band and went home with the worst demo tape in the world! I still can't believe how bad it is even after all of these years. Usually time will be a little forgiving, ha...not in this case! There's a lesson in there somewhere!

Beginning in the spring of 1982 the band's history things get a little sketchy as to who played when and with what line up. There were lots of personnel changes for a while. In trying to secure a lineup to fulfill our gigs Rick Neiz agreed to play with us for a month or so after Bill left and before the two of them would begin work on their new project, "Floppy Disk." I don't remember how we met Skip Zehms, but we did! The funny thing is Skip doesn't remember how he met us either! I won't guess how it happened. It just did. Skip played with Rick on bass for about a month. Rick then left to play with Bill. Got that?! Skip came from a rock background but also had a wide range of musical interests. He was very much aware of the styles of music we were playing and where we were coming from. Skip worked hard to make this project work and brought one of the most likeable personalities you would ever want to meet to the group. We all enjoyed Skip. He fit right in just like he would always been there, a real natural. Skip has been a life long friend of ours. Enjoy his bio!

Back row: Jerry Hebebrand, Rise
Front row: Wayne Skau, Skip Zehms, Rick Niez, Rick Pfeifer

258

Skip Zehms - Drums

Skip: "My grandmother is most responsible for my interest in playing music. When I was only four years old she mailed me a German made Hohner melodic also referred to as a wind piano or keyboard harmonica among other names. Later she gave me a Hammond organ.

I played first-chair trumpet in the grade school symphonic band of which I have a great early memory of being tapped on the shoulder by Carol McDonald, the prettiest blond girl in my school, and being told, "You play the best, Norman." I was smitten, but there was a big problem. No one knew that I had never learned to read music but was able to play good enough by ear to make first chair as long as I didn't have to play first at an audition.

My mother would take me to jazz ensemble recitals in San Francisco and Oakland area music stores so I could watch trumpet players. In actuality this exposed me to drums and drummers. But like a good young man I kept at the trumpet. But when my grandmother came through again, this time with a Sears drum kit for Christmas, the hook was set. From then on I spent a couple hours in the garage every day trying to play what was on the radio: The Beatles, The Monkees, Herb Alpert, Johnny Cash, the theme from Hawaii Five-O, anything and everything.

Our next door neighbor was a professional drummer and regularly had backyard jams with marimbas, kettle drums, and lots of what looked to my young eyes as a great sin as I peeked through the knotholes in the fence. Eventually I got up enough courage to have a peek over the fence. They called me over and invited me to play with them. They had some great parties and played great "homemade" music. A special treat for me was when they reversed the blower on the vacuum and melted beer bottles.

My father spent 26 years in the U. S. Navy and between grade school and junior high he was transferred to the Great Lakes Naval Training Center located north of Chicago. My first week at school I was asked to audition for the school symphony...oops...it was just myself, the music assistant, and a pile of sheet music; Busted! I was taken for a talk with the music

259

director who made an offer; I could stay in the program but would have to start over on first-grade theory books. That particular 12-year old boy had better things to do, so the drums sat abandoned from that day forward for a long time.

I was 18 when Jerry "Rocky" Zellner, a keyboardist and vocalist who was one of the founding members of Skyrock, a semi-regional 50's/60's cover band, moved to Rome, Wisconsin, where I was living. Skyrock had split up and Zellner and a guitarist named "Dash Rip-Rock" (don't recall ever hearing his real name) needed a drummer and a vocalist. Fate intervened as Rocky had heard me practicing in my dad's welding shop with my jamming partner, Toby Hack, a bassist, from Fort Atkinson, Wisconsin. Both of us were hired to cover a bunch of gigs Skyrock had booked at taverns, bars, Eagles Clubs, Grange Halls and festivals throughout Southern Wisconsin and Northern Illinois during the summer of 1977.

We rehearsed for a week. I had never played professionally. It was the first time I ever sang into a mic on backup harmonies for songs like The Beatles' "Please, Please Me," etc. I was having a blast and after playing together for almost a year we were getting pretty good. Somewhere there is a priceless poster from "Kettle Moraine Days" in Eagle, Wisconsin, of us posing on the hood of Dash's '69 GTO convertible wearing red ruffled silk shorts and black vests. Yeehah! Great fun. I'd like to know what became of old Dash Rip-Rock. Not long after my first year as a professional musician Toby Hack, Guy Moon, a high school friend of his also from Fort Atkinson, and I did some garage jamming. Guy eventually ended up in Hollywood and has won Emmy's for writing soundtracks for television shows. He also sat in on sessions with Bonnie Raitt. My memory is not real clear on this but somehow the three of us ended up at the famous "Pfeifer barn," which I believe to be multi-dimensional because nobody ever really leaves. Sometime later I received a phone call from Jerry Hebebrand (Rise's husband). I don't recall any of the conversation as it's all kinda blended and fuzzy now. But in any case I ended up with drums in the back of my Camaro and found myself in the "barn." Next thing I remember is making a beer run for Rick....and the rest is history.

Good memories of playing with Mourning Dayze include the occasional "snow-in" at Alpine Valley and romping around with a few ladies here and there. I recall a few wild nights when playing in the Stoughton/Edgerton area. Those folks lived hard and played hard. I met the girl I should have married there."

The Executives

Skip Zehms, Jeffre James Onsrud, Roxanne Kohlin Miles,
Mark Bushbeck, Kyle Derke

No Toys

Tom Steele   Skip Zehms   Bob Talbot   Scott Kleist

Skip had a good friend he felt would be a positive addition to the band, Scott Kleist from Oconomowoc. Scott played sax, guitar, keyboards, and had interests in recording. Rise and Wayne were enthusiastic and excited about the prospect of having a horn in the group. I was not. It just wasn't part of my musical pallet. I did agree to give the horn a try remembering how much I enjoyed Aaron's horn work but that was in a different context. I also felt some "new blood" in the band would be good and the horn would give us a different sound and open up new musical avenues for us. I was always looking for ways which we could re-invent ourselves for our Alpine audiences. By this time we would been playing there about 14 consecutive winter seasons and we needed to keep ourselves fresh, current and interesting for our audience and management. Scott was just what we needed. This lineup worked together for nearly a year before things began to unravel.

Wayne had a friend, Tom McDermott, that had played bass with him in "Rolling Rock" along side his long time friend and Edgerton rocker, Maynard McIntyre. Maynard also played with Wayne in the legendary "Stoned Hinge" band and is still rockin' today with "Rolling Rock." Maynard exemplifies the heart and soul of rock 'n roll. Wayne suggested we give his friend Tom McDermott a try on bass which we did. Tom was a great guy to be around. He was full of energy and enthusiasm for music and enjoyed playing with this lineup which was Skip on drums, Scott sax and guitar, Tom on bass, Wayne guitar and vocals, Rise keyboards and vocals, and Rick guitar and vocals. Tom loved playing music, worked hard at his craft, and really became part of the Mourning Dayze family. Everyone enjoyed hanging with Tom.

Tom McDermot

Soon after Tom was with us Wayne left the group. Wayne too was part of our family. It's just the way things go within any group. You have to be free to follow your heart and of course it's important that you do or know you can. It's who you are. We continued playing as a five piece group without Wayne.
This group fell apart just before the summer season began at Alpine, 1983. I needed to put a group together to play the summer season. I gave the great drummer Steve Dougherty a call to see if he would be interested in working Alpine for the summer and also bassist Jerry Lehr. This group would be a trio. "Where did Rise go?" you might ask. Well, she was crisscrossing the country in an eighteen wheeler with her husband Jerry. Something both of them longed to do and simply decided to do it.

Rise gettin' ready to hit the road!

Steve Dougherty - Drums/Vocals.
Jerry Lehr - Bass/Vocals.

Steve, Jerry and I had worked together in "Grand Slam" but never did anything together as a trio.

I was very excited about playing with Steve and Jerry. These guys were loaded with talent and our personalities seemed a good fit. I just loved playing with Steve. He brought such a good vibe to the stage and was a real pro on his kit and a fab singer too! Steve also was very tolerant of all the "dumb stuff" you end up having to do when you're a house band. He understood it was a gig and our living. He had been around the block more than once. Steve brought great tunes to the band and turned me on to many giants of the blues: Namely T-Bone Walker, Elmore James and Howlin' Wolf, Surf music (which I'd nearly forgotten about!) Gypsy Jazz and the music of Danny Gatton. all for which I'm forever grateful. Steve has been a good friend for as long as I've known him and always the consummate professional. Steve is a real musical treasure. Jerry was a fine bassist with great chops and a very fine voice, I always felt Jerry should sing more. I felt he had a real personal approach to his singing and very heartfelt.

For some reason I never quite got a handle on what direction this trio would take. I think I was too concerned about keeping the Alpine gig and putting that before the music. These two guys and the Alpine gig really afforded me the chance to play whatever I wanted. Those chances don't come along every day. I just wasn't up to the task to take full advantage of this great musical opportunity.

Jerry Lehr would soon leave the group and Steve and I found ourselves in need of a bass player. We turned to the Milwaukee Journal classifieds and found a wonderful man to play bass with us, Bob Berlyn. Bob had a genuine interest in playing with a group like ours and worked hard on his bass. It was not his primary instrument. He was first a sax player. Bob loved to play and seemed to enjoy the mix of styles we were into even though it was often a bit new to his own "hands on" experience. Bob enjoyed "band life," the personalities, stories and perspectives that came from that well.

Bob Berlyn - Bass. Steve Dougherty - Drums/Vocals. Rick – Guitar/Vocals.

Rick, Bob Berlyn-bass and Steve Dougherty-drums played as a trio for nearly one year.

The timeline of the band and "who's doing what when" is unclear during these years I'll give an rough sketch of events. It is by no means to be considered a "spot on" accurate accounting of our history. If I've left something out, it's not been intentional or due to a lack of effort. Rather, because I simply don't remember or couldn't find out with any kind of certainty who was doing what, when. Steve, Jerry, Rise and I played one season at Alpine somewhere in here. Also, there was a winter season at Alpine somewhere around this time when Jerry Lehr was playing bass as was his friend Chis. He played drums with us and Wayne was back singing and playing as well. I just don't remember where in the timeline. I apologize guys. If you have information that would clear up our timeline, we'll do our bloody best to include it if there is a second edition of the book. Please contribute if you can help us to be accurate and give credit where credit it due. The intent is not to rewrite history! (Smiles)

After nearly a year traveling around the country in their truck Rise returned to the band. It was good to have her singing again. Bob was fascinated with the voice, delivery, and presence of Rise. He recognized she was a gifted, genuine, and talented performer. With Rise with us again we had more options regarding material we could draw on and get it together quickly. Bob was at times surprised by our repertoire and often commented on how we didn't do tunes most bands seemed almost expected to play and played tunes most bands wouldn't touch. He appreciated the risks we took with our choice of material. If there was a tune that caught our ear which we could do with soul and conviction, I saw no reason not to give it a try. I thought that is why we played in the first place. How we present and place tunes in our set in response to our crowd, how the band is playing and where the room was at, is the key to playing music that your audience is unfamiliar with or doesn't expect in a given situation. Music is best played "for" an audience, not "at them."

Bob brought the band into the digital age. Here's how; Rise was singing a dance song by Madonna, "Into the Groove," which happened to have a keyboard based, synth bass line. We have played many tunes in the past that had synth bass lines by having the bass player play them on his bass and thought nothing of it. Well, here we are getting ready to rehearse our tunes for the week in the "barn" and Bob walks in with his electric bass and a small Korg keyboard. Hmmm? What's this? Bob thought he would be more true to the tune and style and played the bass part on his keyboard in true "techno" style. It was great. It gave the tune a modern, poppy and snarkey edge. More important than that, it was the beginning of the bands affair with the world of digital technology. Bob's understanding of how this technology could be applied to live performance would prove to be monumental in the story of the band.

Bob Berlyn diggin' in

1985 - Bob Berlyn – Bass/Sax/Keyboards

Bob: I started playing with Mourning Dayze in 1985 on bass. I'm not sure the rest of the band knew at the time that my main instrument was sax. But I really wanted to play in a rock band. I was a couple years out of college so playing in this context was a welcome change by having no sheet music, just raw rock and roll. Most importantly was playing with musicians who performed with incredible soul. That was the greatest attribute of Mourning Dayze, rock and roll with conviction.

I was introduced to the music of Bonnie Raitt who Rise could emulate with incredible depth. I had such a blast learning all the tunes we ended up playing and eventually I got to play a little sax on a couple numbers. Later we added sequencing with a drum track and horn lines which I played along with.

I worked with the band for nearly five years before I joined a variety band in Milwaukee and started a family. I'll always cherish those years playing with the band; Rick, Rise, Steve, Boom-Boom, Wayne, Skip, and all the others who made it the longest living band in Wisconsin.

Captain's Catch: Wayne, Boom Boom, Bob Berlyn, Rick, Rise

With this line-up of Steve, Bob Berlyn, Rise and I, Bob was able to play sax, (with Rick on bass) keyboards and sing lead too! The flexibility was nice to have. No matter where we played people always enjoyed hearing Bob play his horn. People commented on it all of the time.

Steve had been with the band for nearly five years. When the day came he told us he was leaving the group to play full-time with a man he had worked with before, the great singer-songwriter, performer, and fabulous harp player, Jim Liban, out of Milwaukee. I would sure miss Steve and his exceptional drumming, but I knew and understood the need and desire to play at a high level and on a full time basis. There are never any regrets when people do what they feel they need to do, were intended to do, or have the chance to better themselves. That's always to be encouraged. It only saddens me when we don't do our very best and settle for mediocrity. I was very happy for Steve and I knew I had made a real friend.

Steve Dougherty

Steve Dougherty

Steve: It might seem odd but my initial recollections of working with Rick at Alpine Valley are of the non-playing experiences. (I could play rounds of golf at anytime.) I was able to enter the amphitheater to see the many acts. I would stand stage watching Elton John or see Bill Cosby go on before Sting. I remember the time Jerry Lehr and I got stuck in the snow on the way home from a New Year's Eve gig and had to walk miles to the downtown Delavan police station to wait out the storm.

But, I always come back to the fond memories of the music made with Rick and the band and the great variety of which went from a quiet Friday night fish fry crowd to a roomfull of post-Grateful Dead concert goers.

I'm most grateful that around this time I got clean and sober, and I would be remiss for not thanking Rick. He put up with my antics and stuck with me through the anxious weeks that followed my initial sobriety. Thanks to Rick I was able to continue to play music.

Since then I've been fortunate to work with many world class musicians and have traveled around the country as well as internationally.

My lasting memory of Mourning Dayze will always be Rick's beautiful guitar playing and the ear-opening fret work he possesses."

269

Boom Boom and Skip, one more time...

Rise was not with the band the following year. With Steve and Rise leaving it was time once again to reevaluate our line-up. Bob was really wanting to play his horn, some keys, and stop playing electric bass. After much thought regarding the band's next move, I contacted Skip who was still in the area while going to school at UW- Whitewater to see if he would be interested in playing in the band again. Skip was enthusiastic and agreed to jump on board. It would be nice to have someone playing with us who knew what they were getting themselves into! You did, didn't you Skip? Smiles...

Now what to do about a bass player? My long time friend Bob Jenson and I had been playing together as members of the "Barn Swallows" for years and gigged on the side now and then. It had been about 15 years since Bob had left Mourning Dayze, but we remained best of friends and in constant contact. I explained the situation to Bob and Bob agreed to terms. Bob Jenson aka, B.J. Or Boom Boom, was back in the band. It was like having a member of the family coming back home! Bob wasn't as skilled as many of the guys that proceeded him, but if he worked hard he would be just fine. Bob has a very natural feel and love for music which is clearly expressed when he's loving his bass.

Our line-up was set with Bob, Skip, Boom Boom, and myself. We gigged as a four piece for over a year with one notable exception during our winter gig at Alpine. I asked Wayne if he'd be interested in singing with us on Saturday nights. Wayne was happy to work with us one night a week. We were all glad to have him. It gave us variety and an edge. Everyone enjoyed his talents. Bob Berlyn introduced the famous Korg M-1 synth to the band that season. The realism of the digitally sampled sounds was like nothing we had ever heard before from a keyboard. Wayne particularly enjoyed having a digital "horn section" to sing and play with. Bob did a "sequence" of an "island" tune I was in love with, "Everybody is Somebody" by Taj Mahl. This was the first fully sequenced song we had done. The band's future could be heard in that sequence. Bob recorded a realistic backing track of the tune on his Korg-M1 which included

270

drums, bass, keyboards, horns and backgrounds. It was a realistic recorded version of the tune on separate mixable tracks. The bands musical pallet suddenly seemed endless and only limited by our imaginations. My imagination was hard at work thinking about the possibilities regarding the real-time use and incorporation of digital drums and backing-tracks in a live setting. I was fascinated by this technology. I was that kid in a musical candy store. It was like having an entire big box home improvement center in our musical toolkit!

The Drum Machine/Workstation

This is a peek behind the scenes of how the drum machine/workstation became incorporated in the band: **Rick:** I had been hearing people talk considerably about the use of drum machines on pop recordings and was very aware of their usage in that medium. I had never remotely considered using a drum machine to replace a real drummer with Mourning Dayze. I felt drum machines sucked the life right out of a band much less the song. Drums, drummers and percussionists are the heart and soul of any band from my point of view. I loved playing with a good drummer. There were years where much of my band life was spent working with the rhythm section. It has been my first love. But the times were changing as they always do. I wanted to keep the band current, in the mix, moving forward and provide as many musical options as possible for the listeners, dancers, and ourselves. There is an ever present drive to keep our performances fresh, exciting and fun.

Former bassist Rick Niez had told me I should check out his current band who were proving to be very successful in Milwaukee. Instead of a real drummer they were using a drum machine. I really found that hard to believe. I had to check them out. The night I saw them his band was playing for a huge crowd, the dance floor packed, and the band sounded fab. If you weren't paying close attention, you might not realize they didn't have a real drummer. It was more confirming proof that a drum machine would work reasonably well in a live setting. Not that is was as good as a real drummer or could replace a real drummer, not by any means, just that "it worked." I wasn't convinced that was the direction I wanted to go, but it sure got me thinking more seriously about giving it a try.

One Sunday afternoon Bob Jenson and I were backing up local solo artist and long time friend Dan Reilly at the Showboat in Indianford just outside Edgerton, Wisconsin. Dan was entertaining the crowd while playing his 12string, and singing his heart out and using a drum machine nicknamed, "Marta." (That's because everyone in Edgerton has a nickname, just a fact of life.)

It was my first experience playing with a drum machine in a live setting. It worked. The audience and dancers didn't seem to mind at all. The only trouble we ever had was when a tough "looking for trouble" gang of motorcycle drummers would come to see us play. They had heard about "Marta" and felt they had a score to settle. All hell would break loose with sticks flying everywhere and then they tried to unplug "Marta"! It was ugly!

For Mourning Dayze live performance with the drum machine/sequencer was well received. Not 100% by any means and many in our audience had a very difficult time accepting us using a drum machine. Some club owners would not consider booking us because of it. I do the programming with emphasis on getting the drums to sound the very best I can. Next I lay down bass and keyboard parts, and would add the horns or some frills here and there. Once I had it complete it would always be there for better or worse. In addition it would provide Rise with the opportunity to just sing and would not have to be concerned with playing an instrument. It would allow her to do her thing, just sing!

The drum machine/sequencer was never meant to be used as a musical crutch nor was it intended as a slam to any drummer, anywhere. It has been used to the best of my ability as Bob Berlyn would say occasionally say as "an organic tool." If it didn't have some organic quality to it, I wouldn't use it.

Since 1992, the band has been using sequenced drums and backing tracks. Most of that work has been done by me. I have supplemented the bands song list with sequences produced commercially which I'll arrange, rearrange, edit, and mix so they sound like us. The commercially available tunes have been a real benefit. They are usually contemporary pop tunes which means I don't have to spend every hour I have sequencing tunes and gives the band a few more musical options.

This technology has given Mourning Dayze the opportunity to play reggae, salsa, Motown and horn driven blues as well as rock,swing, pop, dance, and country by using the instrumental flavorings of each style which is provided by the synthesizer. Consequently, the band has been more singer/songwriter/arrangement based these past 18 years. Much different than what I had envisioned, but still fun. Doing the programming for the band has given me a way to share myself with our listeners in ways I never had imagined.

Back to the band...

Bob integrated the sequencer into our live performance very creatively. When Bob would "sequence" (record) a horn section on his Korg-M1, he would sequence the trumpet on one track and trombone on another track, then play the tenor part on his horn which would really give the sound a shot of realism. Adding to that, in between his horn lines, Bob would play keyboards! Cool eh?! Yip! Now, how was the rest of the band going to play along with the unforgiving timing of a sequencer? It sure wasn't going to follow the band! Skip was about to undertake and display a great act of discipline and courage on behalf of the band. What we did, to allow us to "have a horn section," was to have Skip use a "click track" to play along with. Yes, it's exactly like playing along with a metronome. Skip needed to play in perfect time with the sequencer and the band needed to follow Skip, perfectly! There was no room for error, none. Fun eh? That's what was needed if we were going to have a "horn section." Skip busted his butt to make it work. It would prove to be a daunting task. During our breaks Bob patiently taught me how to sequence drum parts using a stand alone Korg drum machine we purchased as a band. We began to combine both machines for a few tunes with Bob sequencing horn parts and I sequencing the drum parts. It worked. The band was able to play along with the sequenced drums just like Boom Boom and I experienced when we played with Dan Reilly at the Showboat a few years earlier.

We added a few tunes to our night using sequenced horns and drums. It was fun to a degree. We could play island tunes, Motown, and R&B tunes creating the illusion we had a horn section, a rock steady drummer, and new sounds.

Wayne was attracted to the fact we now had the ability to add horns to our sound. We could now play R&B and Motown with more of the lines that added spice to the mix. It was an inspiring sound. Soon Wayne began to play with us Friday, Saturday and Sundays once again. Shortly after this Bob Berlyn left the group. Remember, Bob had the Korg-M1 and the technological "know how" to sequence and integrate MIDI into our sound. When Bob left we not only lost a friend, but we also lost the technology, expertise, and hardware (the M1) which very "organically" integrated the synthesizer into the band.

Wayne and his Norwegian Teleprompter!

I had been going to Nashville once a year since 1988 to the Chet Atkins Convention. Due to the inspired acoustic guitar playing I had heard at the convention of Tommy Emmanuel and Pat Kirtley, and because of my long time love of acoustic guitarists, Marcel Dadi and Leo Kottke, I wanted to purchase a quality acoustic guitar that sounded like John Valentine's gorgeous Martin D-18. (The sound of that guitar made a lasting impression on me.) Instead of my "dream" acoustic guitar I bought a Korg-T3 workstation which was the big brother of the Korg-M1. So now I've spent all this money on the Korg. Do ya think I could figure out how to use it? Nope...I gave Bob Berlyn a call. "Bob, I need some HELP!" (It took Bob nearly one complete summer during our breaks to teach me how to use just the drum machine! How long would this take?!) Bob kindly offered to teach me how to use the T3. We spent an afternoon at his home in Milwaukee. He walked me through how to use the machine. I got it! I also asked Bob if he would be willing to sequence some horn parts for the band. Bob was glad to do that for which we were all grateful. You'll still hear some of Bob's sequences when we gig: "Given' it Up For Your Love," "Nobody wants to lose," "Domino," and the first full sequence I'd ever heard, "Every Body is Somebody." Every time we play those tunes it's like Bob is still with us on stage. We know he's there in spirit! Thanks Bob!

Our line-up was Skip, Wayne, Boom Boom, and Rick. Rise was also playing with us again. Rise used the T3 when we gigged so she could access the keyboard's great realistic sounds of pianos, organs and horns. On the keyboard Rise was playing the horn parts to songs we were doing live just like any other keyboard part.

My sequencing skills kept growing on the T3. The force that drove me was that I felt the band could play live using only the drum machine. I felt my skills along with the technology and sounds the T3 offered allowed me to lay down realistic grooving drum tracks that would be very good. You wouldn't know we were using a drum machine instead of a drummer unless you were looking at us. Well...almost anyway. Mourning Dayze was now a part-time band, but I still wished to play at the highest level we could. This was my answer. I knew what it meant to undertake such a project and the time was right for a change.

I told my bandmates that we were going to use the drum machine in the T3 instead of a real drummer for our live performances. I think they were all a little skeptical but agreed to give it a try. And ya, I guess you could say Skip was replaced by a drum machine but not really. This was a call from the music itself. It didn't have a thing to do with anything other than that. I had a mountain of work to do to prepare for our first gig without a real drummer. It takes me between four to eight hours, to sequence one song's drum track. It was work that took up most of my free time for the next fifteen years. I really felt it was worth giving it a solid try and saw many advantages for our band in using this medium and was only too aware of the drawbacks. Here's something to consider and that's our audiences. If our audiences had not responded positively to this change, we would have gone back to using a real drummer. They enjoyed the technological change too. Their needs can never be overlooked or taken for granted, especially all of those beautiful brown eyed girls, eh? Speaking of our audiences, this story needs to take a break from talking about "the band" and spend a little time talking about the amazing town and people of Edgerton. They have their own musical legacy and have supported this band since 1970! Volumes could be written about live music and that fabulous town.

Enjoying this while we can...

Edgerton

Edgerton, Wisconsin, located seventeen miles west of Whitewater and Newville, an unincorporated community sitting only three miles from Edgerton, have been favorite spots for Mourning Dayze for over forty years. Edgerton originally named, Fulton Station, is often called "Tobacco City U.S.A," because of the tremendous historical impact tobacco growing has had on this community. At one time there were forty tobacco warehouses in Edgerton. Edgerton has its famous people as well, Pauline Jacobus, pottery artisan, Sterling North, author of "Rascal," Rich Bickle, NASCAR driver, and Steve Stricker, PGA Tour golfer. It should be noted that Steve Stricker when ever asked by Mourning Dayze would always gladly provide a signed piece of golf memorabilia to be raffled off for a charitable cause. Steve's demonstration of love and support for his home town is genuine and as good as it gets.

Edgerton has a rich musical tradition. It's the home of legendary rocker, guitarist and singer, Maynard McIntyre who has worked with Wayne in two notable groups, "Stoned Hinge" and "Rolling Rock." Maynard rocks like no body else. He's the real thing. Don't miss him if you get the chance. Then there's the great duo Cary and Krud who have also been playing the area for years. There's also "new blood" in town with Luke Tadder and the "Mad Tadders" starting a new tradition . The circle will not be unbroken.

Maynard McIntyre and longtime bandmate Wayne Skau

Bob Jenson and Wayne Skau, both longtime members of Mourning Dayze, are from Edgerton and are living legends. People will come from all over to hear Wayne sing and play and Bob play his bass. Mourning Dayze was almost renamed "Boom Boom Bobby and the Hairdos." (Plugger, owner of the Red Baron in Edgerton sponsored a "Name The Band" contest along with "Boom Boom Bobby and the Hairdos," chosen as the winner. "Skau potatoes and Ham" came in second and "Permanent Rollers" third.) Residents from the town of 5,500 have been loyal friends and fans since the 60's. They all have been following Bob and Wayne in the bands they've played in from their high school days until now. Check out their stories on the included dvd!

Wayne and Bob singing a rare duet!

When Bob joined the band he immediately began booking jobs for us in his home town. We played at the Youth Center. It's a place for teens to go, hang-out, be cool, listen to music and dance. We also played often at the Red Baron's "Cellar." The "Cellar" was in the basement of the Baron. You took a winding staircase down from the main floor to get there. It reminded me of a "folk" club, a place solo acts would play. There was a very small stage with a piano to the side, small bar, and maybe six or seven small tables, small and intimate. Mourning Dayze was a trio back then with Denny Ketterman on drums. We would gig there playing what ever we wanted and always having a fun time.

It was here Bob introduced us to many of his friends and family many of whom have been long time friends of the band with some that have left us way too soon. Most notable having been Tom "the Prez" Jenson. We first saw "the Prez" perform while we were on break in the "Cellar." Tom was doing an impersonation of President Richard Nixon which had the crowd laughing to tears and then would sing "Angry," "You are My Sunshine," "In Heaven there is no Beer" and solo on the kazoo! The whole place was up for grabs with all smiles and belly laughs. No one ever wanted to have "Prez" leave the stage, but he did after leaving us with a few thoughtful words to live by! If

280

you never saw "Prez" perform, you should know that this kind of performance and crowd response was not just a one time thing. Every time Tom performed and once he hit that stage and put that mic in front of him he was full of energy with a burning desire to bring life, joy and happiness to whom ever was in the crowd. He was determined to fire up the crowd and win them over-he always did. If "the Prez" was entertaining his bandmates, the crowd at the Red Baron, Alpine Valley, Summer Fest, or Wisconsin State Fair Tom always delivered the same genuine fun filled performance...yes, always! He put smiles on peoples' faces and filled the room with a vibe that said, "Isn't this great! Life is sooooo good, it's great to be alive! Let's Party!"

"The Prez" playing at Rise's wedding

It's the wonderful, amazing, music loving, caring, hard working, life loving and party hard people of Edgerton that we as a band can never thank enough. We would not be here without you. Your support has been unbelievable these past 45 years. It's been truly remarkable and a real celebration of life, love and music! We are honored to be your band.

The Red Baron has been a place we've been setting up and tearing down in one incarnation or another since 1970! On top of that since 1970 Bob and Rick have played with different lineups every Halloween and every Wednesday before Thanksgiving which is the busiest night of the year for the Red Baron-it's even

281

bigger than New Year's Eve. The Baron was always packed and still is with the children of the children of the children who saw them at the Youth Center! Let that soak in. It's really unbelievable! The Red Baron has had four changes in ownership since their first gig there. I think the first was "Father Tom Lovell." The second was Edgerton's one and only Jeff Schultz who always supported the group and encouraged them to pursue bigger things and lastly Jim "Plugger" whose support for the band had been unfailing and unbelievably kind and currently the Banucshi's who have given the Barron a face lift and carry on the tradition of providing Edgerton with a place to rock. We cannot thank these guys enough. Let's face it. If people didn't come to see us, we wouldn't have a gig.

Rise wasn't with us when we first started gigging in Edgerton but two years later Rise played her first gig at the Baron and is one Bob nor Rick will ever forget or let Rise forget. While setting up on Halloween night a naked man slowly walked through the length of the bar and right by the band. Rise in a voice that said, "what am I doing here?" stated, "I'm never playing here again!" We are all grateful she changed her mind!

Halloween at the Red Baron

     Edgerton and the surrounding area including Indianford and Newville, has had a long history of supporting live music. I know of no locale you would find so many venues supporting live music within a five mile. Newville, known as "the Gateway to Lake Koshkonong," Wisconsin's third largest lake, makes it a popular area for boaters and vacationers. During the summer it has been estimated that thirty to forty thousand people visit this area on weekends. Numerous bars and restaurants are spread out along the lakeside. The Anchor Inn, located on the Rock river in Newville, has supported this band for the past 25 years. The Anchor's current owner, John Kinnett has done a world class job of creating the perfect setting to forget all of your troubles. You can sit back, be pampered, relax, enjoy fabulous service, great food and drinks, and fantastic atmosphere. Sitting outside in the summer is like being transported to the Florida Keys! There's great live music, themed parties, bon fires at night, boat docking and pontoon rental! John has made this getaway a place to thoroughly immerse yourself in the perfect idea of "taking some time off." Many people schedule their summer weekends at Anchor Inn around the dates Mourning Dayze play there. As a band, we appreciate John's efforts in promoting good times and live entertainment. Thanks John!

Dan Reilly

It would be impossible not to mention "Dan Reilly and the Barn Swallows" and their impact on the Edgerton music scene. Dan Reilly is a singer/songwriter/entertainer extraordinaire, who performs throughout southern Wisconsin as a single.

Years ago Dan would occasionally gig using a backup band called "The Barn Swallows." It started simply as a gig that was about having fun to do and include lots of local talent. Rick, Rise, Bob and Wayne have spent many a night pickin' and grinnin, and singing while backing up Dan. Wayne would often introduce Dan as the "Sultan of Fulton" as he came roaring on stage to the sounds of "Sweet Pam." Dan as a songwriter used different incarnations of "The Barn Swallows" to back him up in the studio. *The Flatlander Blues, Cheesehead Song, Bear Fan's Polka* and the heartfelt *Chelsea's Song* not only got significant regional airplay but also directly led to bookings at Milwaukee's Summer Fest, Wisconsin State Fair, as well as opening for national country headliners Johnny Rodriguez, Sweethearts of the Rodeo, Rodney Crowell and Highway 101, The Platters and Cryin' Shames throughout the state.

Bob's cousin Gene was the Swallows rock solid drummer and his brotherTom, known as "the Prez," was an amazing and well loved entertainer who always had a guest spot or two in the show. Tom loved to entertain! Tom would often be brought up on stage

285

to sing some traditional polkas, and then would solo on his kazoo. Man, this always brought the house down. People would laugh, smile and just have a ball with it. After his polkas he would sometimes do a blues tune "Here Come's Mama" which was a favorite and then he would do some comedy with Dan. People loved "I Wanna Spearfish Too" and from Hee Haw, "Gloom, Dispair." Tom would often end his portion of the show with a little good ol' rock-n-roll with support from the Barn Swallows singing "Love Stinks." But when he would put on his yellow wig that was as long as he was tall and sing "Wild Thing." The place went wild! People who had never seen Tom before couldn't believe it or didn't quite know what to think of him. People who had seen him before couldn't wait to see him again. Tom always fired up the crowd, was so well loved, and will always be remembered.

And here he is...The Prez!   *Wild Thing!*

"Dan Reilly and the Barn Swallows" at Alpine Valley

The "Prez" Tom Jenson   Dan Reilly

Curtis T. Anderson

Earl Quigley

Gene Jenson

Earl Quigley Bob Jenson   Gene Jenson

*The "Barn Swallows" at
Milwaukee's Summerfest*

*Rick: accordion, pedal steel
Bob playing his Baldwin bass*

*The "Barn Swallows" at Anchor Inn
Warming up the crowd before bringing Dan on.
Check out that bridge!*

(Other notable Barnswallows are: Dale Goede guitar, Dan Algrim guitar, Earl Quigley, lap steel, the great Curtis T. Anderson, mandolin and vocals, Wendy Halverson vocals, Bill Collins spoons, "little Rick" spoons, Chris Conroy drums, Lance Massey fiddle, Tim Deere banjo, Ed Bauer, bass, tuba and bass harmonica, Sam James pedal steel, Jeff Onsrud bass, Bill Conway drums and the one and only Jeff Bartz. Jeff took care of sound, transported the band and equipment in his motor home "the whale" provided tremendous behind the scenes support and did a fantastic and memorable impression of Elvis and Rodney Dangerfield. Jeff could bring a crown to tears with laughter when he did Rodney.

288

Jeff does the King's thing!

People everywhere just love Dan. He has done so much
for the music and the people of the area. He is truly a legend.
Check this out. It says a lot: Reporter Marcia Nelesen wrote this
article on Dan for the Janesville Gazette, Monday, March 26, 2012;
Dan Reilly was born after his time.
Like Henry David Thoreau, Reilly relishes his solitary time. He lives
off his land and his wits.

Reilly, 56, of Fulton Township also abides by old-fashioned
barn-raising ideals, always ready to help his community.

Jim Linsley, a farmer down the road and longtime friend, said
Reilly is "one of those guys who's always there. If there is some sort
of charity event or fundraiser, he usually has something to do with
it."

Reilly serves his community with his music, time and energy.
Other people donate money or merchandise; he donates his many
talents.

When asked the source of his largess, Reilly searched for an
answer and then simply said: "If we ain't here to help each other,
what are we here for? "Music gives you a chance to give back and

have fun," said Reilly, who plays 12-string guitar and harmonica. "I can't give everybody $500, but I can give a $300 or $500 gig without having it taken out of my pocket. "You go give them music, and that draws the crowds where they can raise money."

Reilly and his wife, Marcia, have had their own share of challenges, friends say, adding that may be another reason for the couple's empathy for others. Their two babies were born premature, and the oldest, Chelsea, is blind as a result.

Those who benefit from Reilly's generosity include private people down on their luck, his former country grade school, low-income children and children with disabilities, wildlife organizations, the Lions Club, veterans, the Wisconsin School for the Visually Handicapped and the local police department. Reilly acts as auctioneer for charity events. He has played his guitar by the bedside of a dying woman after being asked by her family. Last year, Reilly donated to Edgerton Community Outreach more than $1,500 he raised hosting a haunted house on his property. He also donates surplus produce there.

Blaine Larson, an Edgerton police officer, called his friend "Mr. Edgerton." "He doesn't say no," Larson said of Reilly. "When people call, he says 'yes.'"

John Thompson was in the Lions Club with Reilly. "He's just a good 'ol country Irishman who likes to give things to people and doesn't need a lot for himself," Thompson said.

Reilly likes seeing the results of his work come back to the community, whether it's donated food or conservation land bought for the public.

Friends say Reilly could be wealthy if he charged for every event he donated. But Reilly said a short stint in Nashville convinced him he doesn't want that lifestyle.

Instead, the self-taught musician lives off his music here, playing dinner clubs and bars. He earns enough for his needs, and he and his family don't seem to need much. They live on the homestead in a cozy, wood-heated house. They don't have air conditioning, and a friend says Reilly cools off in summer by sprawling under a large willow.

Reilly abhors the thought of working for somebody and supplements his income by farming and selling produce from a *seven-acre garden.*

Linsley described Reilly as an "old-school" person who is always willing to help and expects nothing in return. "Danny always finds value in people and not material things," Linsley said. "He was born a couple hundreds of years too late. That's what his mom always told me." (9)

Why he hasn't made it big?: "I don't want to. Songs that made it to the radio "kind of made it on their own," Reilly said. He's turned down offers to tour: "I don't want to be in no big cities. I don't like life on the road." He'd rather stay near home and play area establishments. An agent from Chicago once called and said he could put Reilly to work every night. "(I told him), I don't want to work every night. Then I'd be calling it work, just like you. Once my music gets into too much business, it's not fun anymore. As long as it is paying the bills, I'll keep it where it's at. I think it's a miracle to get paid to do music in the first place."

Advice to others: Call your own shots. Be self-employed. "Pick something you like to do, and figure out a way to get paid for it."

How he writes his music: Stuff catches in his head. Once, Reilly was having lunch in an Indianford tavern. A fisherman came in and asked a woman there to describe the town. "It's two bars and a bait shop," she said. A song was born.

Some of his favorite things: Hunting. Sitting on a bucket watching the bobber go own. Making music in his basement. Seeing the good that comes from his fundraising. Hauling his guitar around on his travels, singing and partying with the locals in such places as Irish pubs and the streets of Jamaica. "You can go anywhere with music," Reilly said, "Everybody speaks music."

Awards: *The Melvin Jones Fellowship award from the Lions Club, where he is a member*

There have been so many great clubs and bars we've played at in this area. (Who could forget Mike and Deanna Hart's Junkyard parties!) It's really impossible to give each the credit they deserve. I'm not even going to try. Just know this, we're all deeply grateful for all the opportunities you've given us to play for you. We never forget. It's the you, the wonderful people of this area that have made us possible. The people of Edgerton deserve so much of the credit.

We Love The Band Party

Speaking of the people of Edgerton, Will and Sara O'Connel and friends, conceived the idea to organize and throw a "We Love The Band" party. They asked if we would be willing to play for it. We were more than happy to. It was a nice way for us to give something back to the people that support us all year long, year in and year out. As a band we often forget how much we mean to people and how many lives we have touched. The impact we have on others can be quite profound. We often hear about it. Now think about this. The same people that support us all year long are throwing a party for us! How cool is that?!

Will and Sarah had us play in their large and beautiful back yard. They had a good place for us to set up, room to dance, and plenty of space for people to come sit and enjoy the party. (And juice... can't forget Will's generator!) Sounds perfect for a great party eh? It was! Rise adds, "the fun part of the band parties was enjoying the laid back loose feel to them as well as being able to play with no limits. We can play anything we want, talk to people whenever we want and play bunches of requests."

The parties were always great fun with plenty of laughs. Will and Sara had fun themed t-shirts made for every party. A huge WE LOVE THE BAND party banner was hung up on the side of the house. For the third We Love The Band Party a deck was made by Willpower giving the band a solid place to set up and gave dancers plenty of room to shake it. There was always great food and all the beer and drinks in the world! These parties had huge turnouts and were always rockin'. A great deal of the success of these parties has to go to Will and Sarah who were the perfect people to host this event and making everyone feel relaxed, welcomed, and in the groove. We never expected to get paid to play for these parties, but year after year the hat was passed and we were given money we tried to turn down. We always spent the money we were given on anything we felt would improve the band, usually new equipment!

292

The Baseball Bus

We as a band have never had the opportunity to spend much
time with those that came to see us play. We were always setting
up, playing, on break, or tearing down. The group itself rarely
spends any down time together. I really wanted to plan some
kind of "Fan Appreciation Party" to demonstrate our appreciation
for the people that have been so supportive of the band. My first
thought was to have a big picnic with lots of food and beer at
Edgerton's Racetrack Park. We could play a huge game of
baseball choosing sides with everyone who wanted to play. That
sounded great to me, but didn't really go over very well. It was
the idea of baseball however, and how it can bring people
together and often making life long memories that got this party
started. In the 70's Bob, Wally, Turtle, Bob Lee, Paul, Rise, I and
some others would occasionally go to a Brewer game on a
Sunday afternoon and just have a great time. Maybe something
like that would work for the band. One Sunday afternoon while
on break at the Anchor Inn while talking with Colleen Barrett and
Holly Millard the idea of the band taking a Sunday off and going
to a Brewer game with "friends of the band" came up. Colleen
was all over it mentioning that Theresa Reilly who was there as
well had done something similar using Van Galder bus lines.
That's all it took to get this idea off the ground. The band was all
for it. With Colleen's help in taking care of the bus arrangements,
getting people to commit to the date, establishing times,
collecting ticket money and generally helping to organize the

passenger list we were off! Colleen was really like the fifth member of the band in making these trips "happen." We can't thank her enough. On the bus ride to Miller Park there was a dvd of the band playing plus plenty laughs and plenty of beer! Rise, with her strong desire to make things and events "extra special" always came up with some idea to put some sparkle in the event. She had some great commemorative "koozies," Mourning Dayze M&Ms and V.I.P. event tags made. Dr. Mark Irgens even had baseball caps made for the game! We would tailgate in the parking lot at Miller Park enjoying each others company, atmosphere, great food and beer. It brought a big cheer from the group when "Welcome Friends of Mourning Dayze" was flashed on the scoreboard. The baseball bus trips were great fun and always loved and appreciated by everyone. Go Brewers! It was so much fun we did this for three consecutive years.

The pictures say it all! Thank you Edgerton for all of your support! You're Amazing!

OFFICIAL
MOURNING DAYZE

MILWAUKEE
BREWER
BASEBALL
BUS
JUNE 22, 2008

THE BREWERS WELCOME

FRIENDS OF MOURNING DAYZE
FRIENDS OF TIM CARPENTER
GOOD SHEPHERD PARISH
GRANDMA ALICE NOORDYK
GRANDMA DEANNER RORTVEDT
GREAT LAKES RUBBER & SUPPLY
GREIBER FAMILY OUTING
HAPPY 25TH BIRTHDAY LYNDSEY
HAPPY 9TH BIRTHDAY PARKER FRIEDLANDER
HAPPY 90TH B'DAY TONY WINIARSKI

The Derby Party

And........... they're off!

Since 2009, the first Saturday in May, the weekend of the Kentucky Derby, Rick and Rise drive to Valparaiso Indiana to play for the best darn Kentucky Derby party you ever saw! Rick and Rise are guests of Alan Luckett's parents, Bob and Betty, who are absolutely "fab" hosts! Alan is married to Rick's and Rise's sister Renee.

With Alan's family having roots in Kentucky there is a special interest in Derby weekend and "The Two Greatest Minutes in Sports." Bob and Betty throw a huge party for friends and family in their lovely home complete with the house looking like the club house at Churchill Downs complete with women wearing a wide variety of Kentucky Derby hats. All hoping they are to win the "best Derby hat" contest (Which can be as exciting as the race!), do a little wagering, have country ham, rice & peas, mint juleps and fine Kentucky Bourbon. Just great fun!

Rick loves getting the chance to play thumb-style guitar for those who come from the state where thumb picking was born. Muhlenberg County Kentucky is considered to be the birthplace of "thumb-pickin'."

Rick and Rise set up their equipment in the kitchen along with Al who supports the duo with laying down grooves from his electric bass and occasional vocals. Al is always full of energy, fun, and entertaining. Rise loves how the kitchen gives them a backdrop of Betty's beautiful backyard gardens and wildflowers. It truly is a million dollar view. The fine guitarist and local legend

"Little Chris" has come to the party for many years primarily so he and Rick can jam to get the party started. They always share great grins and are loved by the Derby Day crowd. Rick then plays by himself early tunes of Chet Atkins and Merle Travis. Rick: "I'm in a little bit of heaven when I get to play some of Chet and Merle's early music for a great kindred spirit. Al's mother's father, Great Grandpa Bill and I both share a love of that style of music." Rick & Rise then play and sing traditional songs from Kentucky as well as some classic songs about famous horses and horse races. A highlight is when Al's dad, Bob, reads the introduction to Merle Travis' classic mining tune, "Dark as a Dungeon." One year Bob's brother, Harry, who has been a miner his entire life read the intro. It was thrilling. Nephew Roland's singing of "Camptown Races" is always loved by the packed house. (In this case it really is a packed house!) In 2012 Roland persuaded his reluctant mom (come on mom!) to drive last minute from Madison, Wisconsin, to Whitewater to pick up his drum kit and then drive three more hours to Valparaiso to the Derby Party. Roland was ready to rock. We had never played together before. That didn't stop us from having a wonderful time together. The crowd loved Roland. They couldn't get enough of his playing. Niece Rachel likes to get into the spotlight too. Her performance of "You Are My Sunshine" is always a showstopper. Sister Renee will also get up and sing with the band (watch out if she sings "Fever"!) as well as sing gospel tunes unaccompanied with her bro and big sis. It's so nice when they sing together. But no one knocks 'em dead like Betty, mom, when she sings "May I Sleep in your barn tonight Mister?" It's something you will never forget!

It's always a great party. Now don't spoil it by asking, "who won the race?"

Rick & Rise

Rick and Rise have been performing as a duo since the early 70's. Oh, but first, let's clear this up, Rick and Rise are brother and sister, not husband and wife as urban legend has it! They'll sing just about anything that allows them to utilize their personable and beautiful two part harmonies from folk, country, gospel and pop to rock. They like to "stretch" out at times, playing jazz standards and really anything else they feel would work or had a whim to try. As a duo in the 70's, they had often opened up for the band when the opportunity presented itself. This was quite a surprise and sometimes confusing for those who had never seen Mourning Dayze before and expected to hear rock n' roll. During their early years they sang a lot together, with sparkling innovative harmonies to the music of the Everly Brothers, Beatles, Neil Young, Mason Profit, Simon and Garfunkel, Harry Chapin and a fantastic West Side Story medley.

As pop music evolved so did they, displaying no fear of change. They've stayed on top of current trends, always performed a few pop tunes, but more importantly searched for music that was not main stream and overplayed that they could present to their audiences as being fresh and new. A key strength these two have is in delivering the song with honesty and conviction. Rick, "if we aren't energized and aren't honestly into what we're doing, how are we going to energize and win over our audience?"

As the drum machine and sequencer began to be used exclusively with the band, Rick and Rise continued to open up for the band but this time Rick's sequences provided them with bass, drums, and keys, a synthesized band. This allowed them to play a much broader range of material and most importantly dance material that would go over in the venues they traditionally played. Significantly, this gave them the option to play jobs where a full group would be too large or when the group as a whole wasn't interested in playing. This would prove invaluable, because as time moved on Bob and Wayne would not want to work as much as they had in the past, particularly friday nights and weekdays. Rick & Rise continue to gig as much as they're able, staying as active as work and their schedules allow.

Consider the music of some of the well known artists Rise has sung and interpreted through the years-Linda Ronstadt, Carol King, Carley Simon, Bette Midler, Bonnie Koloc, Patsy Cline, Roberta Flack, Aretha Franklin, Pat Benatar, Donna Summer, Diana Ross, Madonna, Stevie Nicks and Bonnie Raitt. Add to that the countless highly talented obscure artists whose songs she has sung throughout her entire career. Look at the stars of contemporary music she's singing today-Pink, Alicia Keys, Beyonce, Duffy, Adele, K.T. Tunstall, Ingrid Michaelson, Michael Jackson, Bruno Mars to name a few. Give yourself a few minutes to think about what she's sung these 45 years, then consider the variety and longevity of her work. It's really quite amazing. I've been so fortunate to have had my sister to sing and work with all of these years. We've shared many magical musical moments together. It's been wonderful. Yea, Rise!

Mourning Dayze
1998-2016

The four of them had played together off and on and in various forms and groups since the late 70's. They began playing as a group in 1998 and continue to be active today. Consider this: the average life of a band is between one and two years. The Mourning Dayze have been together without a change in personnel for over 25-years, their longevity is astounding!

Rise and Wayne's world class vocals have been loved by audiences everywhere. Rick and Bob lay down infectious grooves and get people movin' in their chairs or out on the dance floor. Combine that with a wide range in material delivered with soul and conviction and you've got the formula for a good time. One question the band gets a lot is, "what kind of music do you play?" or "what kind of band are you?". To that, the band simply replies, "we play music you can dance to: it's music we enjoy and want to share with you."To hear them live, you'd understand their answer and oh, by the way, they're not bad to listen to either!

The next time you hear them play, think of the band's beginnings in '65, the culture, the music, the changes in the world. Consider all the one night stands they've played and ya, that means driving to the gig, setting up, tearing down then diving home again with all the history that comes with them to the gig, night after night. There's a lot happening on that stage-this includes the rehearsing one and two nights a week as a group, time invested with their instruments, and the time required to prepare for rehearsals. You've got to set up and tear down for rehearsals too, ya know! During the colder months, the oil burner needs to be started to make sure the barn is warm enough for practice. Someone has got to be sure there's fuel oil to burn. One's personal life always seems to be second to that of the band's-just ask any member's spouse, family or friends. They'll tell you, they know all too well! It takes a special person to partner up and stick with someone playing in a band. We thank our spouses, families and friends for all they've done and given to let us "play." For the people in the band, there's nothing else they'd rather be doing.

The band is thankful as well as grateful to have been able to do what they love these past 50 plus years. Many people ask, "why they've been at it so long?" Well here might be a clue. The band hears this from people all the time. "You guys really look like you're having fun up there." That might be the biggest reason they're still playing, they're still having fun.

The End

One night while sitting at home in front of the computer, with too much time on my hands, Google's search engine box began calling me, like a genie that has granted me an unlimited number of wishes. Asking me if I had anything I'd like it to search for. "Hmmm? Wonder what would pop up if I searched Mourning Dayze? Never tried that before." Until February of 2005, none of us had ever "Googled" the name Mourning Dayze, let alone "Fly My Paper Airplane!" Hard to imagine isn't it?

I typed in Mourning Dayze and hit "search." I almost couldn't believe what I saw. There were many references to Mourning Dayze and one in particular. Gear Fab Records had rereleased the Mourning Dayze 45 "Fly My Paper Airplane," which was recorded in Chicago, on an album called "The Psychedelic States: Illinois in the 60's"! Man, I flew to the phone to call Doug to tell him the story. Then called Steve, who let out a patented "WHAT?" He couldn't believe it either. Doug was as blown away as Steve and I, but with one big difference, as usual, he saw the significance of the moment and all the possibilities it held regarding our history and story. Just like our music, our story could be shared. It was Doug who said we should buy a hearse as well as make a record. I knew he meant this when he said, "we should write a book about the band."

Footnotes

(1) Royal Purple News, "Whitewater loses an icon: Kachel was key asset to campus development" n.d. http://royalpurplenews.com/?p=1420 para. 5, accessed 22 Jan. 2014

(2) University of Whitewater, University News, David Kachel, UW-Whitewater, "David Kachel, UW-Whitewater alumnus and donor, dies at age 83" Feb. 4, 2011, http://www.uww.edu/news/archive/2011-02-kachel, para 2/4, accessed 26 Jan. 2014.

(3) 1960's-Wikipedia, the free encyclopedia n.d., / http://wwwehow.com/how 5771468 footnote.html (accessed 3-31-14)

(4) Psychedelia-Wikipedia, the free encyclopedia. Http://en.wikipedia.org/wiki/Psychedelia...accessed...4-9-2014

(5) E. Vulliamy, "Love and Haight," *Observer Music Monthly* 20 May 2007

(6) P. Braunstein, and M.W. Doyle (eds), *Imagine Nation: The American Counterculture of the 1960s and '70s* (New York, 2002), p.7

(7) Roots of Communal Revival 1962-1966

(8) Hinckley, David (October 15, 1998). "Groovy-The Summer of Love, 1967." *New York Daily News*. Retrieved September 28, 2012.

(5-8) Summer of Love-Wikipedia, the free encyclopedia. http://en.wikipedia.org/wiki/Summer of Love...accessed 4-9-2014

(9) Reprinted with permission of the Janesville Gazette

P. 82 Richard C. Haney's letter used with his permission.